Belarus and Moldova
country studies

Federal Research Division
Library of Congress
Edited by
Helen Fedor
Research Completed
May 1995

On the cover: St. George, patron saint of Belarus, and
antique Moldovan rug

First Edition, First Printing, 1995.

Library of Congress Cataloging-in-Publication Data

Belarus and Moldova : country studies / Federal Research
    Division, Library of Congress ; edited by Helen Fedor. —
    1st ed.
        p. cm. — (Area handbook series, ISSN 1057–5294)
    (DA Pam ; 550–112)
        "Research completed May 1995."
        Includes bibliographical references (pp. 207–223) and
    index.
        ISBN 0–8444–0849–2 (hc : alk. paper)
        ——— Copy 3 Z663.275 .B45   1995
        1. Belarus. 2. Moldova. I. Fedor, Helen, 1957– . II.
    Library of Congress. Federal Research Division. III.
    Series. IV. Series: DA Pam ; 550–112.
DK507.23.B45 1995   95–45993
947'.65—dc20   CIP

Headquarters, Department of the Army
DA Pam 550–112

Reprinted without alteration on recycled acid-free paper.

Bernan
Lanham, Maryland
January 1996

Foreword

This volume is one in a continuing series of books prepared by the Federal Research Division of the Library of Congress under the Country Studies/Area Handbook Program sponsored by the Department of the Army. The last two pages of this book list the other published studies.

Most books in the series deal with a particular foreign country, describing and analyzing its political, economic, social, and national security systems and institutions, and examining the interrelationships of those systems and the ways they are shaped by cultural factors. Each study is written by a multidisciplinary team of social scientists. The authors seek to provide a basic understanding of the observed society, striving for a dynamic rather than a static portrayal. Particular attention is devoted to the people who make up the society, their origins, dominant beliefs and values, their common interests and the issues on which they are divided, the nature and extent of their involvement with national institutions, and their attitudes toward each other and toward their social system and political order.

The books represent the analysis of the authors and should not be construed as an expression of an official United States government position, policy, or decision. The authors have sought to adhere to accepted standards of scholarly objectivity. Corrections, additions, and suggestions for changes from readers will be welcomed for use in future editions.

Louis R. Mortimer
Chief
Federal Research Division
Library of Congress
Washington, DC 20540–5220

Acknowledgments

The authors are indebted to numerous individuals and organizations who gave their time, research materials, and expertise on affairs in Belarus and Moldova to provide data, perspective, and material support for this volume.

The collection of accurate and current information was assisted greatly by the contributions of Stephen R. Burant of the United States Department of State, Professor Thomas E. Bird of Queens College, Valery Kurdzyukou of the Embassy of the Republic of Belarus, A. James Firth of the United States Department of Agriculture, John Mumford of The Washington Group, Eugene Fishel of the United States Department of State, Professor Paul E. Michelson of Huntington College, Professor Ernest H. Latham, Jr., of the American-Romanian Academy, Carmen Kosik, Raymond Milefsky of the Defense Mapping Agency, and Iurie Leanca of the Embassy of the Republic of Moldova. The authors also acknowledge the generosity of all the individuals who allowed their photographs to be used in this study.

Thanks also go to Ralph K. Benesch, who oversees the Country Studies/Area Handbook Program for the Department of the Army. In addition, the authors appreciate the advice and guidance of Sandra W. Meditz, Federal Research Division coordinator of the handbook series. Special thanks go to Marilyn L. Majeska, who supervised editing; Andrea T. Merrill, who performed the prepublication editorial review and managed production; David P. Cabitto, who designed the book cover and the illustrations on the title page of both chapters, provided graphics support, and, together with Thomas D. Hall and the firm of Maryland Mapping and Graphics, prepared the maps; Ihor Y. Gawdiak, who provided historical background information; and Glenn E. Curtis, who critiqued the text. The following individuals are gratefully acknowledged as well: Vincent Ercolano and Janet Willen, who edited the chapters; Barbara Edgerton and Izella Watson, who did the word processing; Francine Cronshaw, who compiled the index; and David P. Cabitto, Stephen C. Cranton, and Janie L. Gilchrist, who prepared the camera-ready copy.

Contents

List of Figures

Preface

At the end of 1991, the formal liquidation of the Soviet Union was the surprisingly swift result of partially hidden decrepitude and centrifugal forces within that empire. Of the fifteen "new" states that emerged from the process, many had been independent political entities at some time in the past. Aside from their coverage in the 1991 *Soviet Union: A Country Study*, none had received individual treatment in this series, however. *Belarus and Moldova: Country Studies* is the second in a new subseries describing the fifteen post-Soviet republics, both as they existed before and during the Soviet era and as they have developed since 1991. This volume covers Belarus and Moldova, two nations on the western border of what was once the Soviet Union.

The marked relaxation of information restrictions, which began in the late 1980s and accelerated after 1991, allows the reporting of extensive data on every aspect of life in the two countries. Scholarly articles and periodical reports have been especially helpful in accounting for the years of independence in the 1990s. The authors have described the historical, political, and social backgrounds of the countries as the background for their current portraits. However, in general, both Belarus and Moldova (especially the former) have been written about to a lesser extent than other former Soviet republics. In each case, the authors' goal in this book was to provide a compact, accessible, and objective treatment of five main topics: historical setting, the society and its environment, the economy, government and politics, and national security.

In the case of Belarus, providing definitive spellings of personal names or place-names has been a challenge. All names have been transliterated according to the transliteration scheme devised by the United States Board on Geographic Names (BGN), which is widely used by the United States government, although not by the Library of Congress or in most scholarly works. According to the BGN system, most Cyrillic letters are transliterated similarly from both Belarusian and Russian. But some letters are transliterated from the two languages differently (for example, "e," which remains "e" in transliterated Russian but becomes "ye" in transliterated Belarusian), and some letters exist in Belarusian but not in Russian.

Because Belarusian names often differ from the Russian versions that have been used predominantly by the Russian Empire, the Soviet Union, and the world in general, the Russian version is given in parentheses at the first occurrence of a name. Otherwise, the Belarusian names have been used throughout. The few exceptions to this are well-known names (such as Moscow) and words (such as *perestroika*) that have acquired a standardized spelling in English usage.

Another problem in writing about Belarus is what to call it and when. In its early history, the region was known as "Belaya Rus'," "Belorussia," "White Ruthenia," or "White Rus'." (A number of explanations have been proffered for the term "white.") As if this were not confusing enough, the terms "Rus'" and "Russia" have often been confused, sometimes deliberately. The original Rus' was Kievan Rus', which existed for centuries before Muscovy (which would later become Russia) gained significance. Russia later claimed to be the sole successor to Kievan Rus' and often blurred the line between the two. In the Russian language, both *russkiy* and *rossiyskiy* mean "Russian."

During the time when Belarus was part of the Russian Empire and the Soviet Union, it was commonly known as Belorussia, and the language was known as Belorussian. Occasionally, nationalist groups would form and take a name that included the word "Belarusian," but this use of the word was the exception. It was only after the Supreme Soviet declared the country independent that the name was changed from the Belorussian Soviet Socialist Republic to the Republic of Belarus, despite the title of the earlier Declaration of State Sovereignty of the Belarusian Soviet Socialist Republic. The policy in this volume has been to use "Belarus/Belarusian" in the earliest historical times; "Belorussia/Belorussian" while it was a part of either the Grand Duchy, Poland, the Russian Empire, or the Soviet Union; and "Belarus/Belarusian" after the country declared independence in August 1991. The exceptions are organization names in which "Belarus/Belarusian" was deliberately chosen over "Belorussia/Belorussian."

For Moldova, the problem of personal names and place-names is somewhat different. When Moldovan, a dialect of the Romanian language, written in the Latin alphabet was designated the official language of Moldavia in 1989, the Cyrillic alphabet (imposed by Joseph V. Stalin) was dropped, thus obviating the need for transliteration. However, the Moldovan names appearing in the text of this volume are missing most of the diacritics used by the language. In this case, it is a matter of lagging technology: the typesetting software being used simply cannot produce the necessary diacritics in the text (although they appear on the maps). For this the authors apologize and hope that by the time this country study is updated, missing diacritics will no longer be the norm.

As was also the case with Belarus, Moldova and the Moldovans are referred to in different ways depending on the period of history. Until the creation of the Moldavian Autonomous Oblast (outside the traditional boundaries of Moldova) by Moscow in 1924, "Moldova" and "Moldovan" were the terms for the region and the language. From 1924 until the legislature changed the country's name officially in 1990, the terms used were "Moldavia" and "Moldavian." As with Belarus, the policy in this volume has been to adhere to these different names during their respective periods of usage, with the exceptions of names of organizations in which "Moldova/Moldovan" was deliberately chosen over "Moldavia/Moldavian."

Measurements are given in the metric system; a conversion table is provided in Appendix A. A Chronology is provided at the beginning of each chapter. To amplify points in the text of the chapters, tables in Appendix A provide statistics on aspects of the societies and the economies of the countries. A Glossary provides information on certain terms in order to explain their background without creating distractions in the text. Chapter bibliographies appear at the end of the book; brief comments on some of the more valuable sources for further reading appear at the conclusion of each chapter.

The body of the text reflects information available as of May 1995. Certain other portions of the text, however, have been updated. The Introduction discusses significant events and trends that have occurred since the completion of research; the Chronologies and Country Profiles include updated information as available; and the Bibliography lists recently published sources thought to be particularly helpful to the reader.

Figure 1. Belarus and Moldova: Geographic Setting, 1995

Introduction

LOCATED ON THE WESTERN BORDERLANDS of the Russian Empire and later the Soviet Union, the regions that would one day become the republics of Belarus and Moldova had long been part of a buffer zone used to protect Russia from Western influences and military forces. The imperial and Soviet governments attempted to fully integrate the two regions' economies into their own and to Russify their people in order to bind them seamlessly into their respective empires. For a long time, these efforts seemed to work, but in 1991 Belarus and Moldova declared their independence from the Soviet Union and began to go their separate, post-Soviet ways. Independence was not a totally new experience for the two countries, however; each of them had existed briefly as a sovereign entity during the previous hundred years, but this time they had much to undo from the previous regime.

The two countries, former republics of the now-defunct Soviet Union, are a study in contrasts. Belarus, mostly ethnic Belarusian (and overwhelmingly Slavic) in population, had long been part of the Russian Empire and subsequently the Soviet Union. The tsars, and later the commissars, sought to meld Belorussia with Russia and the Belorussians with the Russians. They succeeded to a remarkable extent: independent Belarus still identifies closely with Russia, and Belarusian nationalists are in the minority. Soviet-era political and economic structures, and even symbols, have been retained and even reintroduced, as was the case after the May 1995 referendum that brought back the Soviet-era flag and emblem (both slightly modified) and the Russian language.

Moldova, a country that had also been part of both empires since the nineteenth century, has a majority population of ethnic Romanians, who are not Slavs. Despite Russian and Soviet efforts to Slavicize them, most ethnic Romanians were able to maintain their identity and looked to Romania as the source of their culture. When the Soviet Union began to crumble, Moldova asserted first its sovereignty and then its independence, although the population was far from unanimous on either. But the nationalists eventually carried the day, and Moldova sought to distance itself from Russia, despite the wishes of the Transnistrians, who in 1990 proclaimed the "Dnestr Moldavian

Republic," with a pro-Soviet extralegal government, on the east bank of the Nistru River. The Transnistrians want no part of independent Moldova, its ethnic-Romanian nationalists, or a possible reunification with Romania, where they would be a small minority instead of a powerful political force.

In both Belarus and Moldova, there are many who wish to return to the days of the Soviet Union for a variety of reasons, some economic, some nostalgic, and some fearful. In Belarus these conservatives (ethnic Belarusians as well as ethnic Russians) are in the majority and are to be found throughout the population and the government. Their domination is felt not only in the political arena but in the social sphere as well.

In Moldova the conservatives (mainly, but not exclusively, ethnic Slavs) are located throughout society and the government, but their influence is not as overwhelming as in Belarus. Many of the Moldovan conservatives (although not all) live in Transnistria. Here, they believe, they are the keepers of the Soviet ideal from which a reconstituted Soviet Union will one day rise up again. However, time and the course of events have made it clear that they are trying to protect not a way of life but rather their own political and—especially—economic interests, which are often illegal (including sales of arms and illegal drugs).

Both Belarus and Moldova have stated their wish to have free-market economies, but they have proceeded in this direction at different paces. The economies of both countries had been firmly embedded in the Soviet economy, and each had specialized in a certain sector—Belarus in heavy agricultural equipment and goods for the military, and Moldova primarily in agricultural products and consumer goods—while relying on other republics for raw materials. Both republics had been especially dependent on Russia for inexpensive fuels, a fact that continued to haunt them after independence. Subsidized fuels, priced well below world prices, had made the goods produced by the two countries inexpensive and affordable by the other Soviet republics. With the loss of these cheap fuels, both countries were forced to either decrease their fuel consumption (and their output) or improve the efficiency of their industries. Belarus chose the former path, which coincided with the fact that it was selling fewer of its goods because of price and quality considerations, while Moldova tried, sometimes unsuccessfully, to take steps toward improved efficiency.

Both countries initiated privatization, or the sale of state-owned property, and both were having a difficult time reconfiguring their economies. The Moldovan government was changing its laws to make them more compatible with a free market and more friendly toward foreign investment and business in general. However, vested interests sought to maintain the system or, at least, to make large profits during the transition.

The Belarusian government decided that, despite its intention to sell state-owned property, it would leave the agricultural sector under state control. The government's reasoning was that Belarusian large-scale agriculture was best suited to the heavy agricultural equipment that the country continued to produce, despite the fact that fuel for this equipment was often scarce.

Both Belarus and Moldova stated their intention of having democratic political systems, as did many former Soviet republics. However, making the change from a communist government to a real democracy proved difficult, not the least because of officials who wished to maintain the status quo. They viewed democracy as too chaotic and unstable, unlike the predictability that had characterized their previous political lives. They also saw it as risky and feared to lose the perquisites to which they had been entitled and which they wanted to retain.

Belarus's attempts to become a Western democracy often appeared likely to remain out of reach. Although the constitution added the office of the president and declared a separation of powers, government in Belarus often seemed no different from that of the Soviet era. Political apathy among the population remained so strong that a legislature could not be seated after two rounds of elections in 1995; corruption was still widespread despite the fact that the president had campaigned as an anticorruption candidate; and political leaders looked to Moscow for political, military, and financial support, with the president trying to lead the country back into some sort of union with Russia.

Moldova kept its basic Soviet-era governmental structure, while adding a presidency, universal suffrage, and popular elections, as did Belarus. However, the country's first attempt at a democratically elected parliament showed the need for further modification of the system. The unwieldy size of the body and a hardline nationalist majority made legislative compromises among the various ethnic groups in Moldova impossible, and the result was gridlock. A smaller parliament and a larger number of moderates after the 1994 elections have made legislative progress possible despite the disagreements and factions that are still to be found.

Despite the differences between the two countries, the focal point for those who wish to maintain each country's independence is the same—the national language, the same rallying point as in the revolutions of 1848, a series of republican revolts against Western and Central European monarchies. These revolts all failed in their immediate goals, but they eventually led to greater representation of ethnic groups in legislatures and to greater cultural autonomy, including the use of languages that, until then, had been dismissed by the authorities as peasant vernaculars. However, while nationalists in the last century sought to codify (and sometimes even form) a literary language, the task of the nationalists in 1991 was to revive that language and divest it of its Russian and Soviet accretions.

To those who have never undergone forced cultural assimilation, the issue may seem trivial. What difference does it make what language is spoken or what it is called? To those who have had their use of language restricted, however, the matter goes beyond mere defiance. Language is the medium of the culture on which their daily lives and identities are based. To define what language can be spoken is to define the identity not only of the individual but also of the country.

Moldovans kept Russian as a language of interethnic communication but subsequently entered a debate as to what their own language was to be called: was it Moldovan or Romanian? The president explained that the term "Moldovan" was used in the constitution for political reasons—to assuage the fears of those who feared imminent reunification with Romania (despite the fact that Germany and Austria, for example, which both use the German language, are separate countries). Again, politics, language, and emotions were thoroughly entangled.

Belarusians, the majority of whom prefer to use Russian in their daily lives, have dealt with the language issue differently. They returned Russian to its status of official language, alongside the Belarusian language, through their response to a May 1995 referendum question. Thus the Belarusian language policy reflected Belarus's pro-Russian policies in general.

May 31, 1995

* * *

* * *

In the months following preparation of this manuscript, Belarus's president, Alyaksandr Lukashyenka, and his government continued their pro-Russian policies and their Soviet-era mentality. When Aleksey II, Orthodox Patriarch of Moscow and All Russia, visited Belarus in July, Lukashyenka praised the Orthodox Church while reproaching the Roman Catholic Church for its active proselytizing and politicking. When subway workers in Minsk went on strike in August, the government sent special police units and Ministry of Internal Affairs troops against them. In addition, Lukashyenka reacted angrily to information that United States and Polish trade unions, including Solidarity, were providing financial assistance to the striking workers through Belarusian nongovernmental unions. Also in August, the president ordered that books published in 1992–95 be removed from secondary schools and institutes of higher education. In other words, these schools would return to using Soviet textbooks.

Lukashyenka also continued arrogating power to himself. His unilateral decisions, including suspending parliamentary immunity, outlawing strikes in sectors he deemed critical, banning the activity of two trade unions until further notice, withholding the salaries of parliamentary deputies, and making arbitrary changes in the state budget, paint a picture of a leader seeking to replace the separation of governmental powers with one-man rule. However, it was only after Lukashyenka's decision to suspend parliamentary immunity that the Supreme Soviet spoke up and petitioned the Constitutional Court to rule on the constitutionality of his measures. A constitutional crisis appeared unavoidable unless the two sides could come to an agreement.

Perhaps the most dramatic indication that the Soviet mentality is alive and well in Belarus was the hot-air balloon tragedy in September 1995. A yearly international hot-air balloon race starting in Switzerland included three United States balloons that crossed the border into Belarus. Although Belarusian authorities had been notified of the race earlier, the Belarusian military fired at one of the balloons, claiming that it did not have any identification and that sensitive military installations were nearby. The two American pilots of the balloon were killed when a missile caused their hydrogen-filled balloon to explode. The pilots of a second balloon left the country before any problems arose, but authorities detained the pilots of the third balloon for a day before releasing them. The Belarusian government issued an official apology for the shooting that accepted "a certain amount" of blame but nevertheless tried to justify the military's response. Many people were convinced that this would not be the last manifestation of Belarus's Cold War mentality.

At the same time, events in Moldova centered on two men—Lieutenant General Aleksandr Lebed', commander of the Russian 14th Army, and Mircea Snegur, Moldova's president. The Russian 14th Army, previously known as the Soviet 14th Army, remained in Transnistria after the Soviet Union was dissolved to protect the ethnic Russians in what Moscow called "the near abroad." Despite their ostensible status as peacekeepers in Moldova's dispute with Transnistria, the 14th Army supported the extralegal government of the "Dnestr Republic" and was even accused of supplying weapons to it during the worst of the fighting in 1992.

At the beginning of June, Lebed' offered his resignation in protest of Russian government plans to downgrade the status of the 14th Army to that of an operational group. After initially refusing the general's resignation, the Russian Ministry of Defense accepted it and replaced him with Major General Valeriy Yevnevich. The Moldovan government's concern was that the new commander continue to keep the army's large stock of weapons safe while a political solution was sought for the problems in Transnistria. Lebed' was seen by some as a strong candidate for the Russian presidency in 1996, but his popularity began decreasing once he resigned and removed himself from the public eye.

In a surprising move in July, President Snegur resigned his membership in the ruling Democratic Agrarian Party of Moldova and took his supporters with him to form a new presidential party, later named the Party of Rebirth and Conciliation. By dividing the Agrarians and depriving them of a parliamentary majority, as well as by considering an alliance with a pro-Romanian party, the president had made moves that could disrupt Moldova's political stability. The purpose of these actions was twofold. The first was preparation for the December 1996 presidential election in which Snegur will seek to win on the strength of the ethnic Romanian vote. His two challengers, Prime Minister Andrei Sangheli and Parliament chairman Petru Lucinschi, are expected to capture the votes of Moldova's

Russian-speaking population, thus making Snegur dependent on the ethnic Romanians.

Snegur's other purpose in creating the new party was an effort to change the government to that of a personalized presidential regime, a move opposed by Parliament. This regime would be different from the existing government and would be at odds with Moldova's political traditions. Under a presidential regime, the existing balance of power between the legislative and executive branches would be disrupted, and, critics charge, the country's progress toward democracy would be jeopardized.

In Transnistria the economic situation continued to deteriorate. The authorities of the "Dnestr Republic" sought greater political legitimacy in hopes that this would help them garner more political support and financial assistance from Russia. To this end, the authorities began drafting a constitution and election law in August in preparation for parliamentary elections scheduled for late fall 1995. In the meantime, bread rationing was introduced in Tiraspol and its suburbs in late August.

A more important event also began in August—the winddown of the operational group of Russian troops in Transnistria. Withdrawal of these troops is part of a "gentleman's agreement," reached in October 1994 between Russia and Moldova, that sought a political solution to the stand-off between the "Dnestr Republic" and the rest of Moldova, but that was approved only by Moldova. However, until the Russian State Duma (the lower house of the parliament) approves the agreement, matters will remain at a standstill.

In mid-August the commander, Valeriy Yevnevich, now promoted to lieutenant general, began to transfer nonmilitary equipment from the operational group to Transnistrian civilian authorities. Work also began on the destruction of old munitions (some manufactured before 1940) that could not be transported to Russia. Several trainloads of surplus military equipment were to be sent to Russia as well. At the same time, there was a cutback in the number of the operational group's officers and support staff. But because the Russian Duma had not yet ratified the withdrawal of the operational group, military authorities were calling this a "redeployment" of forces and equipment rather than an actual "withdrawal."

In September, Igor' N. Smirnov, president of the "Dnestr Republic," addressed the Russian State Duma and made an appeal for official recognition of the "Dnestr Republic." President Snegur of Moldova protested this move and continued to place his confidence in political negotiations. Smirnov, on the other hand, hoped to drag out talks until after Russian parliamentary elections, scheduled for December 1995, in an effort to get more support from the new parliament, which he hoped would be more sympathetic to the Transnistrians' cause.

September 29, 1995   Helen Fedor

Chapter 1. Belarus

St. George, patron saint of Belarus

Chronology of Important Events

Period	Description
NINTH CENTURY	
Late	Emergence of Kievan Rus', the first East Slavic state, which soon splits into a number of principalities. One, Polatsk, becomes nucleus of modern-day Belarus.
THIRTEENTH CENTURY	
1240	Belarus and part of Ukraine come under control of Lithuania. Resulting state is called Grand Duchy of Lithuania, Rus', and Samogitia.
FOURTEEENTH CENTURY	
1385	Union of Krevo joins Poland and Grand Duchy in a federation.
SIXTEENTH CENTURY	
1569	Union of Lublin unites Poland and Lithuania into a single state, the Polish-Lithuanian Commonwealth.
1596	Union of Brest unites Roman Catholic Church with the part of the Orthodox Church existing within Polish-Lithuanian Commonwealth.
EIGHTEENTH CENTURY	
1772, 1793, and 1795	Russia, Prussia, and Austria carry out three partitions of Poland. Belorussia, formerly part of Poland, now almost entirely within Russian Empire.
NINETEENTH CENTURY	
1839	Tsar Nicholas I abolishes Uniate Church and forces Uniates (three-quarters of Belorussians are members of Uniate Church at this time) to reconvert to Orthodoxy; bans use of name "Belorussia," replacing it with name "Northwest Territory," and bans Belorussian language.
1861	Serfdom is abolished in Russian Empire.
1863	Kastus' Kalinowski inspires uprising in Belorussia in support of Polish-Lithuanian insurrection against Russia. Insurrection fails, and Polish territories are absorbed into Russian Empire.
1864	Kalinowski, considered founding father of Belorussian nationalism, is hanged in Vilnius.
TWENTIETH CENTURY	
1905–18	Ban on Belorussian language is lifted; Belorussian culture flourishes; period of *nashaniwsta*.

Chronology of Important Events

Period	Description
1918 March	Treaty of Brest-Litovsk is signed, putting most of Belorussia under German control. Central Executive Committee of All-Belarusian Congress (Rada) nullifies treaty and proclaims independence of Belarusian Democratic Republic.
1919 January	Belorussian Soviet Socialist Republic (Belorussian SSR) is established by force of arms.
1921 March	Treaty of Riga divides Belorussia among Poland, Belorussian SSR, and Russia.
1922 December	Belorussian SSR is incorporated into Soviet Union.
1928	Forced collectivization starts.
1935	Belorussians in Poland opposing Polish government's policies on ethnic minorities are placed in concentration camp at Byaroza-Kartuzski.
1941	Nazis create Weissruthenische Generalbezirk (Belorussian Military District) in central part of Belorussia, establish German military regime in eastern part, and parcel out remaining Belorussian territory to Lithuanian and Ukrainian administrative divisions and to East Prussia.
1944 Summer	Red Army "liberates" Belorussian SSR from Nazis; Stalin orders sweeping purges and mass deportations.
1986 April	Chornobyl' nuclear power plant in Ukraine explodes; radiation mainly falls on Belorussian SSR. Secrecy surrounding disaster galvanizes Belorussians to mount protests against Soviet regime.
1988 June	Mass graves of Stalin's victims are found at Kurapaty, near Minsk. Discovery of some 250,000 bodies brings denunciation of old regime and demands for reform.
October	Belarusian Popular Front is formed.
1990 June	Supreme Soviet of Belorussian SSR adopts Declaration of State Sovereignty of the Belarusian Soviet Socialist Republic; Belarusian is declared the official language.
1991 April	Demonstrations are held in several cities over economic and political issues.
August	Coup d'état takes place in Moscow; Estonia, Latvia, and Ukraine declare independence from the Soviet Union.
	Supreme Soviet of Belorussian SSR declares independence on August 25 and changes name of country to Republic of Belarus. Communist Party of Belarus is temporarily suspended.
	Moldovan Parliament bans Communist Party of Moldavia. Moldova declares its complete independence from Soviet Union on August 27 and demands withdrawal of Soviet troops.

Chronology of Important Events

Period	Description
December	Belarus signs Minsk Agreement, establishing Commonwealth of Independent States (CIS).
	Eleven former Soviet republics expand CIS by issuing Alma-Ata Declaration; Minsk becomes headquarters of CIS.
1994 March	Supreme Soviet adopts new constitution; office of president is created.
July	Alyaksandr Lukashyenka is elected president.
1995 May	Parliamentary elections are held; results of two rounds of elections are insufficient to seat new Supreme Soviet.

Country

Formal Name: Republic of Belarus (Ryespublika Byelarus).

Short Form: Belarus.

Term for Citizens: Belarusian(s).

Capital: Minsk.

Date of Independence: August 25, 1991.

Geography

Size: Approximately 207,600 square kilometers.

Topography: Hilly landscape with many lakes and gently sloping ridges created by glaciers in north; low-lying swampy plain in south. One-third of country covered by unpopulated forest tracts. Highest point 346 meters.

Climate: Temperate continental. Average annual precipitation ranges from 550 to 700 millimeters and is sometimes excessive.

Society

Population: 10,404,862 (July 1994 estimate), with average annual growth rate of 0.32 percent.

Ethnic Groups: In 1989 census, 77.8 percent Belorussian, 13.2 percent Russian, 4.1 percent Polish, 2.9 percent Ukrainian, and remainder Lithuanian, Latvian, Tatar, and other.

Languages: Belarusian official language; Russian is language of interethnic communication; languages of minorities protected.

Religion: About 60 percent Orthodox (early 1990s). Other denominations include Roman Catholic, Apostolic Christian, Baptist, Muslim, New Apostolic, Old Believer, Pentecostal,

Seventh-Day Adventist, and Uniate.

Education and Literacy: Compulsory attendance ten years; literacy rate 98 percent (1989).

Health: Health care provided by state, mostly free of charge. System overwhelmed by victims of Chornobyl' accident. Infant mortality rate 18.9 per 1,000 live births (1994). Life expectancy (1994) 66.2 years for males and 75.8 years for females. Modern medical equipment and facilities in short supply. In 1994 about 127 hospital beds and forty-two doctors per 10,000 inhabitants.

Economy

General Character: Extremely centralized. Government efforts to privatize and establish market economy weak.

Gross Domestic Product (GDP): In 1992 about US$30.3 billion; real growth rate –10 percent. Agriculture accounted for 23 percent of GDP, industry for 38 percent, and other sectors for 39 percent.

Agriculture: Mainly state and collective farms; sprinkling of small plots for private household use. Primary crops: fodder, potatoes, wheat, barley, oats, buckwheat, potatoes, flax, and sugar beets. Cattle, hogs, and sheep raised.

Industry: Machine- and instrument-building (especially tractors, large trucks, machine tools, and automation equipment), petrochemicals, plastics, synthetic fibers, fertilizer, processed food, glass, and textiles.

Minerals: Small deposits of iron ore, nonferrous metal ores, dolomite, potash, rock salt, phosphorites, refractory clay, molding sand, sand for glass, and various building materials.

Energy: Primary sources: twenty-two thermal power plants (total capacity 7,033 megawatts), additional small power plants (total capacity 188 megawatts), and nine small hydro-electric power plants (total capacity six megawatts). Country's power grid connected to grids of Lithuania, Russia, Ukraine, and Poland. Almost totally dependent on Russia for oil, coal, and natural gas needed to fuel electric-power generation plants.

Foreign Trade: In 1994 about 84 percent of foreign trade conducted with other members of Commonwealth of Independent States. Imports: natural gas, oil and gas condensate, diesel fuel, mazut, wheat, corn, and sugar. Exports: crude and processed oil, heavy machinery, diesel fuel, mazut, chemical and mineral fertilizers, televisions, trucks, tractors, refrigerators and freezers, meat, and milk.

Fiscal Year: Calendar year.

Currency and Exchange Rate: In March 1995, 11,669 Belarusian rubles per US$1.

Transportation and Telecommunications

Roads: In 1994 estimated at 92,200 kilometers, including 61,000 kilometers of paved surfaces.

Railroads: In 1993 estimated at 5,488 kilometers.

Airports: In 1993, 124 airports, of which fifty-five usable and thirty-one with permanent-surface runways. Main airport in Minsk, Minsk International.

Inland Waterways: Extensive and widely used canal and river systems, especially Dnyapro River and its tributaries and Dnyaprowska-Buhski Canal connecting Buh and Prypyats' rivers. Homyel', Babruysk, Barysaw, and Pinsk major river ports. In 1991 some 800,000 passengers and 18.6 million tons of freight carried. No direct access to sea, but relatively close to Baltic Sea ports. Agreement with Poland to use port of Gdynia.

Telecommunications: In 1994 five television channels: two Belarusian (one state-owned, one private) and three Russian. No cable service available. More than thirty-five AM radio stations in seventeen cities; more than eighteen FM radio stations in eighteen cities.

Government and Politics

Government: Democracy, with president and unicameral legislature, Supreme Soviet, both popularly elected. Government composed of president and Cabinet of Ministers.

Procuracy headed by procurator general. New constitution adopted March 28, 1994; went into effect March 30, 1994.

Politics: Political parties and movements generally quite small. Include Belarusian Popular Front, Party of Communists of Belarus, Communist Party of Belarus, United Democratic Party of Belarus, Belarusian Social Democratic Assembly (Hramada), Belarusian Peasant Party, Belarusian Christian Democratic Union, "Belaya Rus'" Slavic Council, and other parties.

Foreign Relations: Recognized by more than 100 countries (late 1992), nearly seventy of which had some level of diplomatic relations. Recognized by United States on December 26, 1991. Belarusian diplomatic presence abroad limited. Relations with Russia overshadow domestic and foreign policy. Relations with Ukraine weak. Relations with Poland, Lithuania, and Latvia friendly.

International Agreements and Memberships: Member of United Nations (founding member), World Bank, International Monetary Fund, Commonwealth of Independent States, Organization for Security and Cooperation in Europe (until January 1995 known as Conference on Security and Cooperation in Europe), North Atlantic Cooperation Council, European Bank for Reconstruction and Development, and General Agreement on Tariffs and Trade (observer status). Declared ineligible for membership in Council of Europe because of election laws and practices.

National Security

Armed Forces: Armed forces under Ministry of Defense. In 1994 totaled approximately 92,400: ground forces (52,500), air force (27,600, including air defense), some 11,000 centrally controlled units, and about 1,300 staff. No navy. Reserves of 289,500 (those who had had military service in previous five years). In accordance with stated goal of becoming a neutral state, plans originally called for reducing number of troops by 60 percent from 243,000 in 1993 to 96,000 in 1995; plans for further reduction. Universal conscription for eighteen months.

Major Military Units: In 1994 ground forces consisted of three corps headquarters, two motorized divisions, one airborne division, one artillery division, three mechanized divisions, one airborne brigade, three surface-to-surface missile brigades, two antitank brigades, one special duties brigade, and seven surface-to-air missile brigades. Air force consisted of two interceptor regiments, three strike regiments, and one reconnaissance regiment. Four regiments had 300 helicopters, and one transport regiment had over forty helicopters.

Military Equipment: Arms from former Soviet stocks. Extensive Soviet-era defense industry has been hit severely by decreased availability of materials and external demands.

Internal Security: Border Guards (8,000 in 1995) under control of Ministry of Internal Affairs. Local assets of former Belorussian Soviet Socialist Republic KGB transferred to new government. Name retained.

Russian Troops: In 1993 about 40,000 troops of Russian air force. Scheduled to leave in 1995, but not likely to do so. Russian troops tending remaining strategic nuclear weapons to remain stationed in Belarus until 2020.

Figure 2. Belarus, 1995

SINCE THE LATE NINETEENTH CENTURY, national activists have based their attempts to create an independent Belorussian state on the Belorussian language, which had been kept alive over the centuries mainly by peasants. The stage was set for the emergence of a national consciousness by the industrialization and urbanization of the nineteenth century and by the subsequent publication of literature in the Belorussian language, which was often suppressed by Russian, and later Polish, authorities. It is ironic, then, that the first long-lived Belorussian state entity, the Belorussian Soviet Socialist Republic (Belorussian SSR), was created by outside forces—the Bolshevik (see Glossary) government in Moscow. And it was those same forces, the communists, whose downfall in 1991 precipitated the existence of an independent Belarus. The new nation has since been torn between its desire for independence and a longing for integration with newly independent Russia.

The population of the Belorussian SSR was jolted into national awareness in the late 1980s by the occurrence of one disaster and the discovery of another. The explosion at the Chornobyl' (Chernobyl' in Russian) nuclear power plant in Ukraine not only entailed the physically damaging radiation carried by the winds but also came to represent the toll taken on the country's sense of its ethnic and cultural identity by years of Russification (see Glossary). These two sets of consequences affected both the daily lives of the Belorussians and national politics: how was the country to remedy the damage?

Belarus's other disaster was the discovery in 1988 of mass graves containing victims of the atrocities of the early Soviet dictator, Joseph V. Stalin. Although this discovery angered a broad spectrum of Belorussians, it energized only a small group of activists to try to overcome the country's political apathy. Seeing Stalin's actions as clear proof of Moscow's attempts to eliminate the Belorussian nation, nationalists wished to ensure that such barbarity could not occur again. For them, a strong, independent Belarus was the first step in this direction.

Historical Setting

Early History

Belarus's origins can be traced from the emergence in the

late ninth century A.D. of Kievan Rus', the first East Slavic state. After the death of its ruler, Prince Yaroslav the Wise, in 1054, Kievan Rus' split into a number of principalities, each centered on a city. One, Polatsk (Polotsk in Russian), became the nucleus of modern-day Belarus.

In 1240, after the Tatar overthrow of Kiev, the dominant principality of Kievan Rus', Belarus and part of Ukraine came under the control of Lithuania. The resulting state was called the Grand Duchy of Lithuania, Rus', and Samogitia (see fig. 3). Because territories inhabited by Slavs made up about 90 percent of the Grand Duchy, they exerted a great cultural influence on the new state. Official business was conducted in a Slavic language (a predecessor of both Belarusian and Ukrainian) based on Old Church Slavonic (see Glossary), and the law code was based on that of Kievan Rus'.

Belorussia, Poland, and Catholicism

The Union of Krevo (1385), which joined Poland and the Grand Duchy in a confederation, hinged on the conversion of Lithuania's Grand Duke Jogaila from paganism to Roman Catholicism and his subsequent marriage to twelve-year-old Queen Jadwiga of Poland. Thus he became Wladyslaw II Jagiello, king of Poland. Poland and Lithuania were later united into a single state, the Polish-Lithuanian Commonwealth, by the Union of Lublin (1569).

When Roman Catholicism became the official religion of Lithuania shortly after Jagiello's conversion, the Lithuanian and Belorussian nobilities began converting from Orthodoxy to Catholicism and assimilating Polish culture (including the language), a process accelerated by the Union of Lublin. As a result, the Belorussian peasantry was ruled by those who shared neither its language nor its religion, Orthodoxy.

The Union of Brest (1596), which united the Roman Catholic Church with the part of the Orthodox Church that was within the Polish-Lithuanian Commonwealth, was viewed favorably by both the Polish king, Sigismund III, and a number of Orthodox bishops, clergy, and faithful. The new Uniate Church (see Glossary) acknowledged the supremacy of the Roman Catholic pope and accepted articles of Roman Catholic religious doctrine. In return, the Uniate Church retained its traditional Orthodox rites and customs as well as a measure of autonomy in nondoctrinal matters; it was also given the same rights and privileges as the Roman Catholic Church. However, fear of the new church becoming Latinized and Polonized (see Glossary) caused many of the Orthodox faithful to reject the union, and the Orthodox Church continued to exist alongside the Uniate Church in an often bitter struggle.

In the aftermath of the Union of Brest, both civil and religious authorities persecuted the Orthodox Church and supported the Uniates in their takeover of Orthodox property. Social conditions deteriorated, a large-scale revolt was waged against Polish landowners in 1648–54 (coinciding with the Khmel'nyts'kyi Rebellion in Ukraine), and many Belorussians fled to the Ukrainian steppes (see Glossary) to join the Cossacks (see Glossary). Little economic development took place in Belorussian lands, and the vast majority of the Belorussian population lived on subsistence agriculture.

The Partitions of Poland

Belorussia remained a part of Poland until Russia, Prussia, and Austria carried out the three partitions of Poland in 1772, 1793, and 1795. After the last partition, the entire territory of Belorussia became part of the Russian Empire (see Glossary), with the exception of a small piece of land in the west, which was held by Prussia (see fig. 4). Orthodox Russia tolerated the Uniate Church to a certain degree, but in 1839, at a time when three-quarters of all Belorussians were Uniates, Tsar Nicholas I (with the support of the Russian Orthodox Church) abolished the Uniate Church and forced the Uniates to reconvert to Orthodoxy. He also banned the use of the name "Belorussia," replacing it with the name "Northwest Territory" (Severozapadnyy kray in Russian), and banned the Belorussian language. Overall, the state pursued a policy of Russification.

At the time serfdom was abolished in the Russian Empire in 1861, Belorussia was essentially a nation of peasants and landlords. Although they had their freedom, the peasants had little else: they remained poor and largely landless. The imposition of the Russian language, the Orthodox religion, heavy taxes, and military service lasting twenty-five years made the past under Polish rule seem better than the present under the tsars.

Early Belorussian Nationalism

It was memories of life under Polish rule that Kastus' Kalinowski (1838–64) tried to evoke in his clandestine newspaper *Muzhytskaya prawda* (Peasants' Truth), which he published to inspire an uprising in solidarity with the Polish-Lithuanian

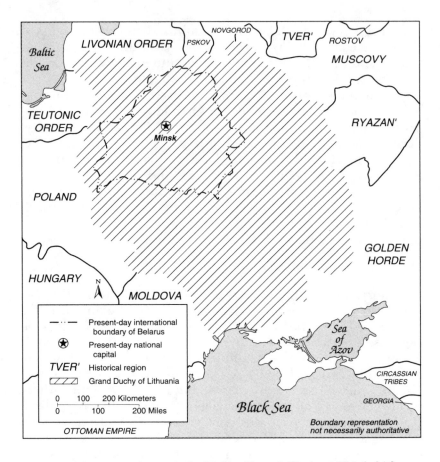

Source: Based on information from Paul Robert Magocsi, *Ukraine: A Historical Atlas*,
Toronto, 1985, 9, 24.

*Figure 3. The Grand Duchy of Lithuania, Rus', and Samogitia at Its
Greatest Extent, Early Fifteenth Century*

insurrection against Russia in January 1863. The insurrection
failed, and the Polish territories and people were absorbed
directly into the Russian Empire. Kalinowski, today considered
the founding father of Belorussian nationalism, was hanged in
Vilnius.

Despite the industrial development that took place in
Belorussia during the 1880s and 1890s, unemployment and
poverty were widespread, giving impetus to large-scale migra-
tions. In the fifty years leading up to the Bolshevik Revolution,
almost 1.5 million persons emigrated from Belorussia to the
United States and to Siberia.

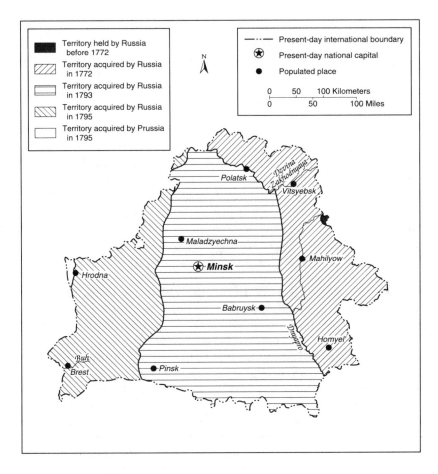

Source: Based on information from Paul Robert Magocsi, *Historical Atlas of East Central Europe*, Seattle, 1993, 71.

Figure 4. Russian and Prussian Acquisitions of Belarusian Territory in the Partitions of Poland, 1772–95

Following the defeat of Russia in the Russo-Japanese War and the Revolution of 1905, strikes and peasant disorders erupted throughout the Russian Empire; to stem the unrest the tsar granted, and then extended, civil liberties. Russian authorities were forced to relax their repressive policies on non-Russian ethnic groups, prompting a national and cultural flowering in Belorussia. The ban on the Belorussian language (and other non-Russian languages) was lifted, although there were still restrictions on its use; education was expanded, and peasants began to attend school for the first time; Belorussian writers published classics of modern Belorussian literature; and the weekly newspaper *Nasha niva* (Our Cornfield), published by the Belorussian Socialist Party, lent the name *nashaniwstva* to this period (1906–18) of Belorussian history.

World War and Revolution

The outbreak of World War I in 1914 turned Belorussia into a zone of strict martial law, military operations, and great destruction. Large German and Russian armies fought fiercely and caused the expulsion or departure of more than 1 million civilians from the country. The Russian government's inept war efforts and ineffective economic policies prompted high food prices, shortages of goods, and many needless deaths in the war. Discontent in the cities and the countryside spread, leading to strikes, riots, and the eventual downfall of the tsarist government.

The two revolutions of 1917—the February Revolution and the Bolshevik Revolution—gave nationally conscious Belorussians an opportunity to advance their political cause. Bolshevism did not have many followers among the natives of Belorussia; instead, local political life was dominated by the Socialist Revolutionary Party, the Mensheviks (see Glossary), the Bund (see Glossary), and various Christian movements in which the clergy of both the Russian Orthodox Church and the Polish Catholic Church played significant roles. The Belorussian political cause was represented by the Belorussian Socialist Party, the Socialist Revolutionary Party, the Leninist Social Democratic Party, and various nationalist groups advocating moderate forms of socialism.

In December 1917, more than 1,900 delegates to the All-Belarusian Congress (Rada) met in Minsk to establish a democratic republican government in Belorussia, but Bolshevik soldiers disbanded the assembly before it had finished its deliberations. The Treaty of Brest-Litovsk in March 1918 put most of Belorussia under German control, but on March 25, 1918, the Central Executive Committee of the Rada nullified the treaty and proclaimed the independence of the Belarusian Democratic Republic. Later that year, the German government, which had guaranteed the new state's independence, collapsed, and the new republic was unable to resist Belorussian Bolsheviks supported by the Bolshevik government in Moscow. The Belorussian Soviet Socialist Republic (Belorussian SSR) was established on January 1, 1919, by force of arms.

For the next two years, Belorussia was a prize in the Polish-Soviet War, a conflict settled by the Treaty of Riga in March 1921. Under the terms of the treaty, Belorussia was divided into three parts: the western portion, which was absorbed into Poland; central Belorussia, which formed the Belorussian SSR; and the eastern portion, which became part of Russia. The Belorussian SSR was incorporated into the Soviet Union (see Glossary) when the Soviet Union was founded in December 1922 (see fig. 5).

The territory of the Belorussian SSR was enlarged in both 1924 and 1926 by the addition of Belorussian ethnographic regions that had become part of Russia under the Treaty of Riga. The area of the republic was expanded from its original post-treaty size of 51,800 square kilometers to 124,320 square kilometers, and the population increased from 1.5 million to almost 5 million persons. Belarus was expanded to its current size of 207,600 square kilometers in 1944.

The New Economic Policy (NEP—see Glossary), established by Vladimir I. Lenin in 1921 as a temporary compromise with capitalism, stimulated economic recovery in the Soviet Union, and by the mid-1920s agricultural and industrial output in Belorussia had reached 1913 levels. Historically, Belorussia had been a country of landlords with large holdings, but after the Bolshevik Revolution, these landlords were replaced by middle-class landholders; farm collectives were practically nonexistent. When forced collectivization (see Glossary) and confiscations began in 1928, there was strong resistance, for which the peasantry paid a high social price: peasants were allowed to starve in some areas, and so-called troublemakers were deported to Siberia. Because peasants slaughtered their livestock rather than turn it over to collective farms (see Glossary), agriculture suffered serious setbacks. However, the rapid industrialization that accompanied forced collectivization enabled the Moscow government to develop new heavy industry in Belorussia quickly.

During the period of the NEP, the Soviet government relaxed its cultural restrictions, and Belorussian language and culture flourished. But in the 1930s, when Stalin was fully in power, Moscow's attitude changed, and it became important to Moscow to bind both Belorussia and its economy as closely to the Soviet Union as possible. Once again, this meant Russification of the people and the culture. The Belorussian language was reformed to bring it closer to the Russian language, and

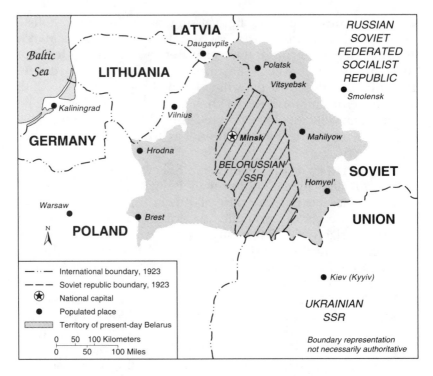

Source: Based on information from Paul Robert Magocsi, *Ukraine: A Historical Atlas*, Toronto, 1985, 9, 24.

Figure 5. Belorussian Soviet Socialist Republic (SSR), 1922

history books were rewritten to show that the Belorussian people had striven to be united with Russia throughout their history. Political persecutions in the 1930s reached massive proportions, causing population losses as great as would occur during World War II—more than 2 million persons.

Belorussian Territory under Poland

Belorussian territory under Poland experienced its own drama. The new Polish state, where ethnic minorities, including Belorussians, Ukrainians, Jews, and Germans, made up one-third of the country's population, began as a democracy. The country's 3.5 million Belorussians were able to open their own primary schools, high schools, and teachers' colleges; the government supported cultural activities; and Belorussians elected three senators and eleven deputies to the Polish parliament, or Sejm, in 1922.

By 1924, however, Poland's policy toward ethnic minorities had changed drastically. Under the guise of combating communism, most Belorussian schools were closed, and publications in the Belorussian language were banned. The government encouraged ethnic Poles (see Glossary) to settle in the Belorussian region, but at the same time it neglected the overall economic development of the area. The Belorussian region became an agricultural appendage to a more industrialized Poland, and unemployment and land hunger were widespread. Between 1925 and 1938, some 78,000 people emigrated from this part of Poland in search of work, mainly to France and Latin America.

In May 1926, war hero Marshal Józef Pilsudski established an authoritarian regime in Poland. The following year, when the Belorussian Peasant-and-Workers' Union spearheaded a widespread protest against the government's oppressive policies in the Belorussian region, the regime arrested and imprisoned the union's activists. Further governmental policies toward the so-called Eastern Territories (the official name for the Belorussian and Ukrainian regions) were aimed at imposing a Polish and Roman Catholic character on the region.

In 1935 Poland declared that it would no longer be bound by the League of Nations treaty on ethnic minorities, arguing that its own laws were adequate. That same year, many Belorussians in Poland who opposed the government's policies were placed in a concentration camp at Byaroza-Kartuzski (Bereza Kartuska in Polish). The Belorussians lost their last seat in the Polish Sejm in the general elections of 1935, and the legislation that guaranteed the right of minority communities to have their own schools was repealed in November 1938. The state then involved itself more deeply in religion by attempting to Polonize the Orthodox Church and subordinate it to the government.

World War II

Germany attacked Poland on September 1, 1939. Two and one-half weeks later, Soviet troops moved into the western portions of Belorussia and Ukraine. Ignorant of, or disbelieving the existence of, mass persecutions under Stalin, most Belorussians hailed the arrival of the Red Army, only to learn quickly of the harsh reality of communism. The flourishing of national culture that the communist party permitted was strictly circumscribed by the party's ideological and political goals. Arrests and deportations were common: about 300,000 persons were deported from western Belorussia to Soviet labor camps between September 1939 and June 1941, when Germany attacked the Soviet Union.

In June 1941, when German tanks swept through Belorussia toward Moscow, many Belorussians actually welcomed the Nazis, thinking that they would free the Belorussian people from their communist oppression. However, the Nazis' designs for the occupied territories became known soon enough: Germanizing and assimilating 25 percent of the Belorussians and either ousting or destroying the remaining 75 percent; parceling out Belorussian territory to the Lithuanian and Ukrainian administrative divisions and to East Prussia, while making the central part of Belorussia the Weissruthenische Generalbezirk (Belorussian Military District); and placing the eastern portion of Belorussia under the German military regime.

Although the front was far to the east, military operations continued within Belorussia. During the three years of Nazi occupation, enormous devastation was caused by guerrilla warfare, retaliatory burnings of entire villages by the occupiers, mass executions of the Jewish population, and two movements of the front through the area. More than 2 million lives were lost and more than 1 million buildings destroyed. An American observer, after six months of travel across Belorussia, called it "the most devastated territory in the world." Major cities, such as Minsk and Vitsyebsk (Vitebsk in Russian), were in ruins.

One of the political consequences of the German occupation was an upsurge of Belorussian nationalism, which the German authorities used for their own ends. Once the Red Army and Soviet administrators fled Belorussia ahead of the Nazis, Belorussians began to organize their own police forces and administration, which the Nazis encouraged. Belorussians living in Belorussia were assisted by Belorussian anticommunist political refugees who were permitted to return from Germany. The Nazis permitted the Union of Belorussian Youth to organize in mid-1943; the Belorussian Central Council (BCC) was formed as a self-governing auxiliary body in December 1943; the BCC mobilized the Belorussian Land Defense in March 1944; and the All-Belorussian Congress was permitted to meet in Minsk to rally resistance to the Russian communists in 1944. However, none of those measures changed the negative attitude of the Belorussians toward the brutal occupation regime.

To counterbalance the Belorussians, the Nazis allowed a number of Russians back from political exile in German-occupied countries in Europe. In addition, they encouraged Poles who had settled in Belorussia during the time of Polish control (and who were frequently at odds with the Belorussians) to become involved in the government.

When the front began moving westward, many Belorussians had to choose between two evils: life with the Soviets or departure into exile. Many Belorussians decided to flee, and tens of thousands of them found themselves in Germany and Austria toward the end of World War II. Some of those who had been deported as forced laborers to Germany agreed to go back to Belorussia, only to be redeported by the communists to Siberia or other remote places in the Soviet Union. All those who fled voluntarily to the West eventually settled in Germany, in other West European countries, or overseas.

Stalin and Russification

The country's misery did not end in the summer of 1944, when the Red Army "liberated" it from the Nazis. Stalin ordered sweeping purges and mass deportations of local administrators and members of the communist party, as well as those who had collaborated with the Nazis in any way, those who had spent the war in slave labor and prison camps in Germany and were now "ideologically contaminated" in Stalin's view, those who were suspected of anti-Soviet sentiments, and those who were accused of "bourgeois nationalism." Only in 1971 did the Belorussian SSR return to its pre-World War II population level, but without its large Jewish populace (see Ethnic Composition, this ch.).

The wartime devastation of Belorussia—the loss of people, homes, animals, public buildings, educational and cultural resources, roads, communications, health care facilities, and the entire industrial base—was complete. To make up for the industrial loss, Stalin ordered the building of new factories and plants, which were more modern and thus more efficient than most of those elsewhere in the Soviet Union.

One of the devices Stalin used to "protect" Belorussia (and the rest of the Soviet Union) against possible Western influences was a program of intensive Russification, thus creating a buffer zone for Russia along the Polish border. Consequently, most key positions in Minsk, as well as in the western provincial cities of Hrodna (Grodno in Russian) and Brest, were filled by

Russians sent from elsewhere in the Soviet Union. The Belorussian language was unofficially banned from use by the government, educational and cultural institutions, and the mass media, and Belorussian national culture was suppressed by Moscow. This so-called cultural cleansing intensified greatly after 1959, when Nikita S. Khrushchev, the leader of the Communist Party of the Soviet Union (CPSU—see Glossary) at the time, pronounced in Minsk, "The sooner we all start speaking Russian, the faster we shall build communism." The resistance of some students, writers, and intellectuals in Minsk during the 1960s and 1970s was met with harassment by the Committee for State Security (KGB—see Glossary) and firing from jobs rather than arrests. Among the best-known dissidents were the writer Vasil' Bykaw, the historian Mykola Prashkovich, and the worker Mikhal Kukabaka, who spent seventeen years in confinement.

The Era of *Perestroika*

The early days of Mikhail S. Gorbachev's *perestroika* (see Glossary) in Belorussia were highlighted by two major events: the Chornobyl' disaster of April 26, 1986 (the Belorussian SSR absorbed 70 percent of the radioactive contaminants spewed out by the reactor), and a December 1986 petition sent by twenty-eight intellectuals to Gorbachev expressing the Belorussian people's fundamental grievances in the field of culture ("a cultural Chornobyl' ").

Whereas the full impact of the physical effects of Chornobyl' was kept secret for more than three years, the "cultural Chornobyl' " became a subject of hot discussion and an inspiration for considerable political activity. The petition pleaded with Gorbachev to prevent the "spiritual extinction" of the Belorussian nation and laid out measures for the introduction of Belarusian as a working language in party, state, and local government bodies and at all levels of education, publishing, mass media, and other fields.

The document embodied the aspirations of a considerable part of the national intelligentsia, who, having received no positive answer from the CPSU leadership either in Moscow or in Minsk, took to the streets. A number of independent youth groups sprang up, many of which embraced the national cause. In July 1988, the Organizational Committee of the Confederation of Belarusian Youth Associations called for "support of the radical restructuring of Belorussia."

In June 1988, mass graves, allegedly with up to 250,000 of Stalin's victims, were found near Minsk at Kurapaty. This sensational discovery fueled denunciations of the old regime and brought demands for reforms. An October demonstration, attended by about 10,000 people and dispersed by riot police, commemorated these victims and expressed support for the Belarusian Popular Front (BPF), which had been formed earlier in the month in hopes of encouraging reform.

The group of activists who called for reform was relatively small; most people, although angry about the mass graves, remained both attached to Soviet ways and politically apathetic, believing that all these public activities would make no difference in the long run. The March 4, 1990, elections to the republic's Supreme Soviet (see Glossary) illustrated the extent of political apathy and ideological inertia. Of the 360 seats in the legislature, fifteen were unfilled (at least eleven remained so more than a year later); of those elected, 86 percent belonged to the Communist Party of Belorussia (CPB). This conservative majority was not alone in slowing the pace of reforms. A majority of the republic's population, 83 percent, also voted conservatively in the March 17 all-union referendum on the preservation of the Soviet Union, even though the Supreme Soviet of the Belorussian SSR adopted the Declaration of State Sovereignty of the Belarusian Soviet Socialist Republic on June 27, 1990 (following the Russian example of some two weeks earlier).

A series of strikes in April 1991 put an end to the republic's reputation as the quietest of the European Soviet republics. The demands were mainly economic (higher wages and cancellation of a new sales tax), but some were also political (resignation of the government and depoliticization of republic institutions). Certain economic demands were met, but the political ones were not. However, increasing dissent within the party led to thirty-three CPB deputies joining the opposition as the Communists for Democracy faction one month later.

Independent Belarus

Following the August 1991 coup d'état (see Glossary) in Moscow and declarations of independence by Estonia, Latvia, and Ukraine, the Supreme Soviet in Minsk declared the independence of Belarus on August 25, 1991, by giving its Declaration of State Sovereignty the status of a constitutional document and renaming the country the Republic of Belarus.

The disorientation that overtook the communists in the wake of the coup was used by liberals and nationalist reformers in various structures to advance their cause: the Supreme Soviet forced the resignation of its chairman, Mikalay Dzyemyantsyey, for siding with the coup leaders and replaced him with his deputy, Stanislaw Shushkyevich; all CPB property was nationalized; the name of the state was officially changed from the Belorussian Soviet Socialist Republic to the Republic of Belarus; and the CPB was temporarily suspended while its role in the coup was investigated.

Shushkyevich's support for the continuation of some kind of union culminated on December 8, 1991, in his signing of the Minsk Agreement (see Appendix B), which established the Commonwealth of Independent States (CIS—see Glossary). On December 21, eleven former Soviet republics expanded the CIS by issuing the Alma-Ata Declaration (see Appendix C). Minsk became the headquarters of the CIS.

After much negotiation and considerable revision, the Supreme Soviet adopted a new constitution, which went into effect on March 30, 1994. The new document created the office of president, declared Belarus a democracy with separation of powers, granted freedom of religion, and proclaimed Belarus's goal of becoming a neutral, nonnuclear state. The winner of the quickly organized election was Alyaksandr Lukashyenka, whose sentiments and policies seemed destined to reunite Belarus with Russia in some way. Treaties were signed with Russia that made political concessions to the latter in hopes of creating economic advantages for Belarus. And there were clashes with parliament over the issue of presidential powers.

In the campaigning for the May 1995 parliamentary elections, continuing censorship of the media's campaign coverage demonstrated the less-than-democratic nature of the state. In response to the lack of information and as a consequence of continued political apathy on the part of the populace, two rounds of elections failed to elect enough deputies to seat a new Supreme Soviet. And Lukashyenka continued to accumulate power through his appointments and dismissals.

Physical Environment

Topography and Drainage

Belarus, a generally flat country (the average elevation is 162 meters above sea level) without natural borders, occupies

Children amusing themselves in a park on a Sunday afternoon, Minsk Courtesy Jim Doran

Young girls in folk costumes Courtesy Anatol Klashchuk

an area of 207,600 square kilometers, or slightly less than the state of Kansas. Its neighbors are Russia to the east and northeast, Latvia to the north, Lithuania to the northwest, Poland to the west, and Ukraine to the south.

Belarus's mostly level terrain is broken up by the Belarusian Range (Byelaruskaya Hrada), a swath of elevated territory composed of individual highlands that runs diagonally through the country from west-southwest to east-northeast. Its highest point is the 346-meter Mount Dzyarzhynskaya (Dzerzhinskaya in Russian), named for Feliks Dzerzhinskiy, head of Russia's security apparatus under Stalin. Northern Belarus has a picturesque, hilly landscape with many lakes and gently sloping ridges created by glacial debris. In the south, about one-third of the republic's territory around the Prypyats' (Pripyat' in Russian) River is taken up by the low-lying swampy plain of the Belarusian Woodland, or Palyessye (Poles'ye in Russian).

Belarus's 3,000 streams and 4,000 lakes are major features of the landscape and are used for floating timber, shipping, and power generation. Major rivers are the west-flowing Dzvina Zakhodnyaya (Zapadnaya Dvina in Russian) and Nyoman (Neman in Russian) rivers and the south-flowing Dnyapro (Dnepr in Russian) with its tributaries, the Byarezina (Berezina in Russian), Sozh, and Prypyats' rivers. The Prypyats' River has served as a bridge between the Dnyapro flowing to Ukraine and the Vistula in Poland since the period of Kievan Rus'. Lake Narach (Naroch' in Russian), the country's largest lake, covers eighty square kilometers.

Nearly one-third of the country is covered with *pushchy* (sing., *pushcha*), large unpopulated tracts of forests. In the north, conifers predominate in forests that also include birch and alder; farther south, other deciduous trees grow. The Belavezhskaya (Belovezhskaya in Russian) Pushcha in the far west is the oldest and most magnificent of the forests; a reservation here shelters animals and birds that became extinct elsewhere long ago. The reservation spills across the border into Poland; both countries administer it jointly.

Climate

Because of the proximity of the Baltic Sea (257 kilometers at the closest point), the country's climate is temperate continental. Winters last between 105 and 145 days, and summers last up to 150 days. The average temperature in January is –6°C, and the average temperature for July is about 18°C, with high humidity. Average annual precipitation ranges from 550 to 700 millimeters and is sometimes excessive.

Environmental Concerns

The most notorious legacy of pollution from the communist era is the April 26, 1986, accident at the Chornobyl' nuclear power plant in Ukraine. Some 70 percent of the radiation spewed was carried by the wind to Belarus, where it affected at least 25 percent of the country—especially Homyel' (Gomel' in Russian) and Mahilyow (Mogilёv in Russian) *voblastsi* (sing., *voblasts'*), or counties, in the south and southeast, and 22 percent of the population. Although more than 2 million people (including 600,000 children) lived in areas affected by fallout from the disaster, the Soviet government tried to cover up the accident until Swedish scientists pressed for an explanation of the unusually high levels of atmospheric radiation in Sweden.

The Belorussian government's request to the Soviet government for a minimum of 17 billion rubles to deal with the consequences was answered with Moscow's offer of only 3 billion rubles. According to one official in 1993, the per capita expenditure on the accident was one kopek in Russia, three kopeks in Ukraine, and one ruble (100 kopeks) in Belarus.

Despite the government's establishment of the State Committee for Chornobyl', the enactment of laws limiting who could stay in contaminated areas, and the institution of a national program for research on the effects, little progress was made in coping with the consequences of the disaster, owing to the lack of money and the government's sluggish attitude. In 1994 a resettlement program for 170,000 residents was woefully underbudgeted and far behind schedule. To assist victims of the Chornobyl' disaster, a Western organization, the Know-How Fund, provided many Belarusian doctors with training in the latest bone-marrow techniques used in Europe and the United States.

The long-range effects of the disaster include an increasing incidence of various kinds of cancer and birth defects. Congenital defects in newborns are reported to be 40 percent higher than before the accident. Tainted water, livestock, farm produce, and land are widespread, and the extensive wetlands retain high concentrations of radiation. Cleanup of the disaster accounted for 14 percent of the state budget in 1995. Other environmental problems include widespread chemical pollution of the soil, which shows excessive pesticide levels, and the industrial pollution found in nearly all the large cities.

Population and Ethnic Composition

Population Characteristics

In July 1994, an estimated 10,404,862 people (fifty persons per square kilometer) lived in Belarus, with additional populations of ethnic Belarusians (see Glossary) living in Poland, Russia, Ukraine, Kazakhstan, Latvia, Lithuania, and Estonia. Ethnic Belarusians in the West (living primarily in Britain, Germany, France, Belgium, the United States, Canada, and Argentina) numbered more than 1 million.

In 1994 the annual population growth rate was estimated at 0.32 percent, resulting from a birth rate of 13.1 births per 1,000 population, a death rate of 11.2 deaths per 1,000 population, and a net migration rate of 1.3 persons per 1,000 population. The birth rate had declined from 15.0 per 1,000 population in 1989, and the death rate had increased from 10.1 (see table 2, Appendix A). The estimated 1994 average life expectancy at birth in Belarus was 66.2 years for males and 75.8 years for females. The annual population growth rate is expected to decrease slowly well into the next century as a result of fears of birth defects caused by the Chornobyl' accident and the difficult economic situation (see The Economy, this ch.).

Population growth in Belarus has declined because of a rapid drop in fertility rates (an estimated 1.9 children per woman in 1994) and because of a sharp increase in infant and child mortality, which had been in decline before the Chornobyl' accident in 1986. Improvements in the infant mortality rate, which was estimated at 18.9 per 1,000 live births in 1994, were further blocked by poor maternal health, poor prenatal care, and frequent use of abortion as a means of birth control. Belarus has instituted a pronatal policy to counteract women's reluctance to have children, but difficult economic conditions and fear of birth defects caused by environmental pollution continue to be major causes of the decline in the birth rate.

Falling birth rates also have contributed to the graying of the population (see fig. 6). This will affect the country in a number of ways, including the allocation of funds from its budget. With fewer workers supporting more pensioners, the administration will be paying more in pensions than it collects in taxes (see Welfare, this ch.).

The population's gender structure was profoundly affected by World War II. The large loss of male lives during the war ensured not only that there would be a surplus of females, but that this surplus would persist for at least another generation.

A law passed in September 1992 gave the entire population of Belarus an automatic right to citizenship. This included all the ethnic Russians (see Glossary) who had moved there over the years, including military personnel and government officials. However, many declined to acquire Belarusian citizenship. As a result, Belarus is sometimes represented abroad or administered by ethnic Russians who are residents, but not citizens, of Belarus.

In 1992 Belarus's largest cities were Minsk, the capital, with 1.7 million inhabitants; Homyel', with 517,000; Vitsyebsk, with 373,000; Mahilyow, with 364,000; Hrodna, with 291,000; and Brest, with 284,000. The republic included more than 100 cities and towns, twelve of which had a population of 100,000 or more. Of the total population, 68 percent lived in cities and 32 percent lived in rural areas in 1994. These figures resemble those for the former Soviet Union as a whole.

Ethnic Composition

The 1989 census of the Soviet Union, its last, showed a mainly Slavic population in Belorussia: Belorussians (77.8 percent), Russians (13.2 percent), Poles (4.1 percent), Ukrainians (2.9 percent), and others (2.0 percent). Other ethnic groups included Lithuanians, Latvians, and Tatars. A large number of Russians immigrated to the Belorussian SSR immediately after World War II to make up for the local labor shortage, caused in part by Stalin's mass deportations, and to take part in rebuilding the country. Others came as part of Stalin's program of Russification.

There has been little conflict with the major non-Belarusian group, the Russians, who account for about 13 percent of the population. The Russification campaign in what is now Belarus used a mixture of subtle and overt coercion. The campaign was widely successful, to the extent that Russian became the language of choice for much of the population. One-third of the respondents in a 1992 poll said they consider Russian and Belarusian history to be one and the same. A large number of

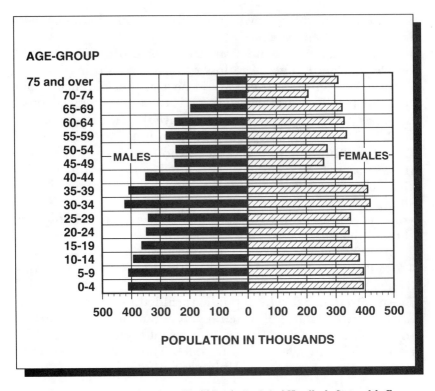

Source: Based on information from World Bank, *Statistical Handbook: States of the Former USSR*, Washington, 1992, 83.

Figure 6. Population of Belarus by Age and Gender, 1990

organized Russian cultural bodies and publications exist in Belarus.

Ethnic Poles, who account for some 4 percent of the population, live in the western part of the country, near the Polish border. They have retained their traditions and their Roman Catholic religion, and this practice has been the cause of friction with Orthodox Belarusians, who also see a decidedly political bent to these cultural activities (see Religion, this ch.).

Ukrainians account for approximately 3 percent of the population. Belarusians and Ukrainians have been on basically friendly terms and have faced similar problems in trying to maintain their ethnic and cultural identities in the face of Russification by Moscow.

Jews have been present in Belarus since medieval times, but by the late eighteenth century they were restricted to the Pale of Settlement and later to cities and towns within the Pale (see Ethnic Composition, ch. 2). Before World War II, Jews were the second largest ethnic group in Belorussia, accounting for more than 50 percent of the population in cities and towns. The 1989 Soviet census showed that Jews made up only 1.1 percent of the population as the result of genocide during World War II and subsequent emigration.

Language, Religion, and Culture

Language

"Language is not only a means of communication, but also the soul of a nation, the foundation and the most important part of its culture." So begins the January 1990 Law About Languages in the Belorussian SSR, which made Belarusian the sole official language of the republic.

The Belarusian language is an East Slavic tongue closely related to Russian and Ukrainian, with many loanwords from Polish (a West Slavic language) and more recently from Russian (see fig. 7). The standard literary language, first codified in 1918, is based on the dialect spoken in the central part of the country and is written in the Cyrillic alphabet (see Glossary). Under Polish influence, a parallel Latin alphabet (*lacinka*) was used by some writers in the eighteenth and nineteenth centuries and is still used today by some Roman Catholics in Belarus and abroad.

One early proponent of the Belorussian language, poet Frantsishak Bahushyevich (1840–1900), the father of modern Belorussian literature and a participant in the 1863 uprising, was inspired by the fact that many 200- and 300-year-old documents written in Belorussian could be read and understood easily in modern times. The concept of the native language as a repository of national identity and an expression of aspiration to nationhood has been the leitmotif of Belorussian literature and polemics beginning in the late nineteenth century.

Although the tsarist government regarded the Belorussians as well as the Ukrainians as another branch of Russians, not as a separate nation, the Belorussian language was registered in the first systematic census of the Russian Empire in 1897. In the early 1920s, Belorussian language and culture flourished, and the language was promoted as the official medium of the communist party and the government as well as of scholarly, scientific, and educational establishments. Most primary and

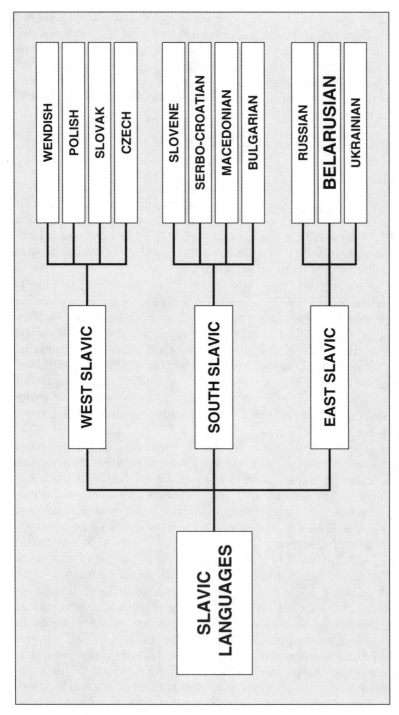

Figure 7. The Belarusian Language in the Family of Slavic Languages

secondary schools switched to instruction in Belorussian, and institutions of higher education gradually made the switch as well. The Belorussian State University was founded in 1921, the Institute of Belorussian Culture was founded in 1922, and a number of other institutions of higher learning also opened. The interests of other minorities in the republic were taken into account in a July 1924 decree that confirmed equal rights for the four principal languages of the republic: Belorussian, Polish, Russian, and Yiddish.

With the advent of *perestroika*, national activists launched a campaign to restore the Belorussian language to the place it had enjoyed during the 1920s. To urge the government to make Belarusian the official language of the republic, the Belarusian Language Society was established in June 1989 with poet-scholar Nil Hilyevich as president.

Belorussia's CPSU leadership, consisting almost exclusively of Russified technocrats, ignored all the government resolutions and decisions on languages. However, it could not ignore the general language trend throughout the non-Russian republics of the Soviet Union, particularly in the neighboring Baltic states and Ukraine, where national movements were stronger and exerted an influence on events in the Belorussian SSR. After months of meetings, rallies, conferences, and heated debates in the press, on January 26, 1990, the Supreme Soviet voted to make Belarusian the official language of the state, effective September 1, 1990. The law included provisions for protecting the languages of minorities and allowed up to ten years to make the transition from Russian to Belarusian.

Despite the provisions, implementation of the law has encountered both active and passive resistance: many people still want their children to be educated in the Russian language rather than in Belarusian, and some government officials agree to give interviews only in Russian. According to data assembled in 1992 by the Sociology Center of the Belarusian State University, some 60 percent of those polled prefer to use Russian in their daily life, 75 percent favor bilingualism in state institutions, and only 17 percent favor having the government declare Belarusian the sole official language. One Western source reported that in the early 1990s, only 11 percent of the population, most of whom lived in the countryside, were fluent in Belarusian.

Since late 1992, there had been a growing demand that the Russian language be given the same official status as Belarusian. The answer to a question of whether Russian should be an official language, one of four questions in a May 1995 referendum, put an end to any uncertainty: the populace voted "yes."

Religion

Before 1917 Belorussia had 2,466 religious congregations, including 1,650 Orthodox, 127 Roman Catholic, 657 Jewish, thirty-two Protestant, and several Muslim communities. Under the communists (who were officially atheists), the activities of these congregations were severely restricted. Many religious congregations were destroyed and their leaders exiled or executed; the remaining congregations were sometimes co-opted by the government for its own ends, as in the effort to instill patriotism during World War II.

In 1993 one Belarusian publication reported the numbers of religious congregations as follows: Orthodox, 787; Roman Catholic, 305; Pentecostal, 170; Baptist, 141; Old Believer (an Orthodox sect; see Glossary), twenty-six; Seventh-Day Adventist, seventeen; Apostolic Christian, nine; Uniate, eight; New Apostolic, eight; Muslim, eight; Jewish, seven; and other, fifteen.

Although the Orthodox Church was devastated during World War II and continued to decline until the early 1980s because of government policies, it underwent a small revival with the onset of *perestroika* and the celebration in 1988 of the 1,000-year anniversary of Christianity in Russia. In 1990 Belorussia was designated an exarchate (see Glossary) of the Russian Orthodox Church, creating the Belarusian Orthodox Church. In the early 1990s, 60 percent of the population identified themselves as Orthodox. The church had one seminary, three convents, and one monastery. A Belarusian theological academy was to be opened in 1995.

Soviet policies toward the Roman Catholic Church were strongly influenced by the Catholics' recognition of an outside authority, the pope, as head of the church, as well as by the close historical ties of the church in Belorussia with Poland. In 1989 the five official Roman Catholic dioceses, which had existed since World War II and had been without a bishop, were reorganized into five dioceses (including 455 parishes) and the archdiocese of Minsk and Mahilyow. In the early 1990s, figures for the Catholic population in Belarus ranged from 8 percent to 20 percent; one estimate identified 25 percent of

*Interior of modern Orthodox
church, Brest
Courtesy John Mumford*

*Religious procession
honoring the icon of the Holy
Mother of God of Zhyrovichy
Courtesy Anatol Klashchuk*

the Catholics as ethnic Poles. The church had one seminary in Belarus.

The revival of religion in Belarus in the postcommunist era brought about a revival of the old historical conflict between Orthodoxy and Roman Catholicism. This religious complexity is compounded by the two denominations' links to institutions outside the republic. The Belarusian Orthodox Church is headed by an ethnic Russian, Metropolitan Filaret, who heads an exarchate of the Moscow Patriarchy of the Russian Orthodox Church. The Roman Catholic archdiocese of Belarus is headed by an ethnic Pole, Archbishop Kazimir Sviontak, who has close ties to the church in Poland. However, despite these ties, Archbishop Sviontak, who had been a prisoner in the Soviet camps and a pastor in Pinsk for many years, has prohibited the display of Polish national symbols in Catholic churches in Belarus.

Fledgling Belarusian religious movements are having difficulties asserting themselves within these two major religious institutions because of the historical practice of preaching in Russian in the Orthodox churches and in Polish in the Catholic churches. Attempts to introduce the Belarusian language into religious life, including the liturgy, also have not met with wide success because of the cultural predominance of Russians and Poles in their respective churches, as well as the low usage of the Belarusian language in everyday life.

To a certain extent, the 1991 declaration of Belarus's independence and the 1990 law making Belarusian the official language of the republic have generated a new attitude toward the Orthodox and Roman Catholic churches. Some religiously uncommitted young people have turned to the Uniate Church in reaction to the resistance of the Orthodox and Roman Catholic hierarchies to accepting the Belarusian language as a medium of communication with their flock. Overall, however, national activists have had little success in trying to generate new interest in the Uniate Church.

The Uniate Church, a branch of which existed in Belarus from 1596 to 1839 and had some three-quarters of the Belarusian population as members when it was abolished, is reputed to have used Belorussian in its liturgy and pastoral work. When the church was reestablished in Belarus in the early 1990s, its adherents advertised it as a "national" church. The modest growth of the Uniate Church was accompanied by heated public debates of both a theological and a political character.

Because the original allegiance of the Uniate Church was clearly to the Polish-Lithuanian Commonwealth, the reestablished church is viewed by some in the Orthodox Church in Belarus with suspicion, as being a vehicle of both Warsaw and the Vatican.

Before World War II, the number of Protestants in Belarus was quite low in comparison with other Christians, but they have shown remarkable growth since then. In 1990 there were more than 350 Protestant congregations in the country.

The first Jewish congregations appeared in Belorussia at the end of the fourteenth century and continued to increase until the genocide of World War II. Mainly urban residents, the country's nearly 1.3 million Jews in 1914 accounted for 50 to 60 percent of the population in cities and towns. The Soviet census of 1989 counted some 142,000 Jews, or 1.1 percent of the population, many of whom have since emigrated. Although Belorussia's boundaries changed from 1914 to 1922, making the area smaller, a significant portion of the decrease in the Jewish population was the result of the war. However, with the new religious freedom, Jewish life in Belarus is experiencing a rebirth. In late 1992, there were nearly seventy Jewish organizations active in Belarus, half of which were republic-wide.

Muslims in Belarus are represented by small communities of ethnic Tatars. Many of these Tatars are descendants of emigrants and prisoners of war who settled in present-day Belarus after the eleventh century. The supreme administration of Muslims in Belarus, abolished in 1939, was reestablished in January 1994.

Culture

Belarusian culture is the product of a millennium of development under the impact of a number of diverse factors. These include the physical environment; the ethnographic background of Belarusians (the merger of Slavic newcomers with Baltic natives); the paganism of the early settlers and their hosts; Byzantine Christianity as a link to the Orthodox religion and its literary tradition; the country's lack of natural borders; the flow of rivers toward both the Black Sea and the Baltic Sea; and the variety of religions in the region (Catholicism, Orthodoxy, Judaism, and Islam).

An early Western influence on Belarusian culture was Magdeburg Law—charters that granted municipal self-rule and were based on the laws of German cities. These charters were granted in the fourteenth and fifteenth centuries by grand dukes and kings to a number of cities, including Brest, Hrodna, Slutsk, and Minsk. The tradition of self-government not only facilitated contacts with Western Europe but also nurtured self-reliance, entrepreneurship, and a sense of civic responsibility.

In 1517–19 Frantsishak Skaryna (ca. 1490–1552) translated the Bible into the vernacular (Old Belorussian). Under the communist regime, Skaryna's work was vastly undervalued, but in independent Belarus he became an inspiration for the emerging national consciousness as much for his advocacy of the Belorussian language as for his humanistic ideas.

From the fourteenth to the seventeenth centuries, when the ideas of humanism, the Renaissance, and the Reformation were alive in Western Europe, these ideas were debated in Belorussia as well because of trade relations there and because of the enrollment of noblemen's and burghers' sons in Western universities. The Reformation and Counter-Reformation also contributed greatly to the flourishing of polemical writings as well as to the spread of printing houses and schools.

During the seventeenth and eighteenth centuries, when Poland and Russia were making deep political and cultural inroads in Belorussia by assimilating the nobility into their respective cultures, the rulers succeeded in associating Belorussian culture primarily with peasant ways, folklore, ethnic dress, and ethnic customs, with an overlay of Christianity. This was the point of departure for some national activists who attempted to attain statehood for their nation in the late nineteenth and early twentieth centuries.

The development of Belorussian literature, spreading the idea of nationhood for the Belorussians, was epitomized by the literary works of Yanka Kupala (1882–1942) and Yakub Kolas (1882–1956). The works of these poets, along with several other outstanding writers, became the classics of modern Belorussian literature. They wrote widely on rural themes (the countryside was where the writers heard the Belorussian language) and modernized the Belorussian literary language, which had been little used since the sixteenth century. Post-independence authors in the 1990s continued to use rural themes widely.

Unlike literature's focus on rural life, other fields of culture—painting, sculpture, music, film, and theater—centered on urban reality, universal concerns, and universal values.

Education, Health, and Welfare

Education

In Belarus education is compulsory for ten years, from ages seven to seventeen. Primary school, generally starting at age seven and lasting for five years, is followed by an additional five years of secondary school. These schools fall into three categories: general, teacher training, and vocational. Institutions of higher education include three universities, four polytechnical institutes, and a number of colleges specializing in agricultural or technical sciences.

In early 1992, some 60 percent of eligible children attended preschool institutions in Belarus. During the 1993–94 school year, Belarus had 1.5 million children in 5,187 primary and secondary schools, 175,400 students in thirty-three institutions of higher education, and 129,200 students in 148 technical colleges. According to the 1989 census, the literacy rate was 98 percent.

During the communist era, education was mainly conducted in the Russian language; by 1987 there were no Belorussian-language schools in any of the republic's urban areas. When Belarusian was adopted as the country's official language in 1990, children were to be taught in Belarusian as early as primary school; Russian language, history, and literature were to be replaced with Belarusian language, history, and literature. However, Russian remains the main language of instruction in both secondary schools and institutions of higher education.

Health

Belarus's health care system is in poor shape and fails to meet the needs of the population, as is common for the former republics of the Soviet Union. The communist era's neglect of this sphere, poorly trained staff, and substandard technology have resulted in a system in which basic medical services are sorely lacking, contributing to the poor health of the population. The added strains of caring for victims of the Chornobyl' accident have overwhelmed the system. In 1994 there were 127 hospital beds and forty-two doctors per 10,000 inhabitants. The country had 131,000 hospital beds at 868 hospitals. The most common causes of death were cardiovascular disease, cancer, accidents, and respiratory disease.

The Republic Center on AIDS was created in 1990 to coordinate all activities for prevention of the human immunodeficiency virus (HIV) and control of acquired immune deficiency syndrome (AIDS). There is mandatory HIV testing of all hospital inpatients and extensive testing of high-risk populations, such as homosexuals, prostitutes, and prisoners. By the end of 1991, seventy cases of HIV-positive individuals were identified, forty of whom were foreigners. However, because HIV testing kits (as well as other medical supplies) had been supplied by Moscow before the breakup of the Soviet Union, there was doubt as to whether testing could continue at the same level.

Welfare

Belarus's social safety net, largely a continuation of what existed in the former Soviet Union, is based on a guarantee of employment and a number of allowances and benefits for particular needs. Benefits were indexed to inflation in January 1991 (benefits are adjusted at the same rate as the minimum wage), and the system was expanded in 1991–92, partly to alleviate the social costs of switching to a market economy. The safety net had been a growing concern to the government because in the early 1990s it accounted for a large share of general government expenditures. Benefits were funded either directly by the budget or by two major social funds.

The government's greatest social expenditures are for pensions. The relatively low retirement age (fifty-five for women and sixty for men) and the country's demographic structure account for the large number of pensioners. In January 1992, the minimum pension was raised to 350 Belarusian rubles (for value of the Belarusian ruble—see Glossary) per month, the same as the minimum wage. The Pension Law of January 1993 based pensions on income earned at the time of retirement and on length of employment; the pensions of those who did not contribute to the Pension Fund during their years of employment are linked to the minimum wage. In January 1994, Belarus had nearly 2 million old-age pensioners and 600,000 persons receiving other types of pensions.

Legislation passed in late 1992 permits families to receive allowances for children above age three only if they meet certain eligibility requirements based on income. Previously, families with children up to sixteen years of age (eighteen years of age for those in secondary schools) had automatically received allowances based on the minimum wage. The program has

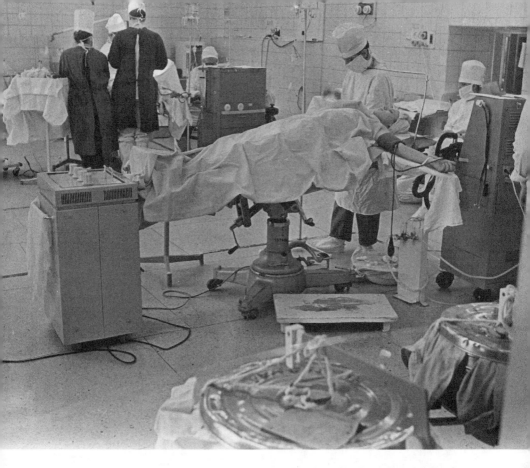

Doctors operating at a specialized medical institute, Minsk
Courtesy Anatol Klashchuk

been hampered by problems in testing for eligibility, however, because of difficulties in assessing income and because of tax evasion by the self-employed.

Unemployment compensation is provided for six months. Benefits are related to earnings for those who work for more than a year and also work continuously for the twelve weeks before separation. For those who work less than a year, benefits are tied to the minimum wage. Because the eligibility criteria for unemployment benefits are quite stringent, half of the registered unemployed are without benefits. In February 1995, some 52 percent of the unemployed received unemployment compensation. In early 1995, women accounted for more than 62 percent of the unemployed.

The government provides a number of other benefits, including lump-sum grants upon the birth of each child; temporary disability allowances; treatment at sanatoria, spas, vacation resorts, and other facilities; and benefits for victims of the Chornobyl' disaster.

Housing

In Belarus about 75 percent of urban housing and many village homes were destroyed during World War II, forcing many people to live in makeshift huts and hovels while housing (along with industrial and public buildings) was reconstructed after the war. This chronic housing shortage was recently exacerbated by the need to resettle Chornobyl' victims. In 1993 per capita housing space was approximately nineteen square meters (slightly less in urban areas), small by Western standards. As is true for most of the former Soviet Union, much of Belarus's urban housing stock consists of drab multistory, prefabricated units. The norm for rural housing is individual homes, which tend to be of a higher quality.

In July 1992, the Law on Privatization of Housing was passed, but little progress was made until mid-1993, when amendments were made to the laws to reassess housing values. Plans called for citizens to receive housing vouchers, which could not be exchanged for cash. In 1993 private housing accounted for 49 percent of the housing stock in Belarus.

The Economy

Belarus is a graphic example of the problems created when an industrial "colony" becomes independent. The Belorussian SSR had imported the bulk of its raw materials, components, and energy from the Soviet Union and exported most of what it produced (much of it for the military-industrial complex) back to the Soviet Union. The country's economy, which had been integrated into that of the Soviet Union, found itself deprived of most of the essential components it needed to function independently when the Soviet system collapsed.

Independent Belarus's economy, like that of the Belorussian SSR, still relies on inefficient, state-supported, industrial facilities, which are increasingly hampered by their need for fuels whose prices are gradually reaching world levels. The economic recession in Belarus intensified in 1994, leading to Belarus's worst economic year to that point. In 1994 the net material product (NMP—see Glossary) had dropped by 21 percent from 1993 (down by more than one-third from its 1989 level), which was worse than in the two previous years; this

Typical modern rural housing in the village of Morach, Kletsk rayon
Courtesy Anatol Klashchuk
Modern urban housing, Maladzyechna
Courtesy John Mumford

45

decline was felt across the board. Agriculture now accounted for 36 percent of NMP, industry for 44 percent, transportation and communications for 3 percent, construction for 12 percent, and the remaining sectors for 5 percent.

Government Policy

Although the government's stated goals during the first years of independence included promoting a market economy, normalizing monetary circulation, and lowering the country's dependence on monopoly suppliers, these goals were not met. Inflation and depreciation in the exchange rate stemmed from the government's compensation for decreased living standards and lower industrial output through subsidies (rather than changes in the country's economic structure and adoption of market reforms).

The government's economic timidity was prompted not only by the wish to maintain the status quo but also by a fear of the social consequences. Years earlier, calls for political action did not stir the populace, but the populace reacted dramatically to sudden price increases. In April 1991, demonstrations occurred in Minsk, Orsha, and other cities, frightening the government into wage concessions, a slowdown of reforms, and promises not to neglect the "social protection net" so as to avoid a repeat of such economically motivated unrest.

As of mid-1995, the government continued to look for easy solutions to its economic problems. It neglected privatization and price liberalization, instead continuing to increase minimum wages to offset minor price increases and to prop up outdated factories.

Privatization

A conservative parliament and a lack of political will have slowed privatization in Belarus in comparison with other former Soviet republics. Although the Law on Privatization of State Property was approved in January 1993, the Supreme Soviet did not approve the 1993 State Program of Privatization and the Law on Privatization Checks (vouchers) until that summer. By the end of the year, less than 2 percent of all republic assets slated for privatization had actually been transferred to the private sector. To speed the pace of privatization, the State Committee on Privatization was converted into a ministry with an expanded staff in March 1994.

The State Program of Privatization calls for two-thirds of state enterprises (see Glossary) to be privatized during 1993–2000. Exemptions include defense-related industries, monopolies (such as utilities), and specialized enterprises working with gems and precious metals. Enterprises of strategic importance can be privatized only with the approval of the Cabinet of Ministers, and agricultural monopolies can be privatized only with the approval of the Anti-Monopoly Committee.

According to the privatization law, 50 percent of each entity slated for privatization will be distributed to the populace via vouchers, and 50 percent will be sold for cash; the prices of the entities will be adjusted for inflation. (There are separate vouchers for housing and property.) Every citizen was eligible to apply for privatization vouchers and to open a voucher account at the Savings Bank (Sbyerbank) as of April 1, 1994. The entitlement is twenty property vouchers per citizen plus one voucher for each year worked, with additional allocations for orphans, the disabled, and war veterans. All vouchers are scheduled to be distributed by January 1, 1996.

In 1995 the practice was quite different from the theory. Privatization of large firms, delayed by the government under various pretexts, had not even started. (Much resistance to privatization also came from factory managers and politicians, particularly at the local level.) At best, some 10 percent of state enterprises had been privatized. Privatization plans for 1995 call for another 500 state-owned enterprises (4 percent of the total) to be privatized.

Agriculture

In 1993 agriculture and forestry accounted for almost one-quarter of the gross domestic product (GDP—see Glossary) and almost 6 percent of the total agricultural output of the former Soviet Union (Belarus has 4 percent of the former Soviet labor force). Agriculture employed 20 percent of the labor force.

During the Soviet era, agriculture in Belarus consisted mainly of state and collective farms, with a sprinkling of small plots for private household use. In the early 1990s, the government based its agricultural policies on that legacy. Instead of disrupting the production of food for both domestic consumption and export, the authorities decided to maintain the large-scale farming for which they believed the existing equipment and capital stock were best suited. In 1994 the Ministry of Agri-

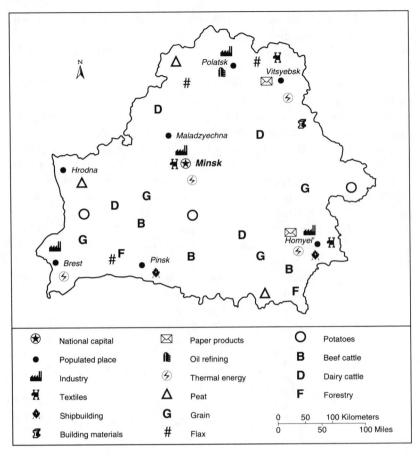

Source: Based on information from Lerner Publications Company, Geography
Department, *Belarus*, Minneapolis, 1993, 46.

Figure 8. Economic Activity in Belarus, 1995

culture planned to transform collective and state farms (see
Glossary) into joint-stock companies that would be agricultur-
ally efficient and would keep providing most of the social services in rural areas.

In March 1993, Belarus added the Law on the Right to Land
Ownership to its Land Lease Law (March 1990). The law on
land ownership limited purchases to small parcels for housing
and orchards, stated that farming would depend on leased
land, and allowed private farmers to lease only up to fifty hectares on long-term leases. This law meant that Belarus would
not develop a private farming sector and that farming would

stay in the hands of the government, which owned the collective and state farms.

In 1993 private agriculture accounted for 37 percent of all agricultural output, reflecting the increase in the number of private farms from eighty-four in 1990 to 2,730 in 1993. However, the average size of private farms remained small: twenty-one hectares in 1993, compared with 3,114 hectares on average for collective farms and 3,052 hectares for state farms. In addition, private plots on large farms in rural areas and garden plots in urban areas continue to provide a significant amount of food, just as they did in the Soviet era.

Belarus can be divided into three agricultural regions: north (growing mainly flax, fodder, grasses, and cattle), central (potatoes and pigs), and south (pastureland, hemp, and cattle). Belarus's cool climate and dense soil are well suited to fodder crops, which support herds of cattle and pigs, and temperate-zone crops (wheat, barley, oats, buckwheat, potatoes, flax, and sugar beets). Belarus's soils are generally fertile, especially in the river valleys, except in the southern marshy regions (see fig. 8).

Despite the progress made by the agricultural sector in 1993, it suffered a setback in 1994. A drought during the summer contributed to a decline of 19 percent in the Belarusian crop. Wheat production declined 35 percent from the previous year, while sugar beet production declined 31 percent and potato production declined 29 percent. Animal products declined 11 percent; the number of cows decreased 2 percent, and the number of sheep declined 30 percent.

The greatest changes in agriculture in the first half of the 1990s were a decline in the amount of land under cultivation and a significant shift from livestock to crop production—because crops had become much more profitable than before (see table 3, Appendix A). The sales price for crops generally increased more than production costs, while inputs for livestock (such as imported fodder) increased in price beyond livestock sales prices. Many private farms faced difficulties, caused partly by inflation, which wreaked havoc on preset contract prices, delayed payments, and budget subsidies.

In early 1993, Belarus's government replaced the system of "recommended" agricultural producer prices with "support" prices, which were intended as minimum guaranteed prices and could be adjusted in accord with price increases in agricultural inputs. Meat prices were deregulated in the summer of

1993, and direct budgetary subsidies were no longer provided to the agriculture sector at all.

Basic foods were watched closely, however, and sometimes "re-protected." For example, prices were reset on rationed sugar in February 1994 in response to a sharp increase in its market price. Another problem was lower food prices in Belarus than in neighboring countries; the government maintained subsidies on food to keep prices low for the people of Belarus. Nonetheless, these subsidies strained the budget while encouraging increased informal exports of food, or "food tourism," from neighboring countries.

Because the agricultural sector is in critical condition, partly the consequence of a drought in the summer of 1994 that reduced agricultural output by nearly 25 percent, the government gave agriculture a special place in the 1995 budget. President Lukashyenka gave collective and state farms credits totaling 520 million rubles to facilitate sowing and to purchase fertilizer. In addition, by implementing sizable price increases for dairy products, pork products, and beef, the government hoped to increase production of these commodities.

Forests cover nearly one-third of Belarus and are the source of raw materials for production of matches, pressboard, plywood, furniture, timbers for coal mines, paper, paperboard, and sections of prefabricated houses. However, during the Soviet era, Belarus's forests were poorly managed and were logged faster than they were replanted. In 1991 the country produced 6.7 million cubic meters of timber.

An ongoing problem facing agriculture is soil depletion, because of a severe fertilizer shortage, and a serious lack of equipment. For many farmers, the answer to the latter, as well as to the cost and shortage of fuel, is a return to horse-drawn ploughs.

The main enduring problem affecting the agricultural and forestry sector is the Chornobyl' disaster of 1986. Belarus absorbed the bulk of the radioactive fallout from the explosion because of weather conditions on the day of the disaster. Long-term radiation affects 18 percent of Belarus's most productive farmland and 20 percent of its forests. Despite the Chornobyl' accident, in 1993 Belarus was still a net exporter of meat, milk, eggs, flour, and potatoes to other former Soviet republics, although its exports were routinely tested for radioactive contamination.

An outdoor flower market at the train station, Minsk
Courtesy Jim Doran
Outdoor market for automobile parts, Minsk
Courtesy Anatol Klashchuk

Industry

In 1985, in the early days of *perestroika,* Belarus specialized mainly in machine building and instrument building (especially tractors, large trucks, machine tools, and automation equipment) and in agricultural production. Because of the vast devastation caused by World War II, the republic's industrial base was of postwar vintage, enabling it to maintain higher labor productivity than many other former republics of the Soviet Union, which were burdened with older, prewar equipment.

In 1992 industry in Belarus accounted for approximately 38 percent of GDP, down from 51 percent in 1991. This figure reflects a decline in the availability of imported inputs (especially crude oil and gas deliveries from Russia), a drop in investments, and decreased demand from Belarus's traditional export markets among the former Soviet republics. Belarus's economy has also been affected by decreased demand for military equipment, traditionally an important sector. Attempts to convert military production to civilian production were largely unsuccessful as of 1995.

By 1993 Belarus also produced petrochemicals, plastics, synthetic fibers, fertilizer, processed food, glass, and textiles (see table 4, Appendix A). Even though Belarus continued its production of electronic instruments and computers, specialties from the communist era, the quality of these goods restricted them mainly for export to former Soviet republics.

In 1994 gross industrial output declined by 19 percent. At the beginning of 1995, every industrial sector had decreased output, including fuel and energy extraction (down by 27 percent); chemical and oil refining (18 percent); ferrous metallurgy (13 percent); machine building and metal working (17 percent); truck production (31 percent); tractor production (48 percent); light industry (33 percent); wood, paper, and pulp production (14 percent); construction materials (32 percent); and consumer goods (16 percent).

Mining

Although not rich in minerals, Belarus has been found to have small deposits of iron ore, nonferrous metal ores, dolomite, potash (for fertilizer production), rock salt, phosphorites, refractory clay, molding sand, sand for glass production, and various building materials. Belarus also has deposits of industrial diamonds, titanium, copper ore, lead, mercury, bauxite, nickel, vanadium, and amber, but little progress has been made in exploiting them.

Energy

Belarus's transition from communism to democracy proved to be more difficult than expected, economically as well as politically. What had once been a boon to industry in the Belorussian SSR—large volumes of inexpensive oil, natural gas, and electricity from the Russian Republic—quickly became a considerable problem for independent Belarus. Under the communist regime, industry had had no incentive to use fuels efficiently, modernize equipment, reduce pollution, maintain factories adequately, recycle, or allot energy resources efficiently. However, once Russian fuel prices began to approach world levels, Belarusian industry had to adjust in order to survive. Logic would seem to call for enterprises to improve their industrial efficiency, but the oil refineries at Navapolatsk (Novopolotsk in Russian) (capacity 22 million tons a year) and Mazyr (Mozyr' in Russian) (capacity 18 million tons a year), as well as many other enterprises, cut their output instead. The 30 percent drop in energy consumption between 1990 and 1993 was the result of a drop in demand for industrial goods produced in Belarus, partly because of the chaotic state of the Soviet economy in the last years of the Soviet Union's existence, and partly because the Soviet Union no longer needed so many goods for its military.

By mid-1993 Belarus's debt to Russia for oil and natural gas had reached US$450 million. After several warnings, Russia temporarily cut off Belarus's supply in August and threatened to do so again on at least two other occasions. In an attempt to head off a crisis, government authorities resorted to allocating energy to priority sectors in 1994.

Russia suspended fuel shipments to Belarus yet again in September 1994 over unpaid fuel bills. This was the impetus for Belarus to sign an agreement giving the Russian state gas company ownership of its Belarusian counterpart, Byeltransgaz, in exchange for the resumption of gas deliveries, but the agreement was not ratified by the Supreme Soviet of Belarus. Byeltransgaz made additional offers of means of repayment, and Russia countered with conditions of its own and hinted that failure to meet these conditions would result in Russia's rerouting of pipelines to Western Europe through either Lithuania or Latvia—a blow to Belarus.

Because delivery of natural gas in 1995 at lower-than-world prices was made contingent on Belarus's timely payment of its bills, Belarus felt the need to diversify its sources of fuels. The government's long-term energy program, in place in early 1995, sought to diversify its sources of fuels from such countries as Poland, Australia, Turkmenistan, and Norway.

In 1993 Belarus imported some 90 percent of its fuel from Russia via the Druzhba (Friendship) oil pipeline and the Northern Lights natural gas pipeline, both of which pass through the country en route to Central Europe. Refineries at Polatsk and Mazyr process some of the crude oil for fuel, and the Polatsk refinery also provides raw material for fertilizer, plastics, and artificial fibers. In 1992 Belarus had 1,470 kilometers of pipeline carrying crude oil, 1,100 kilometers of pipeline carrying refined products, and 1,980 kilometers of pipeline carrying natural gas.

In January 1995, Russia and Belarus signed an agreement under which Russia was to deliver some 66 percent of Belarus's yearly required crude oil at prices that did not exceed domestic Russian prices (which were set to rise significantly over the course of the year). In exchange, Belarus would export products to Russia, although finding enough products that Russia wants could be a problem.

Although Belarus imports most of its fuels, it has small deposits of oil and natural gas close to the Polish border, as well as oil shale, coal, and lignite. Belarus's production of 13 percent (2 million tons) of its crude oil production and 2 percent (2.4 million tons) of its natural gas consumption was stable in 1994.

Belarus also has a large supply of peat (more than one-third of the total for the former Soviet Union), which is used to power industry, heat homes, and fuel boilers at electric power plants. In 1993 thirty-seven factories produced about 2 million tons of peat briquettes.

In 1994 Belarus's twenty-two thermal power plants had a production capacity of 7,033 megawatts and produced 31,400 million kilowatt-hours of electricity. Additional small power plants had a total capacity of 188 megawatts. There were also nine small hydroelectric power plants with a total installed capacity of some six megawatts. All but three plants produced heat as well as electricity.

Harvesting grain on a farm
Courtesy Anatol Klashchuk

The country's power grid is connected to the grids of Lithuania, Russia, Ukraine, and Poland. Most electricity imports come from Lithuania (the Ignalina Nuclear Power Plant) and Russia (the Smolensk Nuclear Power Plant), but even here, Belarus has had problems in paying for its imports. In May 1995, Lithuania resumed electricity exports after more than two years; Belarus agreed to make payment in Russian natural gas.

During the Soviet era, nuclear energy was promoted as an inexpensive source of electricity, but after the Chornobyl' accident, many people in Belarus were opposed to nuclear power. A nuclear power plant was under construction near Minsk in the early 1990s, but the country had no nuclear generating capacity at that time.

Labor Force

The private sector attracted a growing portion of the labor force in 1994, but cooperatives and the state sector continued to account for the bulk of official employment in Belarus. The labor force numbered 4.8 million persons in 1994, or 48 percent of the total population.

A principal reason for Belarus's low official unemployment rate in 1994 (2.2 percent by the end of that year) was underemployment, which had been true during the Soviet era as well (thus keeping down the Soviet unemployment rate). Rather than lay off employees, enterprises often shortened work hours, reduced wages, and even forced employees to take leave without pay instead. Agreements signed by enterprises, labor unions, and the government in 1993 and 1994 called for avoiding declines in output and employment; in return for keeping the same level of employment, labor unions usually refrained from industrial disruptions. At a time when the cost of living was rising dramatically, the social benefits provided by enterprises also acted as a disincentive for voluntary separations: a low-paying job that provided access to clinics, day care, and inexpensive housing was better than cash unemployment benefits alone.

Banking and Finance

Under the communist regime, the currency of the Soviet Union was the Russian ruble, and the banking system was owned and managed by the central government. Gosbank (Gosudarstvennyy bank—State Bank) was the central bank of the country and its only commercial bank as well. It handled all significant banking transactions, including the issuance and control of currency and credit, management of the gold reserve, and oversight of all transactions among economic enterprises. Gosbank had main offices in each of the republics, and, because the banking system was highly centralized, it played an important role in managing the economy.

After independence, Belarus restructured its banks into a two-tier system consisting of the National Bank of Belarus and thirty-six commercial banks (including seven specialized banks: Byelahraprambank, Byelpromstroybank, Byelarusbank, Byelbiznesbank, Priorbank, Byelvnyeshekonombank, and Sbyerbank) with a total of 525 branches in 1994. Of these banks, Sbyerbank is wholly state owned, another bank is owned by an individual, and the rest are organized as either limited liability companies or joint-stock companies.

Belarus's securities market was created at the end of 1992 and is licensed and controlled by the state inspectorate for securities and the stock exchange. The over-the-counter market dominates the securities market, with Russian corporate shares and bonds the most actively traded items. The country has five commodity and stock exchanges.

The Belarusian ruble was introduced in May 1992 in response to a shortage of Russian rubles with which to pay fuel and other debts to Russia. The *zaychyk* (hare), as the Belarusian ruble is known colloquially, was officially tied to the Russian ruble, but Russia would not accept the new unsecured currency in payment, forcing Belarus to dip into its hard-currency reserves. In September 1993, Belarus and five other CIS countries agreed to create a joint monetary system based on the Russian ruble.

Although Belarus and Russia continued to work at creating a monetary and economic union by signing an April 1994 treaty, only a customs union was actually realized. Moscow postponed implementation of the union itself, although it would have given Moscow significant control over the Belarusian economy, for fear of jeopardizing its own fragile economic reforms. Belarus's completely unreformed economy and accompanying high rate of inflation would have forced Russia to print large amounts of money to keep the Belarusian economy going, thereby fueling inflation in Russia.

In early 1995, Belarus's monetary policy was so loose that the National Bank of Belarus came under fire from the International Monetary Fund (IMF—see Glossary) when it lowered the country's key financing rate despite the country's high level of inflation. Belarus was in danger of jeopardizing other IMF loans by its actions. Despite the logic of the IMF's reasoning, President Lukashyenka's view of these difficulties is that they were the result of the IMF's dislike of Belarus's close relationship with Russia.

In November 1994, the Supreme Soviet declared that the country's sole legal tender would be the Belarusian ruble as of January 1, 1995, when the Russian ruble could no longer be circulated. Although the *zaychyk* was convertible, the National Bank of Belarus used multiple exchange rates that depended on the nature of the transaction, thus setting limits on the convertibility of the *zaychyk*.

The government's lax monetary policy failed to support financial discipline, which caused the average monthly inflation rate in 1993 to increase to 45 percent in the last quarter. Even though monthly inflation was down to 10 percent by March 1994, it rose again in 1994 and frightened off investments from abroad, including Russia. The consumer price index rose by 1,070 percent in 1992, by 1,290 percent in 1993, and by 2,221 percent in 1994. In 1995 inflation seemed to abate somewhat, with the average monthly inflation rate of "only" 22 percent through April.

Transportation and Telecommunications

In the former Soviet Union, the central government owned and operated the transportation system of the Belorussian SSR and used it primarily to serve the economic needs of the entire country as determined by the CPSU. Because of the Belorussian SSR's generally flat landscape and its location, building a transportation system there did not entail the difficulties of building on rugged terrain, over permafrost, or in remote areas far from industrial centers.

Railroads were the premier mode of transportation in the Belorussian SSR. Minsk is a major railroad junction, located on the lines connecting the Baltic states with Ukraine to the south and the line connecting Moscow with Warsaw to the west (see fig. 9). In 1993 Belarus had a total of 5,488 kilometers of 1,520-millimeter-gauge railroads; of these, 873 kilometers were electrified. Minsk also has an underground Metro with eighteen stations on two lines (totaling seventeen kilometers).

Belarus's railroads accelerated industrial development and, in wartime, played a significant military role. Well developed compared with those in the other former Soviet republics, the country's railroads continued to play a major role in the early years of independent Belarus. They moved raw materials, manufactured goods, and passengers over long hauls, transporting 30 percent of the country's bulk cargo and 10 percent of its passengers in 1992.

Rail freight transport declined from 71.5 million tons in 1993 to 50.1 million tons in 1994 (see table 5, Appendix A). This drop approximated the decline in gross industrial output over the same period (unlike previous years, when it had been greater). As a result, experts believed that gross inefficiencies of the past had been eliminated and that railroad transportation would not be a bottleneck in the future when industrial output rose.

Because automotive transport is generally not used for long hauls, many roads outside urban areas have gravel or dirt surfaces, especially in the more remote rural areas. The lack of paved roads in these rural areas seriously hampers the movement of agricultural products and supplies. Privately owned automobiles are relatively few per capita and thus have been of limited importance in transportation, although this began to change slowly with the demise of communism. At the beginning of 1994, the country had 92,200 kilometers of roads, two-thirds of which were paved, and many of which were deteriorating. There were no expressways or major national highways. Truck transport of freight declined in 1994 by 41 percent to 122.8 million tons.

In 1994 Belarus received funds and promises of funds from the European Union (EU—see Glossary), Russia, Germany, and Poland to upgrade road and railroad links between Moscow and Berlin. A project funded jointly by Belarus and the European Bank for Reconstruction and Development (EBRD) will upgrade segments of the highway that links Poland to Russia through Belarus.

Belarus has extensive and widely used canal and river systems, especially the Dnyapro River and its tributaries and the Dnyaprowska-Buhski Canal, which connects the Buh (Bug in Russian) and Prypyats' rivers. Homyel', Babruysk (Bobruysk in Russian), Barysaw (Borisov in Russian), and Pinsk are major river ports. In 1991 some 800,000 passengers and 18.6 million tons of freight were carried on the country's inland waterways.

Figure 9. Transportation System of Belarus, 1995

Although Belarus has no direct access to the sea, it is relatively close to Baltic Sea ports and has an agreement with Poland to transport Belarusian goods to the Polish port of Gdynia and to use the port itself. In addition, in 1995 Lithuanian officials were considering giving Belarus access to the Lithuanian port of Klaipeda.

Of Belarus's 124 airports, only fifty-five were usable in 1993, and only thirty-one had permanent-surface runways. Minsk has one airport, Minsk International Airport. In 1994 Belavia, the Belarusian state airline, planned to use US$80 million of a US$220 million credit from Switzerland to build an aircraft service center at the airport.

At the beginning of 1992, Belarus had 1.9 million telephone lines, or about eighteen lines per 100 persons; more than 700,000 applications for household telephones were still pending. Only about 15 percent of the telephone lines were switched automatically. Connections to other former Soviet republics are by landline or microwave, and connections to other countries are by means of a leased connection through the Moscow international gateway switch. An NMT–450 analog cellular telecommunications network was under construction in Minsk in the early 1990s, and approximately 300 kilometers of fiber-optic cable were being added to the city network. Progress in establishing an International Telecommunications Satellite Organization (Intelsat) earth station was slow.

In 1993 four television channels were available in Belarus: Belarus's single state-run television station (Byelaruskaye telyebachannye) and three Russian television stations—Televideniye Ostankino (Ostankino Television, Channel 1), Rossiyskoye televideniye (Russian Television), and Sankt-Peterburg TV (St. Petersburg TV). By 1994 there was one private television station, the Minsk Television Company; its license was suspended during the parliamentary elections of 1994. No cable television service was available. In 1992 an estimated 3.5 million televisions were in use in Belarus.

In 1994 Belarus's state-run radio (Byelaruskaye radyyo) broadcast two national programs, four Russian programs, and various regional programs over thirty-five AM radio stations in seventeen cities and over eighteen FM radio stations in eighteen cities. There was also a shared relay with Voice of Russia. International shortwave radio service broadcasts were in Belarusian, English, German, and Polish. In 1992 an estimated 3.1 million radios were in use in Belarus.

In 1995 the government continued to control television and radio broadcasting in Belarus. In April 1995, when opposition deputies to the Supreme Soviet clashed with President Lukashyenka over questions on the upcoming referendum, Lukashyenka cordoned off the national television and radio building (because of an alleged bomb threat). In the period before voting on both the referendum and parliamentary elections, discussion of the issues disappeared from the media.

Foreign Economic Relations

By mid-1995 Belarus still relied primarily on Russia and other members of the CIS as its primary trading partners (see table 6, Appendix A). But it had started looking to expand its economic ties beyond the CIS. It turned to the EU, with which it signed an agreement with the goal of gradual economic integration of Belarus into the EU, as well as to markets in the east, where it was better able to compete. An example of the latter was Belarus's trade of farm machinery and chemical fibers for Iranian oil in March 1995.

Although the total volume of Belarus's foreign trade declined by nearly one-third in 1994, the proportion of its trade with non-CIS countries increased. Belarus's lack of domestic economic reform, however, has slowed down efforts to improve and expand its foreign economic relations.

In January 1995, Belarus signed a number of agreements in hopes that they would improve its access to foreign markets: trade barriers were lowered between Russia and Belarus, and Kazakhstan joined the agreement to create a free-trade area (however, implementation of the accord was slow). Belarus and the EU signed an agreement to create a free-trade zone between the EU and Belarus. Under its terms, all quantitative limits on imports from Belarus to the EU will be abolished.

Exports

Under communism, the Belorussian SSR had net industrial and agricultural export surpluses within the Soviet Union until 1990, thanks to the relatively high productivity of the Belorussian labor force. The Belorussian SSR shipped trucks, tractors, tractor trailers, elevators, lathes, bearings, electric motors, computer equipment, synthetic yarns and fibers, tires, linoleum, flax, textiles, carpets, potatoes, meat, dairy products, eggs, flour, and various consumer goods to the other republics.

Apart from Belarus's energy situation, little had changed in the direction of independent Belarus's trade from its previous centralized planning system. In 1994 Belarus's major trading partners were still former Soviet republics (mainly Russia, Ukraine, Kazakhstan, Moldova, Lithuania, and Latvia), which accounted for 93 percent of its exports. Exports to these countries totaled approximately US$2.5 billion, a decrease of 36 percent by volume over the previous year. Exports included gasoline (198,000 tons), diesel fuel (147,000 tons), meat and meat products (53,000 tons), milk and milk products (256,000 tons), refrigerators, tractors, and trucks. Belarus had a trade deficit with CIS countries amounting to US$614 million in 1994.

Belarus's main non-CIS trading partners in 1994 were Germany (21 percent of non-CIS trade), Poland (9 percent), the United States (7 percent), Switzerland (4 percent), Austria (4 percent), Italy (3 percent), the Netherlands (3 percent), Hungary (3 percent), China (3 percent), Brazil (3 percent), Britain (2 percent), and Lithuania (2 percent). Exports to non-CIS countries consisted mainly of energy products and heavy machinery. Belarus had a trade surplus of US$434 million with non-CIS countries in 1994.

After independence and continuing into 1995, Belarus's trade deteriorated because import prices for energy and raw materials began to rise to world market levels, and demand for the country's exports by its major trading partners (especially Ukraine and Russia) declined. Payment problems within the former Soviet Union made the situation worse, and limited access to foreign financing caused the domestic economy to decline by further decreasing the volume of trade.

Restrictions on export quantities, imposed by the new government to prevent low-cost Belarusian goods from being sold abroad in large quantities to the detriment of the Belarusian consumer, were relaxed in March 1994, and only certain goods continued to be restricted: oil and gas, electricity, fertilizers, timber and wood products, nonferrous metals, cereals, pharmaceuticals, textiles, and leather. Exports of precious metals and gems had to be licensed by the State Committee on Precious Metals and Precious Stones, and an export ban applied to certain medicinal herbs, animals, and some artworks and antiques. An agreement between Belarus and the EU set export quotas on textiles.

As part of Belarus's pursuit of economic and monetary integration with Russia, interstate trade regulations and taxation were harmonized with those of Russia, and most export and import fees on mutual trade with Russia were abolished by June 1, 1994. In May 1995, Belarus and Russia eliminated customs checkpoints along their common border.

Imports

Both before and after independence, most of Belarus's imports came from Russia (64 percent in 1990) and Ukraine (19 percent in 1990). However, the foreign trade situation worsened for Belarus as the former Soviet Union continued to disintegrate economically. Imports from such countries as Germany, Poland, and the United States increased, so that by 1994 only 76 percent of Belarus's imports came from former Soviet republics. Belarus was now paying higher prices for goods it had previously imported cheaply from former Soviet republics. The greatest drain on its finances now consisted of imports of raw materials and oil, whose prices increased greatly in the early to mid-1990s.

In 1994 Belarus's imports from non-CIS countries decreased by nearly 13 percent from 1993 to US$534 million. Its imports from CIS countries were estimated at US$3.1 billion, a decrease of over 57 percent by volume from the previous year.

In the mid-1990s, Belarus imported oil, natural gas, coal, rolled ferrous metals, nonferrous metals, commercial lumber and sawed timber, chemical products, raw materials for the chemical industry, cement, cotton yarn, silk, machines and equipment, automobiles and buses, sewing machines and washing machines, paper, grain, forage, cooking oil, sugar, tea, fish and fish products, vegetables, and consumer goods. A few items were subject to restrictions for health and security reasons, including chemicals and industrial waste. An improved import tariff structure was introduced in October 1993, partly in line with World Bank (see Glossary) recommendations.

Joint Ventures

A number of foreign companies have set up joint ventures in Belarus to take advantage of its location, its educated (and relatively inexpensive) work force, and its lack of serious ethnic problems. By mid-1995 Belarus had 1,745 joint ventures registered, but only some 30 percent of these were active. Most partners came from Poland, Germany, North America, and Austria. These joint ventures produced only 2 percent of total Belarusian output and employed only 0.4 percent of the total workforce.

Government and Politics

Belarus's declaration of independence on August 25, 1991, did not stem from long-held political aspirations, but rather from reactions to domestic and foreign events. Moscow's slow response to the accident at the Chornobyl' power plant and to the discovery of mass graves of Stalin's victims at Kurapaty led to demands for government accountability and reform. Ukraine's declaration of independence on August 24, in particular, led the Belorussian SSR to realize that the Soviet Union would not last long. Independence nonetheless brought little or no change in the country's political structure.

Prelude to Independence

The series of events that led to Belarus's independence began with the explosion at the Chornobyl' nuclear power plant on April 26, 1986. The foot-dragging of the government in Moscow in even announcing that the accident had occurred, let alone evacuating people from affected areas and providing funds for the cleanup, greatly angered the Belorussian people, most of whom had no political aspirations for independence.

In 1988 Zyanon Paznyak, an archaeologist who would later play a role in national politics, revealed the discovery of mass graves of some 250,000 of Stalin's victims at Kurapaty. Many Belorussians were deeply shaken by this news, and some demanded accountability from the central authorities in Moscow. Reformers created the Belarusian Popular Front (BPF) in October after several mass demonstrations and clashes with the authorities. Paznyak became the spokesman for the reform movement and nationalist aspirations, and he emerged as the BPF chairman.

The March 4, 1990, elections to the republic's Supreme Soviet gave the country a legislature that was little different from previous legislatures: only 10 percent of the deputies were members of the opposition. But for the most part, the populace seemed satisfied with the new deputies, and the BPF's calls for independence and efforts at nation-building failed to stir up the same strong emotions as movements in neighboring Ukraine and the Baltic republics. Although the Supreme Soviet of the Belorussian SSR adopted the Declaration of State Sovereignty of the Belarusian Soviet Socialist Republic on June 27, 1990 (some two weeks after Russia had declared its own sovereignty), the March 1991 referendum held throughout the Soviet Union showed that 83 percent of Belorussians wanted to preserve the Soviet Union.

Political change in the country came about only after the August 1991 coup d'état in Moscow and a display of satisfaction by the Central Committee of the CPB at the coup attempt—it never issued a condemnation of the coup plotters. Following the coup's collapse and declarations of independence by Estonia, Latvia, and Ukraine, Belarus declared its own independence on August 25 by giving its declaration of sovereignty the status of a constitutional document. On August 28, Belarus's prime minister, Vyachaslaw Kyebich, declared that he and his entire cabinet had "suspended" their CPB membership. The next day, both the Russian and the Belarusian governments suspended the activities of the communist party.

Liberals and nationalist reformers used this period of political confusion to advance their cause. On September 18, the parliament dismissed its chairman, Mikalay Dzyemyantsyey, for siding with the coup and replaced him with his deputy, Stanislaw Shushkyevich. The next day, pressed by the small but vocal democratic opposition, the parliament changed the state's name from the Belorussian Soviet Socialist Republic to the Republic of Belarus. A new national flag (three horizontal stripes, white-red-white) was adopted, along with a new coat of arms (a mounted knight, St. George, patron saint of Belarus, with a drawn sword, the emblem of the Grand Duchy of Lithuania, Rus', and Samogitia). On December 8, Belarus joined Russia and Ukraine in signing the Minsk Agreement (see Appendix B) to form the CIS, which formally put an end to the Soviet Union. On December 21, Belarus signed the Alma-Ata Declaration (see Appendix C), which expanded the CIS membership from the original three signatories of the Minsk Agreement to eleven states. And it was agreed that the headquarters of the CIS was to be in Minsk, a move that the government of Belarus welcomed as a means of attracting international attention.

The democratic opposition in the Supreme Soviet, led by the twenty-seven-member BPF faction and some of its allies, continued pressing for a referendum on the dissolution of the Supreme Soviet and for new elections. The electorate seemed to be responsive. More than 442,000 signatures in support of the move were collected within three months, but the initiators had underestimated the conservatism of the Supreme Soviet.

Meeting in mid-October 1992 and encouraged by the electoral victory of former communists in Lithuania and growing resistance to President Boris N. Yeltsin's reforms in Russia, the Supreme Soviet solidly rejected the demand for a referendum. Claiming violations in the signature collection drive, 202 deputies voted against the referendum; only thirty-five deputies supported it, and another thirty-five abstained. In view of the fact that in May 1992 the Central Referendum Commission had validated 384,000 of the 442,000 signatures collected (exceeding the 350,000 signatures required by law), the BPF opposition accused the Supreme Soviet's conservative majority of an open

Interior of metro station, Institute of Belarusian Culture, Minsk
Courtesy Jim Doran

violation of the republic's constitution and of an attempt to retain power by illegal means. Nonetheless, the opposition won a small victory in this tug-of-war: the parliament agreed to shorten its five-year term by one year and scheduled the next elections for the spring of 1994.

The Belarusian government headed by Prime Minister Kyebich consisted of former CPB functionaries and took a very conservative approach to economic and political reforms. Kyebich himself characterized his policy as "traditional" and warned about taking "extreme" positions.

Belarus's conservative Supreme Soviet continued to put obstacles in the path of reform. A privatization law was passed in July 1993, but it allowed collective and state farms to continue to exist and operate. Privatization of state-owned enterprises had barely begun in mid-1995, despite earlier efforts by Shushkyevich, who was largely a figurehead, to move along reform efforts. Conservative Kyebich, who actually controlled the ministries, was a temporary victor when, in January 1994, he survived a no-confidence vote that ousted Shushkyevich and replaced him with a Kyebich crony, Myechyslaw Hryb.

In the meantime, the Supreme Soviet adopted a constitution that went into effect on March 30, 1994, and created the office of president, who would now be the head of government instead of the prime minister. A quickly organized election was held in June, and a runoff election between the two highest vote-getters was held in July; in a surprise result, Kyebich was soundly beaten by anticorruption crusader Alyaksandr Lukashyenka. Both Kyebich and Lukashyenka took pro-Russian stands on economic and political matters, and both supported a quick monetary union with Russia. Lukashyenka even called for outright unification with Russia, but it was his anticorruption stance that won him more than 80 percent of the vote.

After Lukashyenka achieved his victory, the BPF granted him a three-month grace period, during which it did not openly criticize his policies. Because his campaign promises had often been vague, he had great latitude within which to operate. And because Kyebich resigned after the election, taking his government with him, there were no problems in removing ministers.

Lukashyenka's presidency was one of contradictions from the start. His cabinet was composed of young, talented newcomers as well as Kyebich veterans who had not fully supported Kyebich. As a reward to the parliament for confirming his appointees, Lukashyenka supported the move to postpone the parliamentary elections until May 1995.

Lukashyenka's government was also plagued by corrupt members. Lukashyenka fired the minister of defense, the armed forces chief of staff, the head of the Border Guards, and the minister of forestry. Following resignations among reformists in Lukashyenka's cabinet, parliamentary deputy Syarhyey Antonchyk read a report in parliament on December 20, 1994, about corruption in the administration. Although Lukashyenka refused to accept the resignations that followed, the government attempted to censor the report, fueling opposition criticism of Lukashyenka.

Lukashyenka went to Russia in August 1994 on his first official visit abroad as head of state. There he came to realize that Russia would not make any unusual efforts to accommodate Belarus, especially its economic needs. Nevertheless, Lukashyenka kept trying; in February 1995, Belarus signed the Treaty on Friendship and Cooperation with Russia, making many concessions to Russia, such as allowing the stationing of Russian troops in Belarus, in hopes that Russia would return the favor by charging Belarus lower prices for fuels. However, because the treaty included no such provision, there was little hope of realizing this objective.

Lukashyenka had several disputes with parliament, mainly over the limits of presidential power (such as whether the president has the right to dissolve parliament). A hunger strike by opposition deputies, led by Zyanon Paznyak, began on April 11, 1995, after Lukashyenka proposed four questions for a referendum and then stated that the referendum would be held regardless of parliament's vote. The protest ended when the striking deputies, forcibly evicted in the middle of the night during a search for an alleged bomb, found that the national television and radio building had been cordoned off as well because of another alleged bomb threat. After this incident, the parliament gave in on a number of matters, including the four referendum questions, because word of their strike now could not be publicized.

The parliamentary elections held in May 1995 were less than successful or democratic. The restrictions placed on the mass media and on the candidates' expenditures during the campaign led to a shortage of information about the candidates and almost no political debate before the elections. In several cases, no one candidate received the necessary majority of the votes in the May 14 elections, prompting another round on May 28. The main problem in the second round was the lack of voter turnout. After the second round, parliament was in limbo because it had only 120 elected deputies—it was still short of the 174 members necessary to seat a new legislature. Another round of elections was discussed, probably near the end of the year, but the government claimed to have no money to finance them.

Problems of Democratization

Of the 346 seats to the Belorussian Supreme Soviet elected in 1990, fourteen were still vacant three years later, owing to voter apathy. There was also widespread apathy toward the political process and disbelief that what were being advertised as democratic ways would improve the situation. This general political malaise was then, and continued to be in 1995, reflected in the feeble growth, small size, and low popularity of political parties.

Although the 1990 and 1995 parliamentary elections were far from democratic, the predominance of conservatives in the legislature had deeper roots than just the lack of means for free expression and the strictures of the electoral procedure. A widely heard rhetorical question was, "What is more useful, sausage or freedom?" The conservative majority in parliament—largely managers, administrators, and representatives of such groups as war veterans and collective and state farm managers—had successfully slowed the pace of reforms, and the standard of living had decreased dramatically for most of the population.

In view of the tremendous economic difficulties that accompanied the post-Soviet period, the years before *perestroika* looked reasonably good to most citizens. The populace was frustrated by the misuse of a freedom whose benefits were measured predominantly in material terms. Nostalgia for the so-called good old days had been growing stronger ever since the country declared its independence, and the lack of political energy in the country hindered the growth of political parties not tied to the old ways.

An example of political inertia is the debate on relations between Russia and Belarus. This debate has proceeded rather noisily and has been couched in cultural and historical terms, rather than in terms of the state's interests. National interests and foreign affairs are still deemed to be beyond the average citizen's competence, and the idea that the party/government knows best is still prevalent in the popular mind.

The four-question referendum that had prompted the parliamentary hunger strike in April 1994 was held on May 15, 1995. The populace voted "yes" on all four questions: Russian as an official language, the return of a Soviet-era red and green flag, economic integration with Russia, and presidential power to dissolve the Supreme Soviet. The result hardly inspired confidence among aspiring democrats.

Government Structure

The Constitution

A new Belarusian constitution was submitted to the Supreme Soviet in three different versions before it was finally adopted on March 28, 1994, and went into effect on March 30, 1994. The new basic law declares the Republic of Belarus a democracy that operates on the basis of a diversity of political institutions, ideologies, and opinions, with all religions and creeds equal before the law. The official language is Belarusian, although Russian is the language of interethnic communication. Belarus is declared a nuclear-free, neutral state. All persons are equal before the law and are to have their rights, legitimate interests, and freedom protected equally; suffrage is granted to citizens who have reached eighteen years of age. The state also pledges itself to create "the conditions for full employment."

National Government

With the exception of the new office of the president, the government structure of independent Belarus was changed little from that of the Belorussian SSR. Within the government, the communist-era mind-set also persisted, even though the names of office-holders were often different. Because Lukashyenka and the legislature were frequently at odds, there was little agreement on or initiative toward changing or improving the government.

The national government consists of three branches: legislative, executive, and judicial (see fig. 10). Under the constitution, the size of the Supreme Soviet (elected for a term of five years) was reduced from 360 to 260 members. It is the highest legislative body of state power. Its functions include calling national referenda; adopting, revising, and interpreting the constitution; scheduling parliamentary and presidential elections; electing members of high-level courts, the procurator general, and the chairman and members of the board of the National Bank of Belarus; determining guidelines for domestic and foreign policy; confirming the state budget; supervising currency issues; ratifying international treaties; and determining military policy. The role of the Presidium of the Supreme Soviet was reduced to that of an agenda-setting and administrative body. The legislature's two subordinate state committees are the State Customs Committee and the State Security Committee.

Any Belarusian citizen who has the right to vote and is at least twenty-one years old is eligible to stand for election as a deputy. The parliament is elected by universal suffrage.

The president of the republic is elected by popular vote for a five-year term of office and is the head of state and head of the executive branch of government. He adopts measures to guard the country's sovereignty and territorial integrity, appoints and dismisses the prime minister and the members of the Cabinet of Ministers, appoints judges, heads the country's

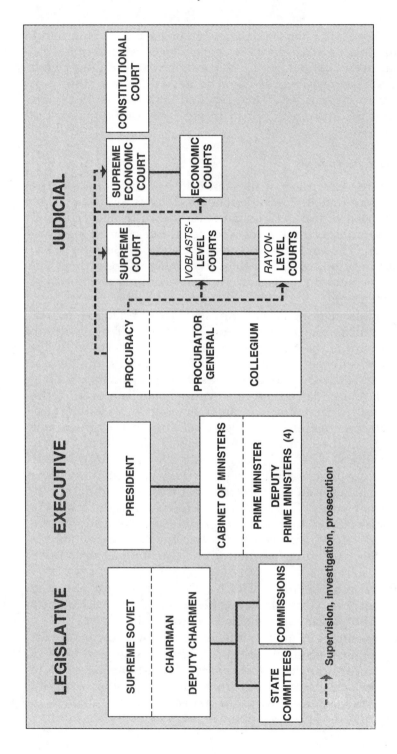

Figure 10. Government Organization of Belarus, 1995

National Security Council, and serves as commander in chief of the armed forces.

The president can be removed by a two-thirds vote in the parliament under certain circumstances, such as violating the constitution or committing a crime. However, the president cannot dismiss the parliament or other elected governing bodies, pending implementation of the referendum on this point.

The executive branch also includes the Cabinet of Ministers, composed of the heads of Belarus's twenty-six ministries: administration of state property and privatization; agriculture; architecture and construction; CIS matters; communications and information; culture and the press; defense; economy; education and science; emergency situations and the protection of the population from the aftermath of the Chornobyl' nuclear power station disaster; finance; foreign affairs; foreign economic relations; forestry; fuel and energy; health care; housing and municipal services; industry; internal affairs; justice; labor; natural resources and environmental protection; social protection; statistics and analyses; trade; and transportation and communications.

Judicial power is vested in a court system that consists of three courts. One court is the Constitutional Court, which consists of eleven judges who are nominated by the president and appointed by the Supreme Soviet. The Constitutional Court receives proposals from the president, the chairman of the Supreme Soviet, the state committees of the Supreme Soviet, at least seventy deputies of the Supreme Soviet, the Supreme Court, the Supreme Economic Court, or the procurator general to review the constitutionality of international agreements or obligations to which Belarus is a party. The Constitutional Court also reviews the constitutionality of domestic legal acts; presidential edicts; regulations of the Cabinet of Ministers; the constitution; laws; legal documents; and regulatory decisions of the Supreme Court, the Supreme Economic Court, and the Procuracy. The Constitutional Court's decisions are final and are not subject to appeal.

Another court is the Supreme Court and its lower-level courts, in which trials are open to all. Cases are first tried in a *rayon*-level court. Either party can then appeal a judicial decision, sentence, or other ruling in a *voblasts'*-level court; final appeal can be made to the Supreme Court. However, an appeal consists merely of a higher court's review of the protocol and other documents of the original trial. In actual practice, decisions are rarely overturned.

The third court is the Supreme Economic Court and its lower-level courts, which have jurisdiction in cases involving economic matters. Such cases include relations between economic entities (such as collective farms) and anti-monopoly cases.

There is a separate system of military courts. Military judges are appointed directly by the president.

The Procuracy functions as a combination of a police investigative bureau and a public prosecutor's office. It investigates crimes, brings criminals to trial and prosecutes them, supervises courts and penal facilities within its jurisdiction, reviews all court decisions in both civil and criminal cases, supervises investigations conducted by other government agencies, and ensures the uniform application of law in the courts.

The Procuracy is headed by the procurator general, who is appointed by the Supreme Soviet. The procurator general then appoints each officer of the Procuracy, known as a procurator. The constitution states that the procurator general and his or her subordinate procurators are to function independently, yet the procurator general is accountable to the Supreme Soviet. Procurators are independent of regional and local government bodies because they derive their authority from the procurator general. Procurators are quite influential because they supervise all criminal investigations; courts are extremely deferential to the procurators' actions, petitions, and conclusions.

Local Government

In 1995 Belarus's local government was arranged in three tiers: six *voblastsi* (sing., *voblasts'*); 141 *rayony* (sing., *rayon*—see Glossary) and thirty-eight cities; and 112 towns and 1,480 villages and settlements (see fig. 11). Large cities were also divided into *rayony*.

Under Belarus's new constitution, local councils of deputies are to be elected by the citizens of their jurisdictions for four-year terms and are to have exclusive jurisdiction over economic and social development programs, local budgets and taxes, management and disposal of local government property, and the calling of referenda. In October 1994, Lukashyenka convinced the Supreme Soviet to amend the law on local self-government, much to the dismay of the opposition, who saw the country's administration come under his control in a single stroke. The local councils in villages, towns, and city districts were to be disbanded and placed under the supervision of local administrations. The head of the regional executives was to be appointed by the president, and the local executives were to be nominated by the regional executives (and approved by the president). Thus, the chain of command would run from the top down, as it had in the days of the Belorussian SSR.

Political Parties

Stanislaw Shushkyevich observed at the beginning of 1993 that almost 60 percent of Belarusians did not support any political party, only 3.9 percent of the electorate backed the communist party, and only 3.8 percent favored the BPF. The influence of other parties was much lower.

In the Soviet era, the Communist Party of Belorussia (CPB), part of the Communist Party of the Soviet Union (CPSU), claimed to rule the Belorussian SSR in the name of the proletariat for the entire duration of the republic's existence. For most of this period, it sought to control all aspects of government and society and to infuse political, economic, and social policies with the correct ideological content. By the late 1980s, however, the party watched as Mikhail S. Gorbachev attempted to withdraw the CPSU from day-to-day economic affairs.

After the CPB was banned in the wake of the August 1991 coup d'état, Belarusian communists regrouped and renamed themselves the Party of Communists of Belarus (PCB), which became the umbrella organization for Belarus's communist parties and pro-Russian groups. The PCB was formally registered in December 1991. The Supreme Soviet lifted the ban on the CPB in February 1993. The CPB was subsequently merged with the PCB.

The most active and visible of the opposition political groups in Belarus in the first half of the 1990s was the Belarusian Popular Front (BPF), founded in October 1989 with Zyanon Paznyak as chairman. The BPF declared itself a movement open to any individual or party, including communists, provided that those who joined shared its basic goal of a fully independent and democratic Belarus. The BPF's critics, however, claimed that it was indeed a party, pointing out the movement's goal of seeking political power, having a "shadow cabinet," and being engaged in parliamentary politics.

The United Democratic Party of Belarus was founded in November 1990 and was the first political party in independent

Figure 11. Administrative Divisions of Belarus, 1995

Belarus other than the communist party. Its membership is composed of technical intelligentsia, professionals, workers, and peasants. It seeks an independent Belarus, democracy, freedom of ethnic expression, and a market economy.

The Belarusian Social Democratic Assembly (Hramada) emerged in March 1991. Its members include workers, peasants, students, military personnel, and urban and rural intelligentsia. Its program advocates an independent Belarus, although it does not rule out membership in the CIS, and a market economy with state regulation of certain sectors. The assembly cooperates with other parties and considers itself part of the worldwide social democratic movement.

The Belarusian Peasant Party, founded in February 1991, is headquartered in Minsk and has branches in most *voblastsi*. The party's goals include privatization of land, a free market, a democratic government, and support of Belarusian culture and humanism.

The Belarusian Christian Democratic Union, founded in June 1991, was a continuation of the Belarusian Christian Democratic Party, which was disbanded by the Polish authorities in western Belarus in the 1930s. Its membership consists mainly of the intelligentsia. It espouses Christian values, nonviolence, pluralism, private property, and peaceful relations among ethnic groups.

The "Belaya Rus'" Slavic Council was founded in June 1992 as a conservative Russophile group. It defends Russian interests in all spheres of social life, vociferously objects to the status of Belarusian as the republic's sole official language, and demands equal status for the Russian language.

In 1995 other parties included the Belarusian Ecological Party, the National Democratic Party of Belarus, the Party of People's Accord, the All-Belarusian Party of Popular Unity and Accord, the Belarusian United Agrarian Democratic Party, the Belarusian Scientific Industrial Congress, the Belarusian Green Party, the Belarusian Humanitarian Party, the Belarusian Party of Labor, the Belarusian Party of Labor and Justice, the Belarusian Socialist Party, the Liberal Democratic Party of Belarus, the Polish Democratic Union, and the Republican Party.

The Media

In late 1992, Belarus had 586 officially approved periodicals: 140 in Belarusian, 159 in Russian, and 241 in both Belarusian and Russian. Other publications combined Russian with another language or were published in English, Polish, or Ukrainian. The only daily newspaper published completely in Belarusian was *Zvyazda* (Star). Other dailies included *Sovetskaya Belorussiya* (Soviet Belorussia) and *Vechernyy Minsk* (Evening Minsk), published in Russian, and *Narodnaya hazyeta* (People's Newspaper), published in both Belarusian and Russian. Belarus's official news agency is BelTA (Belarusian News Agency), and the independent news agency is BELAPAN.

In the mid-1990s, Belarus had a high level of censorship, a carryover from the Soviet period (see Internal Security, this ch.). Works no longer had to be approved before publication, but all nonfiction materials had to be presented to the Inspectorate for the Protection of State Secrets, a small government department subordinate to the Ministry of Communications and Information, which once had been a branch of Glavlit, the Soviet censorship body. Most publishing houses in the country were funded and controlled by the ministry.

Foreign Relations

The United States recognized Belarus on December 26, 1991. By late 1992, more than 100 countries had recognized Belarus, and nearly seventy of them had established some level of diplomatic relations with it. Belarus had a limited number of embassies abroad because its diplomatic activities, as with all other phases of life, were severely constrained by economic hardships. There was also a shortage of experienced diplomats who were Belarusian citizens; international relations had been the purview of Moscow during the Soviet era and continued to be mainly the purview of ethnic Russians residing in, but not citizens of, Belarus.

In 1995 Belarus was a member of a number of international organizations, including the United Nations (UN) (of which it was a founding member), the World Bank, the International Monetary Fund, the Commonwealth of Independent States (CIS), the Organization for Security and Cooperation in Europe (OSCE; until January 1995 known as the Conference on Security and Cooperation in Europe—see Glossary), the North Atlantic Cooperation Council, and the European Bank for Reconstruction and Development (EBRD). Belarus also has observer status at the General Agreement on Tariffs and Trade (GATT) and its successor, the World Trade Organization (WTO). However, the Council of Europe (see Glossary) in 1995 declared Belarus to be ineligible for membership in the council because of shortcomings in its elections and its election laws, including restrictions on mass media coverage of the spring 1995 parliamentary campaign and restrictions on candidates' campaign expenditures.

Belarusian authorities, particularly the Ministry of Foreign Affairs, have been trying to promote the widest possible contacts with Belarusians living abroad (and particularly in the West), with an eye to developing economic and cultural cooperation. The Belarusian domestic media have devoted an increasing amount of space to the life of émigrés, including their past and present activities. A number of cultural exchanges, conferences, and joint ventures took place during the early 1990s; a World Reunion of Belarusians was held in the republic's capital in 1993.

But not everybody in the republic concurs with these initiatives. From the ultraconservatives came denunciations of the émigrés for their alleged collaboration with the Nazis during World War II and their employment by the United States Central Intelligence Agency. However, the democratic opposition groups, including the BPF, have engaged in their own cooperative efforts with Belarusian émigré organizations, through which they have reached out for contacts with Western politicians and governments.

Russia

Even though Belarus's new constitution declared that it is a neutral country, the reality at independence was that Russia was Belarus's neighbor, its military partner, and its largest economic partner. Belarus's heavy economic dependence on Russia, especially for critically needed fuels, has serious political consequences. Russia not only could bring political pressure on Belarus but could also bring the country to its knees economically by withholding oil and natural gas. And with some 1.5 million ethnic Russians living in Belarus and many of the officers in the Belarusian armed forces being ethnic Russians, Russia is in a position to influence Belarus in more subtle ways as well.

The opposition is aware that the government of Alyaksandr Lukashyenka, using economic difficulties as justification, could try to append Belarus to Russia, not only economically but also militarily and politically. Lukashyenka has made it clear from the start that he wants a "special relationship" with Moscow, which, in terms of national security, would mean relying on Russia to ensure Belarus's security and, perhaps, giving Russia a "right of supervision" over Belarusian foreign and security policy.

Some hard-liners have called for closer contacts not only with the CIS but also with Russia itself. Because Belarus is so dependent on Russia already, they argue, it would make sense to be allied with it militarily as well. The Russian troops and missiles still on Belarus's soil would seem to make this alliance the logical choice, but it runs counter to the Belarusian constitution's goal of neutrality. The public itself is divided on the issue.

Nevertheless, although Russia has strong security concerns regarding Belarus, it does not appear interested in taking Belarus under its wing economically. Russia has made a number of changes in its finances and its economy that Belarus has not replicated; many policymakers in Russia see Belarus as a continuing drain on Russia's own financial resources.

The most concrete efforts to date at a close relationship between the two countries lie in the economic and monetary spheres. By June 1, 1994, Belarus had harmonized its interstate trade regulations and taxation schemes with those of Russia; most export and import fees on mutual trade were abolished. In May 1995, Belarus and Russia signed a customs union that eliminated customs checkpoints along their joint border (effective July 15, 1995) and also signed an agreement on cooperation in maintaining state borders.

United States

The United States awarded Belarus most-favored-nation status (see Glossary) for trade on February 16, 1993, and dramatically increased aid (from US$8.3 million under previously signed agreements to US$100 million in January 1994) because of Belarus's agreement to approve the first Strategic Arms Reduction Treaty (START I) and the Nuclear Nonproliferation Treaty (NPT). But the good relations between the United States and Belarus had cooled by 1995, when the reforms and progress toward democracy that had been developing slowly under Stanislaw Shushkyevich were stopped and even reversed by Alyaksandr Lukashyenka. The United States has protested the violations of human rights and democratic reversals under the Lukashyenka administration (see Internal Security, this ch.).

Ukraine

In 1995 Belarus and Ukraine were on good terms and made no territorial claims on each other; nor have their respective minority groups voiced any complaints of discrimination. However, ties between the two countries are weak because of their different relationships with, and views of, Russia. Unlike Belarus, Ukraine is determined to be politically and militarily independent. Kiev complains that whenever Ukraine disagrees with Russia on an issue, Belarus backs the latter.

Perhaps the most important Ukrainian issue for Belarus is the Chornobyl' nuclear power plant. Because Belarus suffered the effects of the 1986 disaster more than any other country, it had a strong interest in the shutdown of the plant. Belarus was therefore alarmed by the Ukrainian parliament's December 1993 vote to keep the plant running, despite the original plans that called for closing it at the end of 1993. Yet Supreme Soviet chairman Shushkyevich's appeals to Ukraine, which was in the midst of an energy crisis, made little difference.

Poland

Once Belarus declared its independence, it signed a number of agreements with Poland, including ones on establishing diplomatic relations and a consular convention, fighting crime, creating a commercial bank to finance bilateral trade, establishing new border-crossing points, and supporting investment opportunities in the two countries. Polish president Lech Walesa and Belarusian parliamentary chairman Stanislaw Shushkyevich signed a bilateral friendship and cooperation treaty during the latter's visit to Warsaw in June 1992. Military and economic agreements were signed in 1993.

In 1994 approximately 300,000 ethnic Belarusians lived in Poland, and 418,000 ethnic Poles lived in Belarus. In neither country are there any obstacles to the ethnic minority's participation in political life. In Belarus most ethnic Poles supported the drive for Belarusian independence and were not seen as a threat to Belarus; the government raised no obstacles to the Poles' acquisition of Belarusian citizenship. The ethnic Belarusians in Poland live mainly in the Bialystok region, one of the poorest areas of the country, but new economic cooperation between Belarus and Poland and specific obligations taken on by Poland are sure to effect changes, if only modestly.

The arena of most disagreements between Poles and Belarusians in the 1990s seemed to be religion. Accusations were made of ethnic Polish dominance of the Roman Catholic Church in Belarus. Polish priests sometimes served in parishes with little or no knowledge of the Belarusian language. But steps were being taken by the Roman Catholic archbishop to counter the more blatant use of Polish political symbols in the churches (see Religion, this ch.).

Lithuania

Although relations between Belarus and Lithuania were generally friendly in the early 1990s, various groups and individuals, and even some elements of the Belarusian government and legislature, cited historical and sociological "facts" about language and ethnicity to claim some of Lithuania's territory, especially around the capital, Vilnius. The two countries signed a border agreement in December 1991 and over the next two years demarcated the previously unmarked border to prevent any further disputes.

During a February 1995 summit, Lithuanian president Algirdas Brazauskas and Belarusian president Lukashyenka signed a friendship and cooperation treaty that resolved all outstanding border issues. No problems were reported in connection with the minorities living in the other country.

Latvia

Belarus's relations with Latvia, one of its major trading partners, have been relatively free of problems. The border is unchanged from that established in 1940; as a result, marking it and establishing normal border controls (so that both countries could deal with smuggling and illegal immigration) were fairly straightforward. Neither the 120,000 ethnic Belarusians in Latvia nor the approximately 3,000 ethnic Latvians living in Belarus reported problems.

Belarus and Latvia have signed a number of agreements. An agreement signed in December 1991 covered respect for the rights of minorities and for national borders. Latvian president Guntis Ulmanis and Belarusian foreign minister Pyotr Krawchanka signed similar accords in August 1993. In May 1995, the transportation ministers of both countries signed an agreement on cooperation in rail transport and communications.

National Security

Belarus's national security interests are couched in conflict. On the one hand, there is the desire by some to protect Belarus's independence and its territory. On the other hand, there is the desire to appease and even actively to cooperate with Moscow, which supplies nearly all of Belarus's fuels and raw materials. Although Belarus's Supreme Soviet signed the CIS Treaty on Collective Security in April 1993, the government also joined the Partnership for Peace program of politico-military cooperation of the North Atlantic Treaty Organization (NATO) in January 1995, but not before waiting to see what Russia would do.

The Armed Forces

Before the dissolution of the Soviet Union, 243,000 Soviet troops were stationed in the Belorussian SSR, with an additional 180,000 troops belonging to the local commands of the strategic rocket and air forces. This situation changed only in May 1992, when Belarus abolished the Belorussian Military District and subordinated all troops on its soil to its own Ministry of Defense.

The Belarusian armed forces officially came into existence on January 1, 1993, the day after all service personnel with Belarusian citizenship, which excluded the great majority of the officers, had taken an oath of loyalty to Belarus. Because there was no stipulation that only Belarusian citizens could serve in the armed forces, they were Belarusian forces in name only, and there was concern among groups such as the BPF that in time of crisis the loyalty of these forces might lie with Russia rather than with Belarus.

A component of this concern was the ethnic composition of the armed forces. At the end of 1992, ethnic Russians accounted for nearly half the Belarusian conscripts and some 80 percent of the officer corps. Since then, the ethnic composition of the officers has been changing gradually in favor of Belarusians as a result of legislative acts, but the process is slow. It will take years before the republic has its own Belarusian-led armed forces that are politically reliable and dedicated to Belarusian nationhood.

Another aspect of the nationality issue was that in 1993 some 40,000 Belarusian natives served as officers in the armed forces of other former Soviet republics. Many of them wished to return home for either patriotic or economic reasons, but such possibilities were limited because of the shortage of housing and the republic's scheduled military reductions in general. What concerned the Belarusian Ministry of Defense, which was dominated by Russians, was an announcement in the spring of 1992 by the Coordinating Council of the Union of Belarusian Soldiers that these officers were willing to fight against Russian military aggression in Belarus.

Because of Belarus's geopolitical importance and its absorption of troops withdrawn from the countries of the former Warsaw Pact (see Glossary), it was the most militarized republic of the former Soviet Union. Even in 1993, it had a ratio of one soldier to forty-three civilians, compared with one to ninety-eight in Ukraine and one to 634 in Russia. In real numbers, this meant an estimated 243,000 troops. In addition, there was a serious imbalance in the officer-to-conscript ratio: three officers for every seven conscripts.

In accordance with its stated goal of becoming a neutral state and in accordance with its new defense doctrine, the government planned to decrease the number of its troops by some 60 percent, from 243,000 to 96,000 (including up to 22,000 officers) by the beginning of 1995. The armed forces employed 64,000 civilians. Further reductions were expected to reduce the total armed forces to a strength of 75,000 or even 60,000. Such a move, however, presents a difficult political problem because of a lack of housing and employment for demobilized service members, who, regardless of their present citizenship, are eligible to become Belarusian citizens and voters.

Women serve in the armed forces as well, although in much smaller numbers than men. They face the same physical and other testing requirements as men. In mid-1995 there were approximately 3,000 servicewomen, many of whom worked at headquarters as secretaries.

As of mid-1995, the armed forces were in the midst of adopting five main reforms. The first was a gradual move toward a goal of 50 percent professional soldiers. By mid-1995 there were 22,000 professional soldiers on contracts of five years or longer and another 9,000 soldiers on contracts of two to five years. These accounted for 32 percent of the uniformed establishment.

The second reform was to redivide the country into military territorial districts whose district commanders would be part of the structure of local government. The Ministry of Defense hoped that after implementing this system, recruits would be able to serve closer to home and that draft avoidance would decline.

The third reform was to create a mobile operational force. Such a force would likely be composed of three brigades: airmobile, helimobile, and airborne/special forces.

The fourth reform was the adoption of a new structure to permit maximum flexibility. The army's new post-Soviet structure, built on corps and brigades, suited Belarus's needs better than the Soviet-era divisions.

Last was the army's increased role in internal security. According to a presidential decree of January 1, 1995, entitled On Reinforcing the Fight Against Crime, troops have been transferred from the Ministry of Defense to the Ministry of

Honor guard at the World War II memorial, Minsk
Courtesy Michael E. Samojeden

Internal Affairs. Belarus's Border Guards are under the control of the Ministry of Internal Affairs. They numbered 8,000 in early 1995.

Ground Forces

In 1994 Belarus had ground forces of 52,500, organized into three corps headquarters, two motorized divisions, one airborne division, one artillery division, three mechanized divisions, one airborne brigade, three surface-to-surface missile brigades, two antitank brigades, one special duties brigade, and seven surface-to-air missile brigades. Equipment included 3,108 main battle tanks (seventy-nine T–54, 639 T–55, 291 T–62, 299 T–64, eight T–80, and 1,800 T–72), 419 medium-range launchers, sixty surface-to-surface missiles, and 350 surface-to-air missiles.

By January 1, 1995, the order of battle for the Belarusian army had changed. Ministry of Defense forces included the 103d Guards Air Assault Division and the 38th Separate Assault-Landing Brigade; the 28th Army Corps (Hrodna and Brest regions), composed of headquarters at Hrodna, the 6th Detached Mechanized Infantry Brigade, the 11th Detached

Mechanized Infantry Brigade, the 50th Detached Mechanized Infantry Brigade, the armament and equipment base, and corps units (missile troops, antiaircraft, chemical and engineer troops, signals, and rear services); the 65th Army Corps (Minsk and Vitsyebsk regions), composed of headquarters at Barysaw, three armament and equipment bases, and corps units; and the 5th Guards Army Corps (Minsk and Mahilyow regions) made up of headquarters at Babruysk, the 30th Detached Mechanized Infantry Brigade, two armament and equipment bases, and corps units.

Air Force

In mid-1994 the Belarusian air force operated two interceptor regiments with MiG–23, MiG–25, and MiG–29 aircraft; three strike regiments with MiG–27, Su–17, Su–24, and Su–25 aircraft; and one reconnaissance regiment with MiG–25 and Su–24 aircraft. Four regiments had 300 helicopters, and one transport regiment had more than forty helicopters. Personnel numbered 15,800.

Belarus also had an air defense force with 11,800 personnel and 200 SA–2, SA–3, SA–5, and SA–10 surface-to-air missiles. The system was being integrated into Russia's air defenses in 1994, owing to Belarus's lack of resources.

Manpower, Education, and Training

In 1995 conscription was for eighteen months, with alternative service available. In 1994 reserve forces numbered approximately 289,500 members, who had had military service in the previous five years.

In the early 1990s, an issue in the training of troops was the teaching and use of the Belarusian language. There was resistance in the Ministry of Defense and in the armed forces themselves to the idea of using the Belarusian language; officials claimed that the Belarusian armed forces were being "politicized." But little progress had been made in 1994 toward the use of Belarusian in the military, as called for by the draft law entitled About the Armed Forces of the Republic of Belarus, which stipulated the use of both the Belarusian and the Russian languages, with a gradual transition to Belarusian.

Expenditures

The defense budget for 1994 was estimated at 686.6 billion Belarusian rubles, accounting for 4.5 percent of GDP and reflecting a slight increase in real terms over the previous few years. One reason for this was that Belarus had obligated itself in a treaty to cover a larger share of the costs in maintaining the army units of other former Soviet republics stationed on its soil. Another was that the government made large outlays in acquiring strategic stockpiles, mostly of fuel reserves.

Nuclear Weapons

When the Soviet Union dissolved, Belarus (along with Russia, Ukraine, and Kazakhstan) technically became a nuclear power because of the eighty-one SS–25 intercontinental ballistic missiles on its soil, even though the republic's Declaration of State Sovereignty declared Belarus to be a nuclear-free state. In May 1992, Belarus signed the Lisbon Protocol to the NPT and, along with Ukraine and Kazakhstan, agreed to destroy or turn over to Russia all strategic nuclear warheads on its territory.

To achieve this objective, the Supreme Soviet had to ratify the START I treaty. For some time, however, the legislature stalled while seeking international guarantees of the republic's security and international funding to carry out the removal. Finally, on February 4, 1993, the START I treaty was ratified, and adherence to the NPT was approved. All tactical nuclear weapons were removed from Belarus by mid-1993, but although the country strove to remove the strategic nuclear weapons (based at Lida and Mazyr) by 1995, there was little hope of meeting this deadline. In February 1995, Lukashyenka decided to stop arms reductions called for by the Conventional Forces in Europe Treaty (CFE Treaty—see Glossary), claiming NATO encroachments on Belarus's territory; in truth, his decision was a matter of finances. These remaining strategic nuclear weapons were tended by Russian troops who would continue to be stationed in Belarus until 2020, according to the customs union agreements reached with Russia in January and February 1995 (see Russian Troops, this ch.).

The Defense Industry

Belarus's large defense industry has been severely hit by the country's cutbacks in imports of fuels and raw materials as well as by decreased demand for military products across the former Soviet Union in general. Because Belarus is now paying higher prices for its fuels and raw materials, the cost of its products has increased, prompting a decrease in purchases not only by Russia but by other former Soviet republics as well. Conversion to civilian industry has not been quick or successful, as is the case across the former Soviet bloc. Belarus is hopeful that its defense industry will get more business from Russia now that Belarus is paying some of the costs of maintaining Russian troops on Belarusian soil. Belarus has also tried to increase its arms markets. In mid-1995 arms deals with Iran and China were pending.

The Commonwealth of Independent States

Geopolitically, Belarus is as strategically important to Russia today as it was in the times of Napoleon Bonaparte and Adolf Hitler. Therefore, repeated invitations were extended to Minsk from the CIS to join in a military alliance. Shushkyevich refused to sign the CIS Treaty on Collective Security that six other CIS states had signed in May 1992. He believed such a move would contravene the Declaration of State Sovereignty, which defines Belarus as a neutral state, and that an independent Belarusian army was essential to maintaining the republic's independence from Russia. The Supreme Soviet in April 1993 nonetheless voted to sign the treaty and eventually took revenge on Shushkyevich for his views on the CIS security treaty by dismissing him in January 1994, officially on charges of corruption. At the same time, accords were also signed on closer economic cooperation with other CIS member states.

Although Belarus joined NATO's Partnership for Peace, it strongly supported Moscow's objections to NATO expansion in Central Europe. The opposition, which realized that Belarus's full membership in NATO would not come about, suggested a Baltic-to-Black Sea zone of economic and political cooperation encompassing Estonia, Latvia, Lithuania, Poland, Belarus, Ukraine, and Moldova. Not only was this idea anathema to pro-Russian elements in Belarusian society, but Poland and the Baltic states would reject it as well if it threatened their prospects for full membership in NATO.

Russian Troops

The removal from Belarusian territory of both strategic nuclear arms and tens of thousands of Russian soldiers is a task as delicate and problematic as it is important if Belarus is to achieve its stated constitutional goal of neutrality.

In 1993 there were an estimated 40,000 troops of the Russian air force in Belarus, comprising one air division with 130 combat aircraft. This consisted of one regiment with thirty Su–

24 fighter-bombers, one heavy bomber division of four regiments with fifteen Tu–22M Backfire bombers and fifty Tu–22 medium-range bombers, and one regiment with twenty Tu–22M Backfire bombers and fifteen Tu–16 medium-range bombers.

Most of these troops were engaged in work related to the seventy-two strategic nuclear missiles based at Lida and Mazyr and were scheduled to leave Belarus in 1995, the anticipated deadline for transferring all nuclear weapons to Russia. This transfer, which depended greatly on housing being built for the troops in Russia, was viewed as unrealistic by mid-1995. An October 1994 announcement stated that two Russian nonnuclear military installations would remain in Belarus.

Despite the creation of a Belarusian army, Belarus had to contend with the fact that the bulk of its officer corps remained composed of ethnic Russians. However, the reduction of troops from 1993 to 1995 included a reduction in the number of officers, which meant fewer ethnic Russian generals.

Internal Security

As with many other Belarusian institutions, the internal security forces were inherited more or less intact when the Soviet Union was dissolved. The local assets of these institutions were transferred to the new government and continued functioning with basically the same policies and, very often, the same personnel. In 1995 the country's security service retained the name KGB.

The former communist, pro-Russian hard-liners still in charge of many of Belarus's institutions are determined to stay in power. One of their methods is censorship. They call newspaper editors in for "chats" about government policy and the subsidies that keep many periodicals afloat. They also enforced the media restrictions on coverage of the May 1995 parliamentary elections, which kept newspapers from publishing interviews with the candidates and stories about the campaign in general.

Crime

A drastic decline in living standards and the general breakdown in law and order throughout the former Soviet Union have contributed greatly to a dramatic rise in crime in Belarus. In the first half of 1993, Belarus's murder rate increased by almost 50 percent and muggings by almost 60 percent. Organized crime is present in Belarus as well. Independent Belarus has also become a transshipment point for illegal drugs intended for Western Europe; locally produced opium and cannabis supply Belarus's own populace.

One of the more public crimes in the republic is corruption in the government. Although Alyaksandr Lukashyenka campaigned on an anticorruption platform, accusations of corruption have stuck to his administration. In December 1994, Syarhyey Antonchyk read a report in the Supreme Soviet charging a number of high-level administration figures with corruption, which led a number of these figures to offer their resignations. Lukashyenka refused to accept the resignations and banned four independent newspapers from publishing the report. Such incidents are generally acknowledged to be just the tip of the proverbial iceberg.

Human Rights

Belarus's transition from the authoritarian institutions of the Soviet era to democratic ones has been spotty, and human rights abuses continue. The government, even before the election of Lukashyenka as president, continued to restrict freedom of speech, press, and peaceful assembly, among other rights.

Although the constitution provides for freedom of speech, this right is observed more in the breach. The government continues to use slander and defamation laws to suppress criticism of its policies and government officials. It also retains a virtual economic monopoly over the press through its ownership of nearly all printing and broadcasting facilities. This absence of independence encourages editors to censor themselves. In other cases, the government simply removes the editor of a publication, cancels a publication's contract for paper, eliminates a publication's government subsidy, or denies a publication access to state-owned printing facilities.

Freedom of assembly is also guaranteed by the constitution, but this too is enforced arbitrarily. Despite the law's explicit statement of procedures for obtaining permission for rallies or marches, officials still deny permission when it suits them or higher levels of the government.

There have been many reports of beatings of prisoners, mainly in the prison in Hrodna, by prison guards or with their complicity. Although such actions are against the law, it is rare for the government to punish perpetrators. Amnesty International has been denied access to the prison routinely, on grounds of security.

In July 1993, Belarus abolished its death penalty for four economic crimes. A revised criminal code under consideration by the parliament would reduce the number of offenses carrying a possible death sentence to eight: preparing and conducting an aggressive war, acts of terrorism against a representative of another state, international terrorism, genocide, premeditated murder, treason, sabotage, and terrorist acts and conspiracy to seize power.

*   *   *

Published materials dealing with Belarus are still somewhat scarce. A standard work, covering Belarus from its earliest history through the mid-1950s, is Nicholas P. Vakar's *Belorussia: The Making of a Nation,* which also covers many aspects of the culture. Another work, which briefly discusses earlier history, despite its title, is Ivan S. Lubachko's *Belorussia under Soviet Rule, 1917–1957,* which emphasizes the Soviet era. A more recent book is Jan Zaprudnik's *Belarus: At a Crossroads in History. Belarus,* an economic review by the International Monetary Fund, provides a picture of Belarus's economy after 1991 and includes tables on a variety of economic performance indicators in the Soviet and post-Soviet periods.

Current information on Belarus, with an emphasis on political, economic, and national security topics, is provided in the Foreign Broadcast Information Service's *Daily Report: Central Eurasia. Transition,* a new biweekly Open Media Research Institute (the successor organization to Radio Free Europe) publication begun in January 1995, tends to have one longer article on Belarus per issue. (For further information and complete citations, see Bibliography.)

Chapter 2. Moldova

Antique Moldovan rug

Chronology of Important Events

Period	Description
SECOND–THIRD CENTURIES	
ca. 105–271	Rome occupies territory of future Romanian lands.
FOURTEENTH CENTURY	
1349	Prince Bogdan establishes Bogdania, later renamed Moldova, stretching from Carpathian Mountains to Nistru River.
SIXTEENTH CENTURY	
1512	Although Stephen the Great (1457–1504) achieves significant victories against Ottoman Empire, Moldova becomes tributary state of empire for 300 years.
SEVENTEENTH CENTURY	
First half	First Moldovan books appear.
EIGHTEENTH CENTURY	
1792	Ottoman Empire cedes all its holdings in Transnistria to Russian Empire under Treaty of Iasi.
NINETEENTH CENTURY	
1812	Bessarabia is incorporated into Russian Empire under Treaty of Bucharest after Russo-Turkish War (1806–12).
1858	Moldovan territory west of Prut River is united with Walachia. Alexandru Ioan Cuza is elected prince of the two regions the following year.
TWENTIETH CENTURY	
1917	February Revolution and Bolshevik Revolution bring down Russian Empire. Bessarabia's newly created National Council declares Bessarabia the independent Democratic Moldovan Republic, federated with Russia.
1918	Bessarabia declares its complete independence from Russia and votes to unite with Romania.
1924	Soviet government creates Moldavian Autonomous Oblast on east bank of Nistru River. Seven months later, oblast is upgraded to Moldavian Autonomous Soviet Socialist Republic (Moldavian ASSR)
1940 June	Bessarabia is occupied by Soviet forces as result of secret protocol attached to 1939 Nazi-Soviet Nonaggression Pact.
August	Soviet government creates Moldavian Soviet Socialist Republic (Moldavian SSR) from most of Bessarabia and portion of Moldavian ASSR.
1941	Germany and Romania attack Moldavian SSR and Ukrainian SSR; Nazi Germany gives Bessarabia, northern Bukovina, and Transnistria to Romania.
1944	Soviet forces reoccupy Bessarabia and Transnistria.
1947	Bessarabia, northern Bukovina, and Transnistria are formally returned to Soviet Union by treaty.

Chronology of Important Events

Period		Description
1950–52		As first secretary of Communist Party of Moldavia, Leonid I. Brezhnev liquidates and deports thousands of ethnic Romanians from Moldavia and institutes forced collectivization.
1986		Mikhail S. Gorbachev announces policy of *perestroika* in Moscow at Twenty-Seventh Party Congress of the Communist Party of the Soviet Union.
1988		Yedinstvo-Unitatea Intermovement is formed by Slavs in Transnistria.
1989		Moldovan Popular Front is formed.
1990	February	Popular Front organizes "Republic's Voters Meeting," attended by more than 100,000 persons. First democratic elections are held for Supreme Soviet of Moldavian SSR. Runoff elections are held in March. Mircea Snegur is elected chairman of Supreme Soviet.
	June	Name of Moldavian Soviet Socialist Republic is changed to Soviet Socialist Republic of Moldova. Supreme Soviet adopts declaration of sovereignty.
	August	Gagauz declare independent "Gagauz Republic."
	September	Slavs in Transnistria proclaim independent "Dnestr Moldavian Republic." Snegur becomes president of Soviet Socialist Republic of Moldova.
1991	May	Soviet Socialist Republic of Moldova is renamed Republic of Moldova. Supreme Soviet changes its name to Moldovan Parliament.
	August	August coup d'état takes place in Moscow. Moldovan Parliament bans Communist Party of Moldavia. Moldova declares its complete independence from Soviet Union on August 27 and demands withdrawal of Soviet troops.
	October	President Snegur announces decision to organize Moldova's own national armed forces.
	December	Stepan Topal is elected president of "Gagauz Republic." Igor' N. Smirnov is elected president of "Dnestr Moldavian Republic." Minsk Agreement establishes Commonwealth of Independent States (CIS). President Snegur signs Alma-Ata Declaration, which expands membership of CIS, but Moldovan Parliament refuses to ratify declaration. Soviet Union is dissolved. United States recognizes Moldova.
1992	March	Government of Moldova declares state of emergency in reaction to mounting violence.
	May	Armed resistance by separatists escalates to full-scale civil war in Transnistria.
	July	An agreement establishing a cease-fire in Moldova is signed by Moldovan president Snegur and Russian president Boris N. Yeltsin.
1993	January	Moldovan Parliament refuses to sign agreement strengthening CIS.
	February	Moldovan Popular Front is re-formed as Christian Democratic Popular Front.
	November	Moldova introduces its own currency, the leu.

Chronology of Important Events

Period		Description
1994	February	Parliamentary elections drastically change Moldovan government. Popular Front majority is gone, and compromises are made with nationalities on various issues.
	March	Public opinion poll is held. Populace votes overwhelmingly to retain independence.
	April	Moldova votes to join CIS.
	August	New Moldovan constitution goes into effect.
	October	Moldova and Russia sign agreement on withdrawal of Russian 14th Army from Transnistria and Tighina (Bendery or Bender in Russian), but only Moldovan government approves it.
1995	March	Students, intelligentsia, workers, and pensioners demonstrate in Chisinau over cultural and educational issues and the name of the language.
	June	Lieutenant General Aleksandr V. Lebed' resigns as commander of Russian 14th Army. Replaced by Major General Valeriy Yevnevich.
		Russian 14th Army is downgraded to an operational group.
		Moldova joins Council of Europe.

Country Profile

Country

Formal Name: Republic of Moldova (Republica Moldova).

Short Form: Moldova.

Term for Citizens: Moldovan(s).

Capital: Chisinau.

Date of Independence: August 27, 1991.

Geography

Size: Approximately 33,700 square kilometers.

Topography: Gently rolling, hilly plain in north; thick deciduous forests in center; numerous ravines and gullies in steppe zone in south. Highest point 430 meters.

Climate: Moderately continental. Average annual precipitation ranges from 400 millimeters in south to 600 millimeters in north.

Society

Population: 4,473,033 (July 1994 estimate), with an average annual growth rate of 0.38 percent.

Ethnic Groups: According to 1989 census, an estimated 65 percent Romanian, 14 percent Ukrainian, 13 percent Russian, 4 percent Gagauz, 2 percent Bulgarian, and remainder Jewish, Belorussian, Polish, Roma (Gypsy), and German.

Languages: Moldovan (a dialect of Romanian) is the official language. Russian retained as language of interethnic communication; areas of non-Romanian ethnic majority may also use local language as means of communication.

Religion: About 98.5 percent of population Orthodox (1991). Other denominations include Uniate, Jewish, Armenian Apostolic, Seventh-Day Adventist, Baptist, Pentecostal, and Molokan (a Russian Orthodox sect).

Education and Literacy: Compulsory school attendance ten years; literacy rate 96 percent (1992). Approximately half of students study in Romanian language and half in Russian language.

Health: Health care provided by state, mostly free of charge. Infant mortality rate 30.3 per 1,000 live births (1994). Life expectancy in 1994 sixty-five years for males and seventy-two years for females. Modern medical equipment and facilities in short supply. In 1990 about 129 hospital beds and forty doctors per 10,000 inhabitants.

Economy

General Character: Centralized. Government efforts to privatize and establish market economy slow.

Net Material Product (NMP): In 1991 about US$13.1 billion; real growth rate –11.9 percent in 1992. Agriculture accounted for 42 percent of NMP in 1991, followed by industry with 38 percent and other sectors with 24 percent.

Agriculture: State and collective farms from Soviet period transformed into joint-stock companies. Primary crops: fruits and berries, grains, grapes, tobacco, vegetables, sugar beets, potatoes, and sunflowers. Cattle, hogs, poultry, and sheep raised.

Industry: Food processing, machinery and metalworking, light industry, building materials, tractors, and wood products.

Minerals: No commercial mineral deposits.

Energy: Primary energy sources (minor hydroelectric and thermal power plants, and firewood) meet only 1 percent of domestic needs. Highly dependent on Russia for nearly all oil, gasoline, coal, and natural gas needed to fuel electric-power generation plants.

Foreign Trade: In 1994 nearly three-quarters of foreign trade with other members of Commonwealth of Independent States. Most imports and vast majority of exports still directed toward territories of former Soviet Union. Imports: industrial raw materials, fossil fuels, and manufactured goods. Exports: wine and spirits, processed foods, and clothing and textiles.

Fiscal Year: Calendar year.

Currency and Exchange Rate: The leu (pl., lei), introduced in November 1993. In January 1995, 4.27 lei per US$1.

Transportation and Telecommunications

Roads: In 1995 estimated at 20,100 kilometers, including 14,000 kilometers of paved surfaces.

Railroads: In 1995 estimated at 1,150 kilometers.

Airports: Major airport in Chisinau.

Inland Waterways: Main river, Nistru, navigable almost entire length, but water transport only of local importance. Only eight rivers extend more than 100 kilometers.

Telecommunications: In 1995 one private television channel and three state television channels: Moldovan, Romanian, and Russian. In 1994 nine AM radio stations in four cities and five FM stations in five cities, as well as a number of private radio stations.

Government and Politics

Government: Democracy, with president and unicameral legislature, Moldovan Parliament, both popularly elected. Government composed of president and Council of Ministers. General Prosecution Office headed by prosecutor general. New constitution went into effect August 27, 1994. Two self-proclaimed republics: "Gagauzia," recognized and granted autonomy; and "Dnestr Moldavian Republic," with an elected, extralegal separatist government.

Politics: Leading parties after 1994 parliamentary elections:

Democratic Agrarian Party of Moldova, Christian Democratic Popular Front, Congress of Peasants and Intellectuals, Gagauz Halkî, and Yedinstvo/Socialist Bloc.

Foreign Relations: First recognized by Romania; as of early 1995, recognized by more than 170 states, including United States (December 25, 1991). Foreign diplomatic presence in Chisinau limited. Relations with Romania influenced by issue of reunification of the two countries. Relations with Ukraine improved as a result of less nationalistic Moldovan policies; presence of Russian 14th Army in Transnistria seen as a common threat. Relationship with Russia very tense.

International Agreements and Memberships: Member of the Organization for Security and Cooperation in Europe (until January 1995 known as the Conference on Security and Co-operation in Europe), United Nations, International Monetary Fund, World Bank, European Bank for Reconstruction and Development, North Atlantic Cooperation Council, and Community of Riparian Countries of the Black Sea. Observer at General Agreement on Tariffs and Trade (GATT) and World Trade Organization (successor to GATT). Alma-Ata Declaration, expanding membership of Commonwealth of Independent States (CIS), signed by president December 1991 but not ratified by Parliament until April 1994. Member of Commonwealth of Independent States as of that date.

National Security

Armed Forces: Armed forces under Ministry of Defense. In 1994 totaled approximately 11,100: ground forces (9,800, including army and Guard Battalion) and air force (1,300, including air defense). No navy. Reserves of 100,000 (those who had had military service in previous five years). Universal conscription, for up to eighteen months.

Major Military Units: In 1994 army consisted of three motor rifle brigades, one artillery brigade, and one reconnaissance assault battalion. Air force consisted of one fighter regiment, one helicopter squadron, and one missile brigade.

Military Equipment: Arms from former Soviet stocks and

undetermined quantities of arms from Romania.

Internal Security: In 1994 national police (10,000). Internal troops (2,500) and OPON riot police (900) under Ministry of Interior. Border Guards under Ministry of National Security. Local assets of former Moldavian Soviet Socialist Republic KGB transferred to new government (along with personnel who wished to transfer) to form new Ministry of National Security.

Russian Troops: In 1994 Russian 14th Army (9,200). "Dnestr Moldavian Republic" forces (5,000) include Dnestr Battalion of Republic Guard and "Cossacks" (approximately 1,000).

Figure 12. Moldova, 1995

THE HISTORY OF THE REPUBLIC OF MOLDOVA is the history of two different regions that have been joined into one country, but not into one nation: Bessarabia and Transnistria. Bessarabia, the land between the Prut and Nistru rivers, is predominantly ethnic Romanian in population and constitutes the eastern half of a region historically known as Moldova or Moldavia (the Soviet-era Russian name). Transnistria is the Romanian-language name for the land on the east bank of the Nistru River; the majority of the population there is Slavic—ethnic Ukrainians and Russians—although Romanians are the single largest ethnic group .

To a great extent, Moldova's history has been shaped by the foreigners who came to stay and by those who merely passed through, including Greek colonists, invading Turks and Tatars, officials of the Russian Empire, German and Bulgarian colonists, communist apparatchiks (see Glossary) from the Soviet Union, soldiers from Nazi Germany, Romanians, and twentieth-century Russian and Ukrainian immigrants. Each group has left its own legacy, sometimes cultural and sometimes political, and often unwelcome.

Moldova's communist overlords, the most recent "foreigners," created the public life that exists in Moldova today. Independence has brought about changes in this public life, but often only on the surface. What further changes Moldova makes will depend partly on how much time it has before the next group of "foreigners" comes to call.

Historical Setting

Early History

Moldova's Latin origins can be traced to the period of Roman occupation of nearby Dacia (in present-day Romania, Bulgaria, and Serbia), ca. A.D. 105–271, when a culture was formed from the intermingling of Roman colonists and the local population. After the Roman Empire and its influence waned and its troops left the region in A.D. 271, a number of groups passed through the area, often violently: Huns, Ostrogoths, and Antes (who were Slavs). The Bulgarian Empire, the Magyars, the Pechenegs, and the Golden Horde (Mongols) also held sway temporarily. In the thirteenth century, Hungary expanded into the area and established a line of fortifications in Moldova near the Siretul River (in present-day Romania) and beyond. The region came under Hungarian suzerainty until an independent Moldovan principality was established by Prince Bogdan in 1349. Originally called Bogdania, the principality stretched from the Carpathian Mountains to the Nistru River and was later renamed Moldova, after the Moldova River in present-day Romania.

During the second half of the fifteenth century, all of southeastern Europe came under increasing pressure from the Ottoman Empire, and despite significant military victories by Stephen the Great (Stefan cel Mare, 1457–1504), Moldova succumbed to Ottoman power in 1512 and was a tributary state of the empire for the next 300 years. In addition to paying tribute to the Ottoman Empire and later acceding to the selection of local rulers by Ottoman authorities, Moldova suffered repeated invasions by Turks, Crimean Tatars, and Russians.

In 1792 the Treaty of Iasi forced the Ottoman Empire to cede all of its holdings in what is now Transnistria to the Russian Empire. An expanded Bessarabia was annexed by, and incorporated into, the Russian Empire following the Russo-Turkish War of 1806–12 according to the terms of the Treaty of Bucharest of 1812 (see fig. 13). In 1858 Moldovan territory west of the Prut River was united with Walachia. And in the same year, Alexandru Ioan Cuza was elected prince of Walachia and the part of Moldova that lay west of the Prut River, laying the foundations of modern Romania. These two regions were united in 1861.

The Beginning of the Soviet Period

In 1917, during World War I and the Bolshevik Revolution, political leaders in Bessarabia created a National Council (Sfatul Tarii), which declared Bessarabia the independent Democratic Moldovan Republic, federated with Russia. In February 1918, the new republic declared its complete independence from Russia and, two months later, voted to unite with Romania, thus angering the Russian government.

After the creation of the Soviet Union (see Glossary) in December 1922, the Soviet government moved in 1924 to establish the Moldavian Autonomous Oblast on land east of the Nistru River in the Ukrainian Soviet Socialist Republic (Ukrainian SSR). The capital of the oblast was at Balta, in present-day Ukraine. Seven months later, the oblast was upgraded to the

Moldavian Autonomous Soviet Socialist Republic (Moldavian ASSR), even though its population was only 30 percent ethnic Romanian. The capital remained at Balta until 1929, when it was moved to Tiraspol (Tiraspol' in Russian) (see fig. 14).

In June 1940, Bessarabia was occupied by Soviet forces as a consequence of a secret protocol attached to the 1939 Nazi-Soviet Nonaggression Pact (see Glossary). On August 2, 1940, the Soviet government created the Moldavian Soviet Socialist Republic (Moldavian SSR), with its capital at Chisinau (Kishinĕv in Russian), by joining most of Bessarabia (see Glossary) with a portion of the Moldavian ASSR (the rest was returned to the Ukrainian SSR). Part of the far northern Moldavian ASSR (Herta—in present-day Ukraine), northern Bukovina (see Glossary), and southern Bessarabia (bordering on the Black Sea) were taken from Romania and incorporated into the Ukrainian SSR, leaving the Moldavian SSR landlocked.

Territorial Changes in World War II

In June 1941, German and Romanian troops attacked the Moldavian SSR and the Ukrainian SSR. Nazi Germany gave Romania, its ally, not only Bessarabia and northern Bukovina but also the land between the Nistru and Pivdennyy Buh (Yuzhnyy Bug in Russian) rivers, north to Bar in Ukraine, which Romania named and administered as Transnistria. This arrangement lasted until August 1944, when Soviet forces reoccupied Bessarabia and Transnistria. A 1947 treaty formally returned Bessarabia, northern Bukovina, and Transnistria to the Soviet Union, and the previous Soviet administrative divisions and Russian place-names were reimposed.

Postwar Reestablishment of Soviet Control

With the restoration of Soviet power in the Moldavian SSR, Joseph V. Stalin's government policy was to Russify (see Glossary) the population of the Moldavian SSR and destroy any remaining ties it had with Romania. Secret police struck at nationalist groups; the Cyrillic alphabet (see Glossary) was imposed on the "Moldavian" (see Glossary) language; and ethnic Russians and Ukrainians were encouraged to immigrate to the Moldavian SSR, especially to Transnistria. The government's policies—requisitioning large amounts of agricultural products despite a poor harvest—induced a famine following the catastrophic drought of 1945–47, and political, communist party, and academic positions were given to members of non-

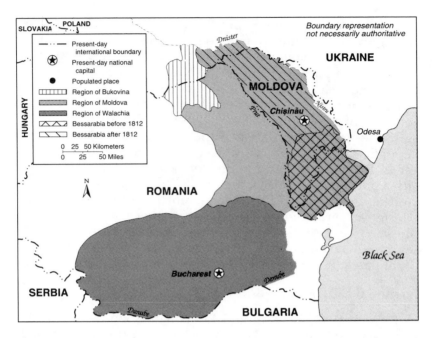

Figure 13. Historical Romanian-Speaking Regions in Southeastern Europe

Romanian ethnic groups (only 14 percent of the Moldavian SSR's political leaders were ethnic Romanians in 1946).

The conditions imposed during the reestablishment of Soviet rule became the basis of deep resentment toward Soviet authorities—a resentment that soon manifested itself. During Leonid I. Brezhnev's 1950–52 tenure as first secretary of the Communist Party of Moldavia (CPM), he put down a rebellion of ethnic Romanians by killing or deporting thousands of people and instituting forced collectivization (see Glossary). Although Brezhnev and other CPM first secretaries were largely successful in suppressing "Moldavian" nationalism, the hostility of "Moldavians" smoldered for another three decades, until after Mikhail S. Gorbachev came to power. His policies of *glasnost* (see Glossary) and *perestroika* (see Glossary) created conditions in which national feelings could be openly expressed and in which the Soviet republics could consider reforms.

Increasing Political Self-Expression

In this climate of openness, political self-assertion escalated

Figure 14. Moldavian Autonomous Soviet Socialist Republic (ASSR) and Transnistria, 1924–95

in the Moldavian SSR in 1988. The year 1989 saw the formation of the Moldovan Popular Front (commonly called the Popular Front), an association of independent cultural and political groups that had finally gained official recognition. Large demonstrations by ethnic Romanians led to the designation of Romanian as the official language and the replacement of the head of the CPM. However, opposition was growing to the increasing influence of ethnic Romanians, especially in Transnistria, where the Yedinstvo-Unitatea (Unity) Intermovement had been formed in 1988 by the Slavic minorities, and in the south, where Gagauz Halkî (Gagauz People), formed in November 1989, came to represent the Gagauz, a Turkic-speaking minority there (see Ethnic Composition, this ch.).

The first democratic elections to the Moldavian SSR's Supreme Soviet (see Glossary) were held February 25, 1990, and runoff elections were held in March. The Popular Front won a majority of the votes. After the elections, Mircea Snegur, a communist, was elected chairman of the Supreme Soviet; in September he became president of the republic. The reformist government that took over in May 1990 made many changes that did not please the minorities, including changing the republic's name in June from the Moldavian Soviet Socialist Republic to the Soviet Socialist Republic of Moldova and declaring it sovereign the same month.

Secession of Gagauzia and Transnistria

In August 1990, the Gagauz declared a separate "Gagauz Republic" (Gagauz-Yeri in Gagauz) in the south, around the city of Comrat (Komrat in Russian). In September, Slavs on the east bank of the Nistru River proclaimed the "Dnestr Moldavian Republic" (commonly called the "Dnestr Republic"; see Glossary) in Transnistria, with its capital at Tiraspol. Although the Supreme Soviet immediately declared these declarations null, both "republics" went on to hold elections. Stepan Topal was elected president of the "Gagauz Republic" in December 1991, and Igor' N. Smirnov was elected president of the "Dnestr Republic" in the same month.

Approximately 50,000 armed Moldovan nationalist volunteers went to Transnistria, where widespread violence was temporarily averted by the intervention of the Russian 14th Army. (The Soviet 14th Army, now the Russian 14th Army, had been headquartered in Chisinau under the High Command of the Southwestern Theater of Military Operations since 1956.) Negotiations in Moscow among the Gagauz, the Transnistrian Slavs, and the government of the Soviet Socialist Republic of Moldova failed, and the government refused to join in further negotiations.

In May 1991, the country's official name was changed to the Republic of Moldova (Republica Moldova). The name of the Supreme Soviet also was changed, to the Moldovan Parliament.

Independence

During the 1991 August coup d'état (see Glossary) in Moscow, commanders of the Soviet Union's Southwestern Theater of Military Operations tried to impose a state of emergency in Moldova, but they were overruled by the Moldovan government, which declared its support for Russian president Boris N. Yeltsin. On August 27, 1991, following the coup's collapse, Moldova declared its independence from the Soviet Union (see Appendix D).

In October, Moldova began to organize its own armed forces. The Soviet Union was falling apart quickly, and Moldova had to rely on itself to prevent the spread of violence from the "Dnestr Republic" to the rest of the country. The December elections of Topal and Smirnov as presidents of their respective "republics," and the official dissolution of the Soviet Union at the end of the year, led to increased tensions in Moldova.

Violence again flared up in Transnistria in 1992. A cease-fire agreement was negotiated by presidents Snegur and Yeltsin in July. A demarcation line was to be maintained by a tripartite peacekeeping force (composed of Moldovan, Russian, and Transnistrian forces), and Moscow agreed to withdraw its 14th Army if a suitable constitutional provision were made for Transnistria. Also, Transnistria would have a special status within Moldova and would have the right to secede if Moldova decided to reunite with Romania.

Progress Toward Political Accommodation

New parliamentary elections were held in Moldova on February 27, 1994. Although the elections were described by international observers as free and fair, authorities in Transnistria refused to allow balloting there and made efforts to discourage the inhabitants from participating. Only some 7,500 inhabitants voted at specially established precincts in right-bank Moldova.

The results of a public opinion poll held on March 6 further reinforced the new Parliament's mandate to preserve Moldova's independence. Moldovans were asked if they wanted Moldova to remain an independent state, and the answer was a resounding—94.5 percent—"yes." Transnistrians did not participate.

The new Parliament, with its Democratic Agrarian Party of Moldova majority, did not face the same gridlock that characterized the old Parliament with its majority of Popular Front hard-line nationalists: legislation was passed, and changes were made. President Snegur signed the Partnership for Peace agreement of the North Atlantic Treaty Organization (NATO) in March 1994, and in April Parliament approved Moldova's membership in the Commonwealth of Independent States (CIS—see Glossary) and in a CIS charter on economic union. On July 28, Parliament ratified a new constitution, which went into effect August 27, 1994, and provided substantial autonomy to Transnistria and to Gagauzia.

Russia and Moldova signed an agreement in October 1994 on the withdrawal of Russian troops from Transnistria and Tighina (Bendery or Bender in Russian), but the Russian government balked at ratifying it, and another stalemate ensued. Although the cease-fire was still in effect at the beginning of 1995 and further negotiations were to include the Conference on Security and Cooperation in Europe (CSCE—see Glossary) and the United Nations, there was little hope for progress in the near future toward settling the dispute and getting the Russian troops to leave.

In March and April 1995, Moldovan college and secondary-school students staged a series of strikes and demonstrations in Chisinau to protest the government's cultural and educational policies. The students were joined by segments of the local intelligentsia and later by workers and pensioners who were protesting for economic reasons. The most emotional issue was that of the national language: should it be called Moldovan, as named in the 1994 constitution, or Romanian, given that most experts regard Moldovan as a dialect of Romanian (see Language, this ch.).

In an April 27 speech to Parliament, President Snegur asked it to amend the constitution and change the name of the language to Romanian. The final decision was postponed until the fall because of the stipulation that six months must pass before a proposed change to the constitution can be made. The student demonstrators declared a moratorium on further strikes until September 6.

In 1995 Moldova was still faced with substantial domestic social and economic problems, but it seemed to be on the road to making progress toward the ideal of a free-market democracy. The country's complex ethnic makeup and the political legacy of the Soviet period continued to contribute to the government's difficulties, but the fall from power of the extreme nationalists in the 1994 parliamentary elections lowered ethnic tensions and allowed compromises to be made with the major ethnic groups. With Russia now a partner in negotiations on Transnistria and with pledges by the new government to respect the rights of the country's Russian-speaking populace, the threat of international hostilities has been greatly reduced.

Physical Environment

Located in southeastern Europe, Moldova is bordered on the west by Romania and on the north, south, and east by Ukraine. Most of its territory lies between the area's two main rivers, the Nistru and the Prut. The Nistru (Dnister in Ukrainian; Dnestr in Russian) forms a small part of Moldova's border with Ukraine in the northeast, but it mainly flows through the eastern part of the country, separating Bessarabia and Transnistria. The Prut River forms Moldova's entire western boundary with Romania.

Topography and Drainage

Most of Moldova's approximately 33,700 square kilometers of territory (about the size of Maryland) cover a hilly plain cut deeply by many streams and rivers. Geologically, Moldova lies primarily on deep sedimentary rock that gives way to harder crystalline outcroppings only in the north, where higher elevations are found on the margins of the foothills of the Carpathian Mountains.

The gently rolling Balti Plain (Stepa Balti in Romanian; Bel'tskaya ravnina in Russian) in northern Moldova (lying at ninety to 600 meters in elevation in the north) gives way to thick, deciduous forests in the Codri Hills (Podisul Codrilor in Romanian; Kodry in Russian), averaging 350 to 400 meters in elevation, where the most common trees are hornbeam, oak, linden, maple, wild pear, and wild cherry. The country's highest point, Mount Balanesti (Balaneshty in Russian), is located in the west-central portion of the country and reaches 430 meters.

The Bugeac Plain (Budzhak in Russian) in the south has numerous ravines and gullies. Transnistria has spurs of the Volyn-Podolian Upland (Podisul Podolie in Romanian; Volyno-Podil's'ka vysochyna in Ukrainian), which are cut into by tributaries of the Nistru River.

About 75 percent of Moldova is covered by a soil type called chernozem (see Glossary). In the northern highlands, more clay-textured soils are found; in the south, red-earth soil is predominant. The soil becomes less fertile toward the south but can still support grape and sunflower production. The uplands have woodland soils, while southern Moldova is in the steppe (see Glossary) zone, although most steppe areas today are cultivated. The lower reaches of the Prut River and the southern river valleys are saline marshes.

Drainage in Moldova is to the south, toward the Black Sea lowlands, and eventually into the Black Sea, but only eight rivers extend more than 100 kilometers. Moldova's main river, the Nistru, is navigable throughout almost the entire country, and in warmer winters it does not freeze over. The Prut River is a tributary of the Danube River, which it joins at the far southwestern tip of the country.

Climate

Moldova's climate is moderately continental: the summers are warm and long, with temperatures averaging about 20°C, and the winters are relatively mild and dry, with January temperatures averaging –4°C. Annual rainfall, which ranges from around 400 millimeters in the south to 600 millimeters in the north, can vary greatly; long dry spells are not unusual. The heaviest rainfall occurs in early summer and again in October; heavy showers and thunderstorms are common. Because of the irregular terrain, heavy summer rains often cause erosion and river silting.

Environmental Concerns

Moldova's communist-era environmental legacy, like that of many other former Soviet republics, is one of environmental degradation. Agricultural practices such as overuse of pesticides, herbicides, and artificial fertilizers were intended to increase agricultural output at all costs, without regard for the consequences. As a result, Moldova's soil and groundwater were contaminated by lingering chemicals, some of which (including DDT) have been banned in the West.

Such practices continue in Moldova to the present day. In the early 1990s, per hectare use of pesticides in Moldova averaged approximately twenty times that of other former Soviet republics and Western nations. In addition, poor farming methods, such as destruction of forests to plant vineyards, have contributed to the extensive soil erosion to which the country's rugged topography is already prone.

Population and Ethnic Composition

Population Characteristics

In July 1994, Moldova's population was estimated at 4,473,033, with an average annual growth rate of 0.38 percent. In 1992 the population's birth rate was 16.1 per 1,000 population (compared with Romania's fourteen per 1,000), the death rate was 10.2 per 1,000 (the same as Romania's), and the rate of natural population increase was 0.6 percent per year (0.9 percent for Romania) (see table 7, Appendix A). The instability that had occurred throughout the Soviet Union at the time of its dissolution had a significant impact on these figures, as is seen by comparing them with the figures for 1989. In 1989 the birth rate was 18.9 per 1,000 population, the death rate was 9.2 per 1,000, and the rate of natural population increase was 1.0 percent. In 1992 the infant mortality rate was thirty-five per 1,000 live births (compared with Romania's twenty-two per 1,000 live births). In 1989 the size of the average Moldovan family was 3.4 persons.

In 1991 about 28 percent of the population was under fifteen years of age, and almost 13 percent was over sixty-five years of age (see fig. 15). Life expectancy in 1994 was sixty-five years for males and seventy-two years for females.

Although Moldova is by far the most densely populated of the former Soviet republics (129 inhabitants per square kilometer in 1990, compared with thirteen inhabitants per square kilometer for the Soviet Union as a whole), it has few large cities. The largest and most important of these is Chisinau, the country's capital and its most important industrial center. Founded in 1420, Chisinau is located in the center of the republic, on the Bîc (Byk in Russian) River and in 1990 had a population of 676,000. The city's population is slightly more than 50 percent ethnic Romanian, with ethnic Russians constituting approximately 25 percent and ethnic Ukrainians 13 percent. The proportion of ethnic Russians and ethnic Ukrainians in the capital's population decreased in the years immediately after 1989 because of the emigration resulting from Moldavia's changing political situation and civil unrest.

The second largest city in the republic, Tiraspol, had a population of 184,000 in 1990. Located in Transnistria, Tiraspol

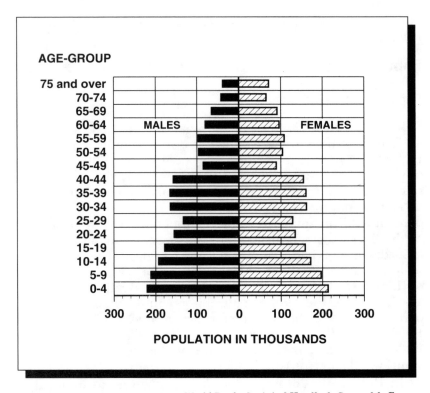

AGE-GROUP

Source: Based on information from World Bank, *Statistical Handbook: States of the Former
USSR,* Washington, 1992, 279; and United Nations, Department for Economic
and Social Information and Policy Analysis, *Demographic Yearbook (Annuaire
démographique), 1992,* New York, 1994, 184.

*Figure 15. Population Distribution of Moldavia by Age and Gender,
1990*

served as the capital of the Moldavian ASSR from 1929 to 1940.
It has remained an important center of administration, transportation, and manufacturing. In contrast to Chisinau, Tiraspol had a population of only some 18 percent ethnic Romanians, with most of the remainder being ethnic Russians (41
percent) and ethnic Ukrainians (32 percent).

Other important cities include Balti (Bel'tsy in Russian),
with a population of 162,000 in 1990, and Tighina, with a population of 132,000 in the same year. As in Tiraspol, ethnic Romanians are in the minority in both of these cities.

Traditionally a rural country, Moldova gradually began
changing its character under Soviet rule (see table 8, Appendix
A). As urban areas became the sites of new industrial jobs and

of amenities such as health clinics, the population of cities and towns grew. The new residents were not only ethnic Romanians who had moved from rural areas but also many ethnic Russians and Ukrainians who had been recruited to fill positions in industry and government (see Ethnic Composition, this ch.).

In 1990 Moldova's divorce rate of 3.0 divorces per 1,000 population had risen from the 1987 rate of 2.7 divorces per 1,000 population (see table 9, Appendix A). The usual stresses of marriage were exacerbated by a society in which women were expected to perform most of the housework in addition to their work outside the home. Compounding this were crowded housing conditions (with their resulting lack of privacy) and, no doubt, the growing political crisis, which added its own strains.

Ethnic Composition

One of Moldova's characteristic traits is its ethnic diversity. As early as the beginning of the eighteenth century, Moldovan prince and scholar Dimitrie Cantemir observed that he "didn't believe that there [existed] a single country of the size of Moldova in which so many and such diverse peoples meet."

At the time of the 1989 census, Moldova's total population was 4,335,360. The largest nationality in the republic, ethnic Romanians, numbered 2,795,000 persons, accounting for approximately 65 percent of the population. The other major nationalities were Ukrainians, about 600,000 (14 percent); Russians, about 562,000 (13 percent); Gagauz, about 153,000 (4 percent); and Bulgarians, about 88,000 (2 percent). The remaining population consisted of Jews, about 66,000, and smaller but appreciable numbers of Belorusssians, Poles, Roma (Gypsies), and Germans (see fig. 16). By contrast, in Transnistria ethnic Romanians accounted for only 40 percent of the population in 1989, followed by Ukrainians (28 percent), Russians (25 percent), Bulgarians (2 percent), and Gagauz (1 percent) (see fig. 17).

In the early 1990s, there was significant emigration from the republic, primarily from urban areas and primarily by Romanian minorities. In 1990 persons emigrating accounted for 6.8 percent of the population. This figure rose to 10 percent in 1991 before dropping sharply to 2 percent in 1992.

Ethnic Romanians made up a sizable proportion of the urban population in 1989 (about half the population of Chisinau, for example), as well as a large proportion of the rural

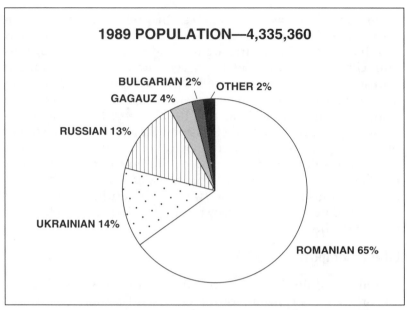

Figure 16. Estimated Population Distribution of Moldavia by Ethnic Group, 1989

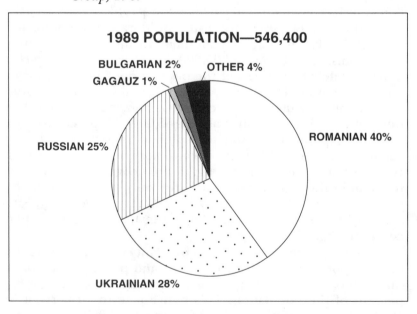

Source: Based on information from Vasile Nedelciuc, *The Republic of Moldova*, Chisinau, June 1992, 23.

Figure 17. Estimated Population Distribution of Transnistria by Ethnic Group, 1989

population (80 percent), but only 23 percent of the ethnic Romanians lived in the republic's ten largest cities. Many ethnic Romanians emigrated to Romania at the end of World War II, and others had lost their lives during the war and in postwar Soviet purges. As a consequence of industrial growth and the Soviet government's policy of diluting and Russifying ethnic Romanians, there was significant immigration to the Moldavian SSR by other nationalities, especially ethnic Russians and Ukrainians.

Unlike ethnic Romanians, ethnic Russians tend to be urban dwellers in Moldova; more than 72 percent of them lived in the ten largest cities in 1989. Many of them came to the Moldavian SSR after it was annexed by the Soviet government in 1940; more arrived after World War II. Ostensibly, they came to alleviate the Moldavian SSR's postwar labor shortage (although thousands of ethnic Romanians were being deported to Central Asia at the time) and to fill leadership positions in industry and the government. The Russians settled mainly in Chisinau and Tighina and in the Transnistrian cities of Tiraspol and Dubasari (Dubossary in Russian). Only about 25 percent of Moldova's Russians lived in Transnistria in the early 1990s (see fig. 18).

Ethnic Ukrainians in Moldova are more evenly distributed between rural and urban areas. Forty-seven percent of them resided in large cities in 1989; others lived in long-settled villages dispersed throughout the region, but particularly in the north and in Transnistria.

The Gagauz, Turkic-speaking Orthodox Christians (unlike most Turks, who are Muslims), are concentrated in rural southern Moldova, mainly around the cities of Comrat, Ciadîr-Lunga (Chadyr-Lunga in Russian), and Vulcanesti (Vulkaneshty in Russian). Their ethnic origin is complex and still debated by scholars, but it is agreed that they migrated to Bessarabia from Bulgaria in the late eighteenth and early nineteenth centuries. Shortly after Moldova declared its sovereignty, in August 1990 the Gagauz declared their own independent "Gagauz Republic" in the southern part of the country. The 1994 constitution accorded them a measure of autonomy, and a decree later that year officially established Gagauzia (Gagauz-Yeri in Gagauz).

Ethnic Bulgarians in Moldova live mainly in the southern part of the country. Most of them are descendants of eighteenth-century settlers who came to the region because of persecution by the Turks. Others came to Bessarabia when the

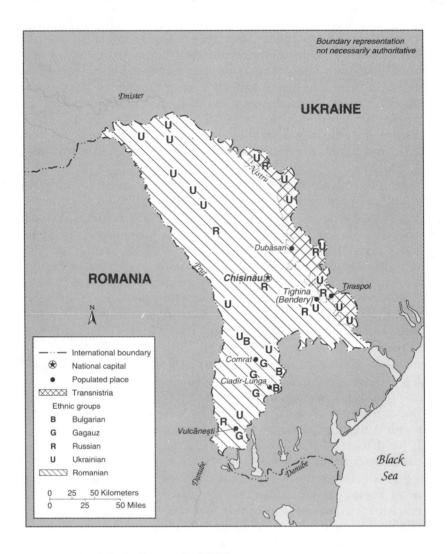

Figure 18. Ethnic Groups in Moldova

Russian Empire encouraged their emigration in the nine-teenth century. Their numbers declined from 177,000 when the Moldavian SSR was formed in 1940 to 88,000 in the 1989 census.

Although considered a religious affiliation in the West, "Jew-ish" was considered a nationality by Soviet authorities, even though Judaism was suppressed as a religion. Although Jews had lived in Bessarabia and the region of Moldova for centuries before Empress Catherine II of Russia established the Pale of Settlement, Jews in Russia were restricted to living and traveling solely within the Pale as of 1792. By the nineteenth century, the Pale included Russian Poland, Lithuania, Belorussia, most of Ukraine, Crimea, and Bessarabia. It was only in the second half of the nineteenth century that exceptions were made and Jews were permitted to live outside the Pale.

Most of the prolonged military conflict of World War I and the Russian Civil War took place in the Pale, inflicting heavy losses of life and property on Jews. When it was created in 1940, the Moldavian SSR (mainly Chisinau) held more than 200,000 Jews. However, their numbers plummeted to only several thousand as a result of emigration. Their ranks increased again during the 1960s and 1970s, only to decline afterward, mainly the result of emigration.

In general, Jews in independent Moldova are not discriminated against. But problems in Transnistria (home to almost one-quarter of Moldova's Jews) and the anti-Semitic attitudes of the "Dnestr Republic" authorities have prompted many Transnistrian Jews to think of emigration.

Language, Religion, and Culture

Language

The Moldovan dialect of Romanian, a Romance language descended from Latin and spoken by the majority of the people of Bessarabia, was viewed by both the Russian Empire and the Soviet Union as an impediment to controlling the local populace. Under the tsars, Romanian-language education and the Romanian press were forbidden as part of a process of forced Russification.

Stalin justified the creation of the Moldavian SSR by claiming that a distinct "Moldavian" language was an indicator that "Moldavians" were a separate nationality from the Romanians in Romania. In order to give greater credence to this claim, in 1940 Stalin imposed the Cyrillic alphabet on "Moldavian" to make it look more like Russian and less like Romanian; archaic Romanian words of Slavic origin were imposed on "Moldavian"; Russian loanwords and phrases were added to "Moldavian"; and a new theory was advanced that "Moldavian" was at least partially Slavic in origin. In 1949 Moldavian citizens were publicly reprimanded in a journal for daring to express themselves in literary Romanian. The Soviet government continued this type of behavior for decades.

Proper names were subjected to Russianization (see Glossary) as well. Russian endings were added to purely Romanian names, and individuals were referred to in the Russian manner by using a patronymic (based on one's father's first name) together with a first name.

In 1989 members of most of the Moldavian SSR's nationalities claimed their national language as their mother tongue: Romanians (95 percent), Ukrainians (62 percent), Russians (99 percent), Gagauz (91 percent), Bulgarians (79 percent), and Roma (82 percent). The exceptions were Jews (26 percent citing Yiddish), Belorussians (43 percent), Germans (31 percent), and Poles (10 percent).

Although both Romanian written in the Cyrillic alphabet (that is, "Moldavian") and Russian were the official languages of the Moldavian SSR, only 62 percent of the total population claimed Romanian as their native language in 1979. If ethnic Romanians are subtracted from this number, the figure falls to just over 1 percent. Only 4 percent of the entire population claimed Romanian as a second language.

In 1979 Russian was claimed as a native language by a large proportion of Jews (66 percent) and ethnic Belorussians (62 percent) and by a significant proportion of ethnic Ukrainians (30 percent). Proportions of other nationalities naming Russian as a native language ranged from 17 percent of ethnic Bulgarians to 3 percent of ethnic Romanians (urban Romanians were more Russianized than rural Romanians). Russian was claimed as a second language by a sizable proportion of all the nationalities: Romanians (46 percent), Ukrainians (43 percent), Gagauz (68 percent), Jews (30 percent), Bulgarians (67 percent), Belorussians (34 percent), Germans (53 percent), Roma (36 percent), and Poles (24 percent).

On August 31, 1989, the Supreme Soviet of Moldavia passed the Law on State Language, which made Moldovan written in the Latin alphabet the state language of the Moldavian SSR. Because of pressure exerted by non-Romanian ethnic groups, Russian was retained as the language of interethnic communication. In areas where non-Romanian ethnic groups were the majority, the language of that majority could also be used as a means of communication. Because of strong objections raised by the non-Romanian nationalities, implementation of the law was delayed.

The new Moldovan constitution, adopted August 27, 1994, designates Moldovan written in the Latin script as the official language, but provisions are made for Russian and other languages to be used in areas of minority concentration. Russian is designated the language of interethnic communication.

On April 27, 1995, President Snegur asked Parliament to change the name of the language in the constitution, from Moldovan to Romanian, in response to demonstrations and strikes led by students. According to Moldovan law, it would be six months before a proposed change to the constitution could be made.

Religion

Most of Moldova's population are Orthodox Christians. In 1991 about 98.5 percent of the population belonged to this faith.

The Soviet government strictly limited the activities of the Orthodox Church (and all religions) and at times sought to exploit it, with the ultimate goal of destroying it and all religious activity. Most Orthodox churches and monasteries in Moldova were demolished or converted to other uses, such as warehouses, and clergy were sometimes punished for leading services. But many believers continued to practice their faith in secret.

In 1991 Moldova had 853 Orthodox churches and eleven Orthodox monasteries (four for monks and seven for nuns). In addition, the Old Russian Orthodox Church (Old Believers— see Glossary) had fourteen churches and one monastery in Moldova.

Before Soviet power was established in Moldova, the vast majority of ethnic Romanians belonged to the Romanian Orthodox Church (Bucharest Patriarchate), but today the Russian Orthodox Church (Moscow Patriarchate) has jurisdiction in Moldova. Russian, Romanian, and Turkic (Gagauz) liturgies are used in the church. After the recent revival of religious activity, most of the clergy and the faithful wanted to return to the Bucharest Patriarchate but were prevented from doing so. Because higher-level church authorities were unable to resolve the matter, Moldova now has two episcopates, one for each patriarchate. In late 1992, the Patriarch of Moscow and All Russia issued a decree upgrading the Eparchy of Chisinau and Moldova to a metropolitan see (for definition of eparchy—see Glossary).

Moldova also has a Uniate minority, mainly among ethnic Ukrainians, although the Soviet government declared the Uniate Church (see Glossary) illegal in 1946 and forcibly united it with the Russian Orthodox Church. The Uniate Church survived underground, however, outlasting the Soviet Union itself.

Despite the Soviet government's suppression and ongoing harassment, Moldavia's Jews managed to retain their religious identity. About a dozen Jewish newspapers were started in the early 1990s, and religious leaders opened a synagogue in Chisinau; there were six Jewish communities of worship throughout the country. In addition, Moldova's government created the Department of Jewish Studies at Chisinau State University, mandated the opening of a Jewish high school in Chisinau, and introduced classes in Judaism in high schools in several cities. The government also provided financial support to the Society for Jewish Culture.

Other religious denominations in Moldova are the Armenian Apostolic Church, Seventh-Day Adventists, Baptists, Pentecostals, and Molokans (a Russian Orthodox sect).

Citizens in independent Moldova have much greater religious freedom than they did under the Soviet regime. Legislation passed in 1992 guaranteed religious freedom but did require that all religious groups be officially recognized by the government. In 1992 construction or restoration of 221 churches was under way, but clergy remained in short supply.

Culture

Moldova's cultural tradition has been influenced primarily by the Romanian origin of its majority population and cannot be understood outside of the development of classical Romanian culture, in which it played a significant role. The roots of Romanian culture reach back to the second century A.D., the period of Roman colonization in Dacia. During the centuries following the Roman withdrawal in A.D. 271, the population of the region was influenced by contact with the Byzantine Empire, with neighboring Slavic and Magyar populations, and later with the Ottoman Turks. Beginning in the nineteenth century, a strong West European (particularly French) influence was felt in Romanian literature and the arts. The resulting mélange has produced a rich cultural tradition. Although foreign contacts were an inevitable consequence of the region's geography, their influence only served to enhance a vital and resilient popular culture.

The regional population had come to identify itself widely as "Moldovan" by the fourteenth century but continued to maintain close cultural links with other Romanian groups. The eastern Moldovans, however, those inhabiting Bessarabia and Transnistria, were also influenced by Slavic culture from neighboring Ukraine. During the periods 1812–1917 and 1944–89, the eastern Moldovans were influenced by Russian and Soviet administrative control, as well and by ethnic Russian immigration.

Bessarabia was one of the least-developed and its population among the least-educated in the European regions of the Russian Empire and later of the Soviet Union. In 1930 its literacy rate was only 40 percent, according to a Romanian census. Although Soviet authorities promoted education (not the least to spread communist ideology), they also did everything they could to break the region's cultural ties with Romania. With many ethnic Romanian intellectuals either fleeing, being killed, or being deported both during and after World War II, Bessarabia's cultural and educational situation worsened.

To fill the gap, Soviet authorities developed urban cultural and scientific centers and institutions that were subsequently filled with Russians and with other non-Romanian ethnic groups, but this culture was superimposed and alien. Urban culture came from Moscow; the rural ethnic Romanian population was allowed to express itself only in folklore or folk art.

Although the folk arts flourished, similarities with Romanian culture were hidden. Music and dance, particularly encouraged by Soviet authorities, were made into a showcase but were subtly distorted to hide their Romanian origins. An example is the national folk costume, in which the traditional Romanian moccasin (*opinca*) was replaced by the Russian boot.

Moldova's folk culture is extremely rich, and the ancient folk ballad known as the "Miorita" plays a central role in the traditional culture. Folk traditions, including ceramics and weaving, continue to be practiced in rural areas. The folk culture tradition is promoted at the national level and is represented by, among other groups, the republic's dance company, Joc, and by the folk choir, Doina.

The first Moldovan books (religious texts) appeared in the first half of the seventeenth century. Prominent figures in Moldova's cultural development include prince and scholar Dimitrie Cantemir (1673–1723), historian and philologist Bogdan P. Hasdeu (1836–1907), author Ion Creanga (1837–89), and poet Mihai Eminescu (1850–89).

Prominent modern writers include Vladimir Besleaga, Pavel Botu, Aureliu Busioc, Nicolae Dabija, Ion Druta, and Grigore Vieru. In 1991 a total of 520 books were published in Moldova, of which 402 were in Romanian, 108 in Russian, eight in Gagauz, and two in Bulgarian.

In the early 1990s, Moldova had twelve professional theaters. All performed in Romanian except the A.P. Chekhov Russian Drama Theater in Chisinau and the Russian Drama and Comedy Theater in Tiraspol, both of which performed solely in Russian, and the Licurici Republic Puppet Theater (in Chisinau), which performed in both Romanian and Russian. Members of ethnic minorities managed a number of folklore groups and amateur theaters throughout the country.

Education, Health, and Welfare

Education

In the decades prior to independence, the Moldavian SSR's education system made substantial progress toward being available to all citizens. At the beginning of the twentieth century, illiteracy had been common among Moldova's rural population. But by 1992, the adult literacy rate had risen to 96 percent. In 1990 the mean duration of schooling was six years, and 30 percent of the population aged fifteen and older had completed general secondary education.

Under the Soviet education system, the Moldavian SSR had parallel systems of Romanian-language and Russian-language education through secondary school, although Russian was seen as the key to advancement. In 1990 a total of 614 preschools were taught in Romanian, 1,333 were taught in Russian, and 373 were taught in both Romanian and Russian. There were 1,025 Romanian-language primary and secondary schools with 399,200 students; 420 Russian-language schools with 239,100 students; and 129 mixed-language schools with 82,500 students studying in the Russian and Romanian languages (more than half of the students studied in Russian). Change occurred slowly at the university level, however, and 55 percent of students continued to study in the Russian language as of 1992.

Under Moldova's education system, ten years of basic education are compulsory, followed by either technical school or further study leading to higher education. In the early 1990s, the Moldovan government restored the Romanian language in schools and added courses in Romanian literature and history to the curriculum. The governments of Romania and Moldova established strong ties between their education systems; several thousand Moldovan students attended school in Romania, and the Romanian government donated textbooks to Moldova to replace books from the Soviet era.

As Moldovan society became more industrialized and more complex under the Soviet regime, the role of higher education also expanded (although ethnic Russian and Ukrainian students were given preference in university admissions during the Soviet era). Although there were only ten students per 10,000 population enrolled in institutions of higher education in 1940, this number increased to 120 per 10,000 population in 1992. In early 1995, Moldova had ten institutions of higher education; four of these institutions had been established since independence. The republic also maintained institutes of agriculture, economics, engineering, medicine, the arts, pedagogy, and physical education.

Health

Although the Soviet government had built health care facilities in the Moldavian SSR, modern equipment and facilities were in short supply in the early 1990s. In 1990 there were 129 hospital beds and forty doctors per 10,000 inhabitants. The 1991 state budget allocated approximately 12 percent of the total budget to health care, most of which was provided to citizens free of charge.

The leading causes of death in Moldova are cardiovascular diseases, cancer, respiratory diseases, and accidents. Other major health problems are high levels of alcohol consumption and illnesses resulting from the extensive and indiscriminate use of herbicides and pesticides (see Environmental Concerns, this ch.).

Welfare

Although Moldavia's official standard of living had long been below the average for the Soviet Union, there were two mitigating factors. The rural character of the country accounted for many households receiving goods (mainly food) as well as cash wages. In addition, Moldavian industry was based on consumer goods (including textiles, consumer appliances, and processed agricultural goods), making them relatively plentiful throughout the republic (see table 10, Appendix A).

The hostilities in Transnistria and the turmoil surrounding the demise of the Soviet Union were the major reasons for the falling standard of living in Moldova in the early 1990s. The outbreak of hostilities in Transnistria interrupted not only the flow of fuels and goods from former Soviet republics through Transnistria into right-bank Moldova but also cut off valuable inputs (for example, fertilizer) that were produced in Transnistria. These shortages of inputs, in turn, indirectly affected such indicators as food consumption, a sign that everyday life was affected (see table 11, Appendix A).

In 1991 Moldova set up the Social Assistance Fund (to provide assistance to the needy) and the Social Security Fund (SSF). The SSF is composed of the Pension Fund, the Social Insurance Fund, the Unemployment Fund, and the Reserve Fund. Funding for the SSF comes mainly from a payroll tax and from direct budget transfers.

The Pension Fund provides old-age pensions (age fifty-five for women who have worked at least twenty years, and age sixty for men who have worked for twenty-five years), pensions for invalids, pensions for women who have raised three or more children, military and special merit pensions, and pensions for people of retirement age or for people who receive disability pensions yet continue to work.

In early 1994, approximately 900,000 people (about 20 percent of the total population) received pensions. Legislation increased both benefits for dependent children and the minimum pension in 1992, and a law was passed to index benefits to inflation, but the law had not been fully implemented by the end of the year. Many felt that passage of this legislation would add significantly to the demands on an already overburdened budget.

Housing

Even before independence, much of Moldova's housing stock was in private hands because of the country's strong tradition of private home ownership, especially in rural areas. In 1994 some 90 percent of rural and 36 percent of urban apartments were held privately.

At the time of Moldova's independence, housing construction was hampered by severe shortages of building materials and disruptions in deliveries. However, the housing stock continued to expand in both rural and urban areas. In 1990 private builders accounted for only 26 percent of construction in urban areas but for 95 percent of construction in rural areas. In 1990 per capita housing space averaged eighteen square meters (fourteen square meters in urban areas and twenty-one square meters in rural areas).

All state-owned housing was scheduled for privatization, in stages, beginning in May 1993 and using government-issued vouchers. Apartments that did not exceed state norms for per capita space utilization were to be turned over to their occupants free of charge. People living in apartments that exceeded space norms would have to pay the state a premium based on the average cost per square meter of housing construction. Privatization using vouchers was scheduled to be completed in the summer of 1995, at which time there would be an open housing market (see Postindependence Privatization and Other Reforms, this ch.).

The Economy

Historically, the region now encompassed by the Republic of Moldova was poorly developed. Economic activity was principally agricultural, rural poverty was endemic, and the urban economy, such as it was, was based almost entirely on commerce, food processing, and the production of consumer goods. Development prior to the mid-eighteenth century lagged for a variety of reasons, but principally because of limited resources and political instability. The region of Moldova was relatively backward in comparison with the rest of Romania.

The Economy in the Soviet Period

Under Soviet rule, the Moldavian ASSR (1924–40) experienced considerable industrial development between the two world wars, particularly in and around Tiraspol, the site of new manufacturing activity. After World War II, substantial industrialization occurred throughout the Moldavian SSR (1940–91), especially in Chisinau, but with a continuing focus on Transnistria as well. In addition to further developing the food-processing industry, the government introduced the textile, machine tool, and electronics industries (see fig. 19).

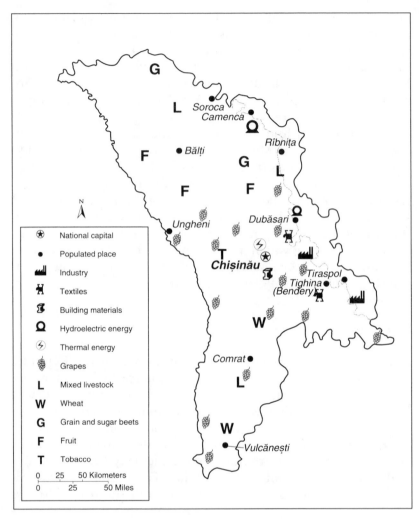

Source: Based on information from Lerner Publications Company, Geography
     Department, *Moldova*, Minneapolis, 1993, 44.

Figure 19. Economic Activity in Moldova, 1995

Until independence, Moldavia's economy was organized
along standard Soviet lines: all industry was state owned, as
were commerce and finance. Approximately one-third of all
enterprises (see Glossary) were subordinate to the economic
ministries of the Soviet Union, and two-thirds were subordinate
to republic-level authorities. Agriculture was collectivized, and
production was organized principally around state farms (see
Glossary) and collective farms (see Glossary).

The Moldavian economy, robust in the 1970s, slowed down somewhat in the early 1980s and contracted sharply in 1985, mainly as a result of declining activity in the wine sector, a casualty of Gorbachev's anti-alcohol campaign. In the late 1980s, the economy briefly regained strength and grew faster than the economy of the Soviet Union as a whole.

Postindependence Privatization and Other Reforms

Once independence was achieved, Moldova's government undertook measures to begin privatization, which included passing a law mandating privatization and establishing the State Department for Privatization to direct the process. The overall reform policy was guided by the Draft Economic Reform Program of the Government of Moldova, a 1991 document calling for establishment of a market economy but permitting significant provisions for government intervention.

In late 1992, the government presented Parliament with a more market-oriented policy in its Program of Activity of the Government of Moldova for 1992–1995. Its goal was to form a new social pact as a basis for a new society and economy for Moldova. The two-part program would first aim at stabilizing the country and then provide for the economy's recovery and growth by such means as agrarian and trade reform, social protection, and a legal framework for a market economy. The direction of the new government was elaborated in the Program of Activity of the Government of the Republic of Moldova for 1994–1997, which was adopted by Parliament. The program focuses on restructuring the economy, reorganizing enterprises, privatizing small and medium-sized enterprises, promoting entrepreneurship, decreasing the budget deficit, implementing an efficient fiscal policy, and formulating new mechanisms to create a market economy. Another bill, the Program for Privatization for 1995–1996, was approved by Parliament in March 1995. It focuses on foreign investment, privatization of agricultural land, the introduction of cash auctions, mass privatization, and the development of capital markets. More than 1,450 state enterprises are to be auctioned off.

During 1992 enterprise privatization committees inventoried assets at each enterprise in the republic; the aggregate result of this inventory became the basis of calculations of Moldova's total industrial wealth. Each citizen was to be provided with patrimonial bonds (vouchers) in 1993, endowing him or her with a share of this total wealth based on years of employment in the economy. Citizens would receive one voucher point per year of work in the republic. Enterprise employees were to be allowed to purchase up to 30 percent of the value of their enterprises at nominal value. By special arrangement, 40 percent of the value of enterprises in the food-processing sector was to be allocated to suppliers. The program was to be completed by the summer of 1995. As of the beginning of 1995, Moldova had 4,400 state and 57,000 private enterprises.

Employees of collective and state farms were also to be provided with vouchers based on the length of their employment in the agricultural sector. In January 1992, Moldova expanded the amount of free land that eligible families would receive from state farms to 0.5 hectare per family, with an additional 0.1 hectare to be added for fourth and subsequent family members up to a maximum of one hectare per family, on the condition that it not be resold before 2001 (although it could be bequeathed).

Collective and state farms were to be converted into joint-stock companies first, and the land and property were to be allocated later. In 1993 Moldova had 481 small private farms; by 1995 this number had increased to 13,958. In 1995 about 1.5 percent of agricultural land in Moldova was held by these small farmers. The reasons for slow privatization of the agricultural sector include slow privatization of large organizations, the use of outmoded production methods and equipment, poor accounting practices, and a shortage of processing facilities.

At the same time that privatization plans were under way, actual reform efforts were halting and relatively ineffectual, and Moldova's economy declined. A number of factors contributed to the decline, including the complicated political situation in the republic (which had seen several changes of leadership in its first years of existence) and the political and military conflict with Transnistria. Substantial industrial capacity is located in Transnistria, and the disruption of traditional economic ties with enterprises there has had a negative effect on the economy of right-bank Moldova.

Further, because Moldova's economy was firmly embedded in the broader economic structures of the former Soviet Union, it also suffered damage from the breakdown in interrepublic trade, abrupt increases in external prices, and inflation resulting from the Russian government's policy of printing large amounts of money. (Moldova retained the Russian ruble as its currency until November 1993.) The consequence of all these factors has been a substantial economic downturn in both industry and agriculture, accompanied by increased unemployment and a decline in labor productivity. In 1991 Moldova's national income was only at 1985 levels. Moldova's industrial output in early 1995 was half that of 1990. Moldova's gross domestic product (GDP—see Glossary) declined by 30 percent in 1994 (and by 5 percent in 1993 and 28 percent in 1992), and its industrial output declined by 34 percent (and by 12 percent in 1993 and 27 percent in 1992).

Labor Force

Moldova's labor force still reflects the structure of the economy under communism. In 1991 about 78 percent of the population who were employed outside the home worked in the state sector, 19 percent worked on collective farms, and 3 percent worked in the private sector. The private sector employed 9 percent of the workforce in 1995. In early 1995, the official unemployment rate was 1 percent, but experts put the real rate at between 10 and 15 percent.

Agriculture

At the time of Moldova's independence, agriculture continued to play a major role in the country's economy, as it had during the Soviet period. In 1991 agriculture accounted for 42 percent of the net material product (NMP—see Glossary) and employed 36 percent of the labor force (see fig. 20).

The organizational backbone of independent Moldova's agriculture continues to be its system of former state and collective farms, one-quarter of which were transformed into joint-stock companies by 1994 and are now owned in shares by the people who work them. In 1993 Moldova's 600 collective farms covered 16.2 million hectares of land and employed 401,300 persons; in the same year, its 389 state farms encompassed 600,500 hectares of land and employed 168,200 persons. Agricultural output from private farms increased from 18 percent in 1990 to 38 percent in 1994.

Moldova possesses substantial agricultural resources; its climate and fertile soils (1.7 million hectares of arable land in 1991) support a wide range of crops. The country is an important regional producer of grapes and grape products, and its orchards produce significant amounts of fruit, including plums, apricots, cherries, and peaches. Fruit production is con-

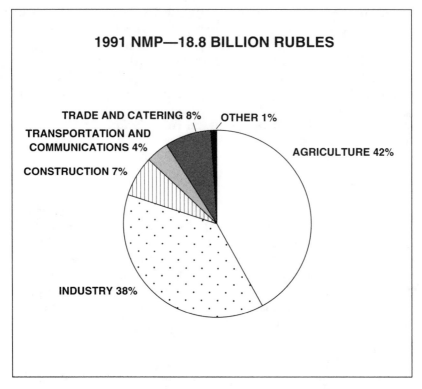

1991 NMP—18.8 BILLION RUBLES

Source: Based on information from International Monetary Fund, *Moldova*,
        Washington, 1993, 31.

Figure 20. Net Material Product (NMP) of Moldova by Sector, 1991

centrated in the north, in the central region, and in the Nistru
River area. Tobacco is also an important commercial crop.
Sugar beets are grown throughout the republic and provide
raw material for a substantial (although antiquated) sugar-
refining industry, and sunflowers are grown for their oil. Cereal
crops, including wheat, are grown widely (corn is the leading
grain) and are used for domestic consumption, export, and
animal feed.

Meat accounts for less than half of total agricultural production. In 1991 about half of total meat output was accounted for
by pork (145,000 tons), followed by beef and veal (97,000
tons), chicken (56,000 tons), and lamb (5,000 tons). From
1990 to 1994, the amount of arable land used for livestock production decreased by some 25 percent; the number of livestock
in 1994 was 400,000.

Probably the most widely known products of Moldova are its wines, sparkling wines, and brandies, which were recognized as among the finest in the former Soviet Union. In 1991 these accounted for 28 percent of the output of the food-processing sector, followed by meat processing with 22 percent of production, and fruit and vegetable processing (including the production of canned fruits and vegetables, jams, jellies, and fruit juices) with 15 percent. Moldova also produces sugar and sugar products, perfume, vegetable oils, and dairy products.

Approximately half of Moldova's agricultural and food production is sold to former Soviet republics. Traditional markets are Russia, Ukraine, and Belarus.

Agricultural production has been in serious decline since the late 1980s, both in terms of overall production levels and in terms of per-hectare production of most crops (see table 12, Appendix A). Overall agricultural output in 1991 was at 1970 levels. A number of factors contributed to the decline, including difficulties in providing necessary inputs and agricultural machinery, disruption of the transportation system, failures in the incentive system, difficulties related to political instability in Transnistria, Gorbachev's anti-alcohol campaign, and, not the least, Moldova's variable weather. In 1990 a drought resulted in a serious decline in production. On the heels of the drought, 1991 saw a spring freeze, severe summer flooding, and then the worst drought in some fifty years. Overall agricultural output in 1993 was down 15 percent from the previous year; grain production, one-third less than in 1991, was particularly affected (especially corn, which was down over 50 percent on average). The trend continued into 1994, when drought and storms with hurricane-force winds caused agricultural output to decline 58 percent from 1993 levels. Although Moldova was traditionally a wheat exporter, it had to import 100,000 to 200,000 tons of wheat as a result of a 1994 harvest that was 800,000 tons less than the harvest of 1993.

In fiscal year (FY—see Glossary) 1992, Moldova participated in the United States Department of Agriculture's P.L. 480 Title I program, which provided US$7 million in long-term credit for government-to-government concessional sales, offered repayment terms of ten to thirty years (with grace periods of up to seven years), and provided low interest rates. Moldova's line of credit was scheduled to increase to US$10 million in 1993.

By the beginning of 1994, total United States assistance to Moldova included approximately US$12 million in technical assistance in support of Moldova's transition to a market economy and democracy and US$68 million in humanitarian assistance. In 1995 the United States was scheduled to provide US$22 million in technical assistance for economic restructuring and privatization. This amount brings total United States assistance to Moldova since 1992 to more than US$200 million.

Industry

In 1991 industry accounted for approximately 38 percent of NMP and employed 21 percent of the work force. Some of the main products of Moldova's industry include electrical motors and equipment, pumps for industrial and agricultural use, and agricultural equipment, including tractors and automobile parts. There is also a small chemical industry, which produces plastics, synthetic fibers, paint, and varnish, and a construction industry, which produces cement and prefabricated reinforced-concrete structures.

The Moldovan consumer goods industry in the early 1990s was faced with the same problems affecting the rest of the Moldovan economy. The supply of cheap fuels and raw materials, provided to Moldavia under the Soviet economic system (under which Moldavia specialized in consumer goods and agricultural products), dried up with the demise of the Soviet Union and the hostilities in Transnistria. Together with high inflation, the cost of goods went up tremendously, sometimes doubling in the course of one year.

In 1991 consumer goods accounted for 22 percent of Moldova's industrial output; the textile industry accounted for approximately 50 percent of this, and food processing accounted for 40 percent. Clothing manufacturing made up another 29 percent of total production.

In 1994 Moldova had eleven enterprises producing military goods. Attempts were being made to convert ten of them to civilian production. However, these facilities were operating at only 15 to 20 percent of capacity, as compared with the industry-wide average of 40 percent of capacity. As a result, conversion prospects were not bright.

Moldova's heavy industry is almost entirely the result of development during the Soviet period. Machine building predominates within heavy industry, accounting for 16 percent of total industrial production.

Sunday afternoon flower market, Chisinau
Courtesy Tom Skipper
Private housing under construction, Stauceni
Courtesy Charles King

Energy and Fuels

Among the most pressing difficulties facing the republic's economy is a near total lack of energy resources. Moldova's own primary energy sources consist of small hydroelectric power plants on the Nistru River at Dubasari and Camenca (Kamenka in Russian); minor thermal electric power plants at Balti, Rîbnita (Rybnitsa in Russian), Ungheni (Ungeny in Russian), and Chisinau; and firewood, all of which combine to meet only 1 percent of domestic needs. A coal-fired power plant was under construction at Cuciurgan (Kuchurgan in Russian), in Transnistria, in 1995.

Another source of problems is the fact that almost 90 percent of power and 100 percent of power transformers are produced in politically troubled Transnistria. In addition, Transnistria's adversarial "government" has frequently disrupted the flow of fuels into Moldova from Russia and Ukraine.

Moldova has an electric-power production capacity of 3.1 million kilowatts, and it produced 11.1 billion kilowatt-hours of electricity in 1993. By 1994 electricity production had decreased 14 percent in comparison with 1993. Over the same period, thermal electric production decreased 22 percent.

Despite its lack of energy resources, the country continues to export some of the electricity it generates to Romania and Bulgaria. However, these exports have been cut back (the countries receive electricity only to the extent to which they supply fuel). Some electricity shortages have occurred in Moldova, mostly in winter, and have been dealt with by rationing. Much of the country's generating equipment (which is not produced by Moldova) and approximately one-quarter of its transmission and distribution lines are in need of repair.

In the early 1990s, energy shortages were prevalent, and energy availability was sporadic, leading to disruptions in economic activity. Imports of coal, natural gas, diesel fuel, and gasoline declined by an estimated average of 40 percent from 1991 to 1992. In 1994 the picture was somewhat different. Gasoline imports were up 33.6 percent, and coal imports increased 15.4 percent, while imports of diesel fuel, mazut, and natural gas fell 25 percent, 51.5 percent, and 3.1 percent, respectively.

In 1994 Moldova was dependent on Russia for 90 percent of the fuel needed for its electric-power generation plants: diesel oil (88,000 tons), gasoline (65,000 tons), fuel oil (365,000 tons), and natural gas (2.8 billion cubic meters). By March

1995, Moldova owed Russia US$232 million for fuel, with half of this amount owed by the "Dnestr Republic."

Moldova had started paying off this debt in goods, including agricultural products, but beginning in late 1994 the government instead gave Gazprom, the Russian state-controlled gas company, equity stakes in key Moldovan enterprises. In January 1995, Moldova gave control of Moldovagas, the state-owned gas company, to Gazprom.

Banking and Finance

Moldova's banking system, part of the Soviet system during the communist era, underwent major changes in 1991. The National Bank of Moldova (NBM), established in June 1991 and modeled on the Bank of Romania, is subordinate to Parliament. It has an extensive set of monetary policy instruments (such as maximum lending rates and reserve requirements) and is legally responsible for bank supervision. However, shortages of trained staff and a lack of experience in making and executing monetary policy caused the NBM difficulties in its early years.

In 1995 Moldova's banking system was composed of the NBM and twenty-six private, joint-stock commercial banks, including the Joint Bank for Export and Import (Banca Mixta Pentru Export si Import). In 1995 the largest commercial banks were Moldindconbanc, Banca de Economii, Banca Sociala, Agroindbanc, Victoriabanc, and Interprinzbanca. The banking system also includes four branches of foreign (Romanian and Russian) banks.

After Russia enacted economic reform measures in January 1992, Moldova liberalized prices for most of its commodities (except bread, milk, energy, utilities, and transportation) and raised other prices by 200 to 425 percent. Price controls were eliminated gradually, with none left after May 1994.

In early 1995, the average monthly rate of consumer inflation was estimated at under 5 percent. This represented a major improvement, as the annual inflation rate had been 105 percent in 1994, 415 percent in 1993, and a staggering 1,500 percent in 1992.

In the early years of its independence, Moldova used both the Russian ruble and the Moldovan coupon (issued only to residents of Moldova) as its currencies. The leu (for value of the leu—see Glossary) was introduced in November 1993 to replace these currencies and to escape the inflation in other former Soviet republics. It has remained reasonably stable against major hard currencies despite the country's high rates of inflation.

Transportation and Telecommunications

In 1995 the main means of transportation in Moldova were railroads (1,150 kilometers) and a highway system (20,100 kilometers overall, including 14,000 kilometers of paved surfaces) (see fig. 21). The major railroad junctions are Chisinau, Tighina, Ungheni, Ocnita (Oknitsa in Russian), Balti, and Basarabeasca (Bessarabka in Russian). Primary external rail links connect the republic's network with Odesa (in Ukraine) on the Black Sea and with the Romanian cities of Iasi and Galati; they also lead northward into Ukraine. Highways link Moldova's main cities and provide the chief means of transportation within the country, but roads are in poor repair, and gasoline shortages make interurban motor transportation difficult. The country's major airport is in Chisinau.

Shipping is possible on the lower Prut and Nistru rivers, but water transportation plays only a modest role in the country's transportation system. In 1990 a total of 317 million ton-kilometers of freight were carried on inland waterways as compared with 15,007 million ton-kilometers on railroads and 1,673 million ton-kilometers on roads (see table 13, Appendix A).

The movement of manufactured goods and of passengers on all means of transportation started to decline in 1989. From 1993 to 1994, for example, the total amount of transported goods fell by 31 percent, passenger traffic decreased by 28 percent, and the number of passengers declined by 24 percent. The main causes for these declines are the high cost of transportation, a lack of fuels, and the poor state of Moldova's transportation infrastructure: approximately 20 percent of Moldova's roads are considered in a critical state.

Moldova's telecommunications facilities are poor, but they were being upgraded in 1995. In 1990 Moldova had an average of twelve telephones per 100 inhabitants (heavily concentrated in urban areas), and there were more than 200,000 unfilled orders for telephone installation. In 1994 Moldova installed 23,800 telephone lines, which included public telephones with direct international dialing capabilities. Some 10,000 digital lines in Chisinau were upgraded by a German company. In 1994 a new company in Chisinau, a joint venture with partners from Greece and Italy, was soon to produce automatic telephone exchanges at the rate of 50,000 lines a year.

Moldova is connected to Ukraine by landline and to countries outside the former Soviet Union via Bucharest rather than via the switching center in Moscow, as was previously the case.

As of 1993, three television channels were widely available in Moldova: Moldova's two national channels (Radioteleviziunea Nationala), Romanian state television (Televiziunea Româna), and Russian state television (Ostankino Television Channel 1). Radioteleviziunea Nationala's daily fifteen hours of broadcasting included five hours of Russian-language broadcasts. Broadcasting in other minority languages was more limited: Ukrainian (three hours per month), Gagauz (three hours per month), Bulgarian (three hours per month), and Hebrew and Yiddish (1.5 hours per month). Televiziunea Româna broadcast fifteen hours per day, and Ostankino Television broadcast nineteen hours per day. In 1995 there was one private television station in Chisinau (whose coverage included most of the republic).

In 1994 nine AM radio stations were reported broadcasting, in four cities: four in Grigoriopol (Grigoriopol' in Russian), three in Chisinau, one in Cahul (Kagul in Russian), and one in Edinet (Yedintsy in Russian). Separatists in the self-proclaimed "Dnestr Republic" had taken over the radio facility in Grigoriopol and broadcast on two of the AM frequencies. The cities of Balti, Cahul, Edinet, Straseni (Strasheny in Russian), and Ungheni each had one FM radio station broadcasting on the same frequencies used when Moldova was part of the Soviet Union. International shortwave radio service was broadcast in English, Russian, Spanish, French, and Romanian. Four private radio stations operated in Moldova in 1994, one of which was funded by an American Christian group. The others broadcast music, mostly for young people.

Foreign Trade

Within the Soviet economy, Moldavia was an importer of industrial raw materials, fossil fuels, and manufactured goods. Its primary exports to other Soviet republics included wine and spirits, processed foods, clothing and textiles, and small amounts of electrical equipment.

Since independence, Moldova has struggled to reorganize its domestic economy and at the same time to reorient its foreign trade, finding new markets for its products and new

141

Figure 21. Transportation System of Moldova, 1995

sources of the essential imports it traditionally obtained from the Soviet Union. In 1991, however, 73 percent of Moldova's imports and 96 percent of its exports were still directed toward territories of the former Soviet Union. In addition, Moldova had a surplus of 572 million rubles in its trade with the former Soviet republics but a deficit of 875 million rubles in its trade with the rest of the world. This disparity clearly suggested the difficulty Moldova faced in restructuring its trade relationships, given that in 1994 about 73 percent of Moldova's foreign trade was with other members of the CIS and only 27 percent was with the West. In 1994 exports totaled 2,397 million lei (US$580 million), up 20 percent from 1993, and imports totaled 2,704 million lei (US$662 million), down 12 percent from 1993, resulting in a trade deficit of 307 million lei.

By 1992 Moldova had established joint ventures with Bulgaria, Germany, Hungary, Poland, Romania, Turkey, Vietnam, and the United States, and it had signed bilateral trade agreements with China, Denmark, Italy, the Netherlands, Spain, Sweden, Serbia and Montenegro, and ten of the former Soviet republics. In 1995 Moldova's major CIS trading partners were Russia, Ukraine, and Belarus, and its major non-CIS trading partners were Romania, Germany, the United States, Bulgaria, Hungary, and Italy. Barter accounted for over 41 percent of Moldova's total volume of foreign trade in 1994.

By the end of 1992, the United States government had signed several agreements with Moldova and had granted Moldova most-favored-nation status (see Glossary). A bilateral investment treaty was signed with the Moldovan government in April 1993. The Overseas Private Investment Corporation (OPIC) had signed a bilateral agreement with Moldova authorizing OPIC to provide loans, loan guarantees, and investment insurance to United States companies investing in Moldova. As of September 1994, 314 joint ventures had been established (partners included more than fifty from Romania, more than thirty from the United States, twenty-five from Germany, and twenty from Bulgaria), but only one-third were operational as of early 1995. Joint ventures account for only 2.3 percent of Moldova's industrial output and substantially less than 1 percent of Moldova's employment.

In 1992 Moldova became a member of the International Monetary Fund (IMF—see Glossary) and the World Bank (see Glossary), making it eligible to receive financing for capital infrastructure projects. (The Moldovan government consulted with the IMF on a plan of economic reform that year and immediately implemented a number of reform measures.) Moldova and United States companies investing in Moldova are also eligible to receive loans from the European Bank for Reconstruction and Development (EBRD), which emphasizes programs and activities that support privatization, financial reform, industrial restructuring, the creation and strengthening of infrastructure, inflows of foreign investment, and environmental remediation. In addition, the Moldovan government has signed the Group of Seven (see Glossary) external debt agreement; its share of the external debt of the former Soviet Union was determined to be US$1.7 billion. An agreement was signed in 1993 by Moldova and Russia transferring this debt to Russia and renouncing any claims by Moldova on properties of the former Soviet Union. In November 1994, Moldova signed a partnership and cooperation agreement with the European Union (EU—see Glossary).

In 1992 the Moldovan Parliament adopted the Law on Foreign Investment (amended in July 1994). This law was developed in cooperation with representatives of foreign enterprises and the World Bank and is recognized as the best of all such laws in countries belonging to the CIS. Together with changes in the tax law, the Law on Foreign Investment has made Moldova a much easier place for foreign companies to do business.

By 1995 the government of Moldova had relaxed most of its restrictions on the country's foreign trade. Importers and exporters no longer need to be registered, but export licenses are still needed for certain goods, such as grains, energy resources, animal hides, and special products (including arms, precious metals, and chemical products).

Government and Politics

On August 27, 1991, the Republic of Moldova declared its independence from the Soviet Union and became a sovereign state, an act that consummated the process of escalating political self-assertion under way since 1988. Behind this phenomenon were *glasnost* and *perestroika*, the general movement toward reform initiated by Mikhail Gorbachev in the second half of the 1980s.

Gorbachev's more permissive approach to political life in the Moldavian SSR enabled Moldovan nationalists to participate in the campaign for election to the Soviet Union's Congress of People's Deputies (see Glossary) in 1989 and to form the Moldovan Popular Front. On February 25, 1990, the first democratic elections for the Supreme Soviet of the Moldavian SSR resulted in a Popular Front majority.

In May 1991, the country changed its name from the Soviet Socialist Republic of Moldova to the Republic of Moldova. The name of the Supreme Soviet was changed to the Moldovan Parliament. It declared Moldova's complete independence on August 27, 1991 (now Independence Day). This pursuit of independence by Moldova's government put it increasingly at odds with Moscow and at the same time led to growing tensions between the ethnic Romanian majority and the non-Romanian minorities in the republic.

Those tensions led to sporadic violence throughout the first half of 1992, until a cease-fire agreement was negotiated by presidents Snegur and Yeltsin in July. The conditions for withdrawing the Russian 14th Army were negotiated and were dependent on constitutional provisions that were to be made after the parliamentary elections of early 1994.

On February 27, 1994, parliamentary elections were held. In the elections, the Democratic Agrarian Party of Moldova won a majority, marking a turning point for Moldovan politics. The new Parliament was able to make compromises between ethnic Romanians and ethnic Slavs, thus enabling it to pass legislation and set a more moderate tone for governing the country. Without a majority of Popular Front extreme nationalists in Parliament, a solution to the problem of Transnistria began to be more than just a futile hope.

Governmental System

On July 28, 1994, the Moldovan Parliament approved a new constitution, which went into effect August 27, 1994. Moldova's previous constitution was that of the old Moldavian SSR (1979), with amendments. The new document defines Moldova as an independent, democratic, "single" state and declares the country's permanent neutrality. The Moldovan language written in the Latin alphabet is designated as the official language, but guarantees are made for the use of Russian and other languages. The new constitution includes a ban on the stationing of foreign troops on Moldova's territory.

Parliament

Moldova is a democracy with a unicameral legislature, the Moldovan Parliament (see fig. 22). Following the earlier Soviet model, called the Supreme Soviet, the Moldovan Parliament maintains a Presidium, which performs legislative functions when the larger body is not in session. Parliament has 104 members elected by universal suffrage for a four-year term. Any citizen eligible to vote (eighteen years of age and not prohibited by law) is eligible for election to Parliament. The next parliamentary elections will be held in 1998.

Parliament ordinarily meets in two sessions per year. The first session starts in February and may not go beyond the end

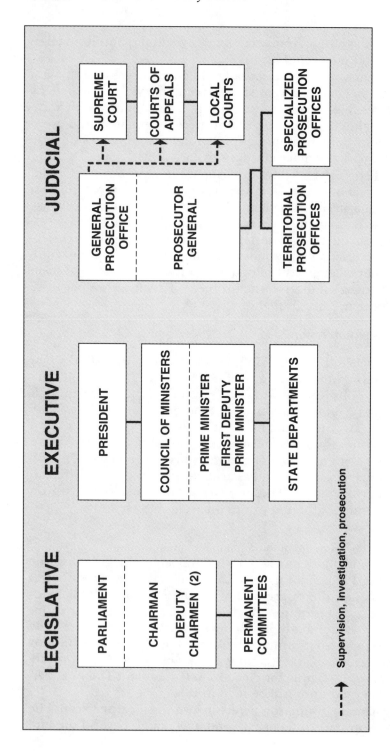

Figure 22. Government Organization of Moldova, 1995

of July. The second session starts in September and may not go beyond the end of December.

Parliamentary leadership consists of a chairman and two deputy chairmen elected by the delegates. The work of Parliament is carried out by fifteen permanent committees, which have purview in the following areas: agriculture and rural social development, crime prevention, culture and religion, ecology, the economy and the budget, foreign affairs, health and social assistance, human rights and relations among nationalities, law, legislative ethics, local administration and the local economy, public relations and the mass media, science and education, state security and military affairs, and women and family issues.

The Presidency

Moldova's head of state is the president of the republic, who shares executive power with the Council of Ministers. Under constitutional arrangements prevailing at the time of the 1990 national elections, the president was elected by members of the Supreme Soviet, but provisions introduced in 1991 called for the president's direct election by all members of the population over eighteen years of age. The president, who must be over thirty-five years old, a resident of Moldova for at least ten years, and a speaker of the state language, is elected to a four-year term of office. The next election is set for December 1995. In mid-1995 the president was Mircea Snegur, named president by the Supreme Soviet in September 1990 and confirmed by popular election in December 1991.

The president's duties include nominating the prime minister and members of the Council of Ministers, taking part in Parliament's proceedings and debates, dissolving Parliament under certain conditions, negotiating and concluding international treaties, serving as commander in chief of the armed forces, granting political asylum, and iniating national referendums.

Council of Ministers

The activities of the government are directed by the cabinet, or Council of Ministers, headed by the prime minister and the first deputy prime minister. In mid-1995 the prime minister was Andrei Sangheli, appointed in July 1992 and reappointed in March 1994. Candidates for the Council of Ministers are nominated by the president (on the prime minister's recommendation) and must be confirmed by Parliament before taking office. In 1995 there were eighteen ministries: agriculture and food; commercial services and housing; culture; defense; economy; education; finance; foreign affairs; health; industry; information and communication; interior; justice; labor and social and family protection; national security; parliamentary relations; privatization and administration of state property; and transportation and road assistance.

In addition to these ministries, the government has state departments subordinate to the Council of Ministers. In 1995 there were nine state departments: architecture and construction; customs control; energy, energy resources, and fuel; environmental protection; national relations; standards, metrology, and technical assistance; statistics; trade; and youth and sports.

The Judicial System

Independent Moldova's judicial and legal systems are carryovers from the Soviet period and conform to practices that were standard throughout the former Soviet Union. The most powerful legal institution is the General Prosecution Office, formerly called the Procuracy (see Glossary). Headed by the prosecutor general, the General Prosecution Office directs investigations, orders arrests, and prosecutes criminal cases. It is also charged with administering the judicial system and ensuring the legality of government actions. In the early 1990s, the Procuracy's corruption and political ties to the Communist Party of Moldavia made it the subject of substantial controversy in discussions on constitutional reform. A significant element of political opinion advocated the abolition or radical transformation of the Procuracy.

Moldova's judicial system is based on a network of local courts and higher-level appeals courts, with the highest court being the Supreme Court (Curte Suprema). Judges do not have a tradition of political impartiality and independence, and the role of defense attorneys is limited. The government of Moldova has initiated reform efforts, but corruption and a lack of organization continue to plague the legal system. Many former Soviet-era judges and chief prosecutors were replaced in 1990 and 1991 during a parliamentary review, but an independent judiciary was still not realized. The system was being reviewed in 1995.

Local Government

Below the central government, Moldova is divided administratively into forty *raioane* (sing., *raion; rayony/rayon* in Russian; see Glossary), as in the Soviet period (see fig. 23). Each *raion* is governed by a locally elected council. *Raion* councils elect executive committees from among their members. The heads of these executive committees are the chief executive officers of the *raioane.* City and village governments are organized much like the *raion*-level governments. In addition to the *raioane*, Chisinau (the national capital), Balti, Tighina, and Tiraspol are designated municipalities and are directly subordinate to the national government.

In 1991 the national government began work on an administrative reorganization intended to alter this structure and to reintroduce a system of counties (*judete*), communes, and villages similar to the one that had been in effect during the interwar period, and one that was still in use in Romania. Under the new system, the counties would consolidate functions carried out by the smaller *raioane*, and local executives would be elected directly. However, this effort was stalled by the secession of Transnistria and the declaration of sovereignty by the Gagauz region, and the Parliament elected in 1994 put the matter aside.

Political Parties

In 1993 more than twenty political parties and movements were registered in Moldova. Until 1990 the Communist Party of Moldavia (CPM) was the dominant political force in the republic. It had controlled the administrative, economic, and cultural affairs of the Moldavian SSR from its establishment until 1990. During that period, CPM officials monopolized virtually all politically significant government positions. However, once democratic elections were decided upon, the party's power disintegrated swiftly. The CPM was formally banned in August 1991, following the abortive August coup d'état against Soviet president Gorbachev, but former communists continued to participate actively in politics through their membership in a variety of successor organizations. The CPM was revived as the Moldovan Party of Communists in 1994.

In the wake of the 1990 elections, the Moldovan Popular Front, founded in 1989 and consisting of an association of independent cultural and political groups, moved into a commanding position in the country's political life. It emerged as

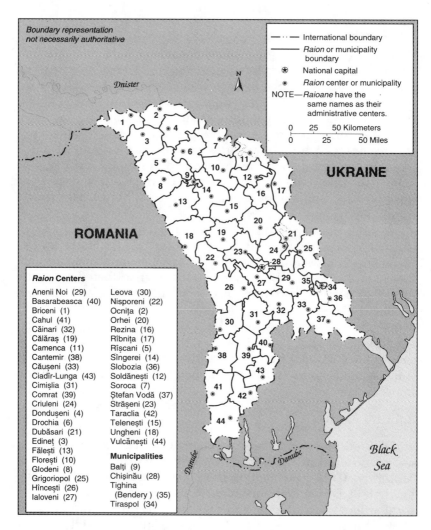

Source: Based on information from Soviet Union, Ministerstvo geologii i okhrany nedr SSSR, "Po Moldavii, turistskaya karta," Moscow, 1989.

Figure 23. Administrative Divisions of Moldova, 1995

an advocate of increased autonomy from the Soviet Union and of the rights of the Moldavian SSR's ethnic Romanian population. Popular Front delegates were able to dominate proceedings in the Supreme Soviet and to select a government made up of individuals who supported its agenda. The Popular Front was well organized nationally, with its strongest support in the capital and in areas of the country most heavily populated by ethnic Romanians. Once the organization was in power, however, internal disputes led to a sharp fall in popular support, and it fragmented into several competing factions by early 1993. In February 1993, the Popular Front was re-formed as the Christian Democratic Popular Front (CDPF).

Several other parties, primarily composed of ethnic Romanians, were organized after 1990. The largest and most influential of these ethnically based parties is the Democratic Agrarian Party of Moldova, which is a coalition of former communists and moderate-to-status-quo supporters of Moldovan statehood and closer economic ties with Russia. The party's support comes mainly from the rural populace, economic conservatives, and ethnic minorities opposed to reunification with Romania. The Democratic Agrarian Party of Moldova won a majority of the votes in the 1994 parliamentary election.

A much smaller but still influential political group is the Social Democratic Party of Moldova. Most of the Social Democrats' leaders originally participated in the Popular Front but later formed their own organization in response to what they perceived as the increasingly nationalistic position of that party. The Social Democrats are multiethnic, and their constituency consists mainly of educated professional and managerial groups. Their support is strongest in the republic's capital.

Another independent formation committed to promoting a less nationalistic agenda for the republic, the Democratic Party for the Rebirth and Prosperity of Moldova, was formed in late 1990. The party draws its support primarily from among ethnic Romanian intellectuals and is active primarily in the capital.

At the other extreme of the political spectrum is the National Christian Party (NCP). The NCP is more expressly nationalistic than the Popular Front and its other competitors—the Congress of the Intellectuals (which is a component of the Congress of Peasants and Intellectuals, a bloc in the 1994 elections), the Democratic Party, and the Democratic Labor Party—and it campaigned openly for reunification with Romania during the 1994 elections. Other parties active in the 1994 campaign for Parliament were the Reform Party, the Yedinstvo/Socialist Bloc, the Republican Party, the Democratic Labor Party, the Green Alliance, the Women's Association of Moldova, and the Victims of Totalitarian Repression.

In late 1993, former Prime Minister Valeriu Muravschi, along with several other leading members of Parliament unhappy with the direction of policy under the existing government, formed yet another party, the Socialist Workers' Party, in order to counter what they saw as the excessively conservative influence of the Democratic Agrarian Party of Moldova. Non-Romanian ethnic communities have also formed political organizations representing their interests. In the early transition period, the most influential of these was the Yedinstvo-Unitatea Intermovement. Yedinstvo, whose members include not only Russians but also Ukrainians, Bulgarians, and other Russian-speaking residents of the republic, is politically conservative in its support of the pre-1990 status quo. Based primarily in Trans-nistria, it is strongly pro-Russian. In Parliament, its positions are represented by the Conciliere legislative club.

Yedinstvo emerged in 1988 from the mobilization of Russian-speaking workers responding to efforts to alter the republic's language laws and demote the status of the Russian language. During the transition period, Yedinstvo was the most effective and influential minority nationalist organization. Its representatives walked out of the first session of the democratically elected Moldavian Supreme Soviet in 1990. In local elections, its adherents won control over local and *raion* governments throughout Transnistria.

Gagauz Halkî (Gagauz People) is a second pivotal minority political group, formed to represent Moldova's population of approximately 153,000 Gagauz. Like the Russian-speaking community in Transnistria, with whom they had been close political allies, Gagauz nationalists gained control over local government (in five *raioane* in the south), where their numbers continue to be concentrated. Like the Transnistrians, the Gagauz declared themselves sovereign in 1990.

The 1990 Elections

The first democratic elections for the Supreme Soviet were held in February and March 1990. Delegates were elected for terms of four years in 380 single-member electoral districts (by early 1993 this number had decreased to 332 following removals and resignations). Electoral rules called for candidates to be nominated by electoral districts rather than by "social organizations," as had been the practice previously. Meetings of work collectives of 100 persons and residents' meetings of fifty or more persons were empowered to nominate candidates.

In order to be elected, candidates had to receive more than 50 percent of the votes cast in an electoral district. When there was no victor in the first round of elections, the two candidates

*Statue of Stephen the Great
(1457–1504), the
Moldovan king who fought
the Ottoman Empire
Courtesy
Paul E. Michelson*

*Newly renovated Ciuflea
Orthodox church, Chisinau
Courtesy
Ernest H. Latham, Jr.*

with the highest number of votes competed against each other in a second round.

In 1990 the republic was divided by the secession of separatist regions and by the outbreak of widespread fighting in Transnistria. At the same time, economic crisis loomed, a result of the collapse of the economic institutions of the Soviet Union. The Moldovan government pursued reforms to address this crisis, but progress toward a market economy was slow, partly as a result of the government's preoccupation with the conflicts among the ethnic groups and partly because of resistance to reform on the part of those with vested interests in the communist system.

In contrast to the artificial quiescence that characterized previous contests, the 1990 elections had considerable controversy. While national CPM officials, including then-First Secretary Petru Lucinschi, promoted open access to the political process, local communist officials in many areas used traditional means to retain power. Reformers complained that local electoral commissions were controlled by "enemies of restructuring" and that the administrative apparatus was being used to subvert the nominating process.

Just as important as bureaucratic resistance in determining the outcome of the elections, however, was the Popular Front's organizational weakness in many localities outside the capital, especially in comparison with the local strength of the CPM's rural party apparatus. Despite these difficulties, Popular Front-approved candidates were on the ballot in 219 out of Moldova's 380 electoral districts by the February 25 election date. Meanwhile, the CPM, enjoying a rebound in popularity and effectiveness under Lucinschi's direction, accounted for 86 percent of all candidates.

A high degree of cooperation between the Popular Front and reformers within the CPM hierarchy was also evident during the early transition period. On February 11, 1990, the Popular Front, with the support of government authorities, had organized a "Republic's Voters Meeting" in Chisinau. This was attended by more than 100,000 people and was addressed by Lucinschi and other high-level communist officials.

Among the candidates supported by the Popular Front were ranking CPM members such as Mircea Snegur. A Central Committee secretary since 1985, Snegur was appointed chairman of the Presidium of the Moldavian Supreme Soviet by the staunchly antireform CPM leader Simion Grossu in July 1989.

By early 1990, however, Snegur had realigned himself with the Popular Front and its political program.

The results of the first round of elections in February confirmed the main trends that had appeared during the nominating process. Competitive races were held in 373 of the 380 districts, and turnout was 84 percent of the electorate. In the 140 contests decided without a runoff, reformers claimed victory for fifty-nine of the candidates, although 115 of the total elected were CPM members (some of whom were supported by the Popular Front). As during the nominating phase, reformers alleged that significant violations of the election law had occurred, despite the Central Electoral Commission's finding of no major infractions.

The second round of elections, held on March 10, 1990, filled the bulk of positions in the republic's Supreme Soviet and had a decisive impact on the country's political life. A fall in turnout for the second round, to 75 percent of the electorate, appears to have hurt the performance of the Popular Front, which won in only forty-two out of 237 districts, a considerably weaker showing than in the February contest. With the conclusion of the runoff, 305 of the deputies to the new Supreme Soviet were CPM members; 101 of the Supreme Soviet deputies were selected from the list supported by the Popular Front. With the support of deputies sympathetic to its views, however, the Popular Front could control more than half of the votes in the new Supreme Soviet.

Political Developments in the Wake of the 1990 Elections

As the political influence of the Popular Front increased in the wake of the elections, the powerful faction of ethnic Romanian nationalists within the organization became increasingly vocal in the pursuit of their agenda. The nationalists argued that the Popular Front should immediately use its majority in the Supreme Soviet to attain independence from Russian domination, end migration into the republic, and improve the status of ethnic Romanians.

Yedinstvo and its supporters within the Supreme Soviet argued against independence from the Soviet Union, against implementation of the August 1989 Law on State Language (making Moldovan written in the Latin alphabet the country's official language), and for increased autonomy for minority areas. Hence, clashes occurred almost immediately once the new Supreme Soviet began its inaugural session in April 1990.

Popular Front representatives, for example, entered a motion to rename the Supreme Soviet the National Council (Sfatul Tarii, the name of the 1917 legislature), in keeping, they argued, with national tradition. Although this motion failed, it provoked an acerbic public exchange among the deputies, which made subsequent cooperation difficult at best. A second controversial motion, on establishing a Moldovan flag (three equal vertical stripes of bright blue, yellow, and red, like the Romanian flag, but with Moldova's coat of arms in the center), passed in the Supreme Soviet but was widely and conspicuously disregarded by its opponents.

The selection of a new legislative leadership also provoked political confrontation. Those appointed to high-level posts were overwhelmingly ethnic Romanians, a situation that left minority activists little hope that their interests would be effectively represented in deliberations on key issues. Ethnic Romanians accounted for only 70 percent of the Supreme Soviet as a whole but for 83 percent of the leadership. All five of the top positions in the Supreme Soviet were held by ethnic Romanians, as were eighteen of twenty positions in the new Council of Ministers.

Faced with what they considered a concerted effort by ethnic Romanian nationalists to dominate the republic, conservatives and minority activists banded together and began to resist majority initiatives. Organized in the Supreme Soviet as the Soviet Moldavia (Sovetskaya Moldaviya) faction, the antireformers became increasingly inflexible.

As confrontation grew among legislative leaders, initiatives undertaken at the local level drew the republic into worsening interethnic conflict. In the minority regions, local forces actively resisted what they considered to be discriminatory legislation from Chisinau. May Day celebrations in Tiraspol became mass protests against the republic's Supreme Soviet. The Tiraspol, Tighina, and Rîbnita city councils, as well as the Rîbnita *raion* council, each passed measures suspending application of the flag law in their territories.

Deputies from Tiraspol and Tighina, unable to block legislation they considered inimical to their interests, announced their intention of withdrawing from the Supreme Soviet. Pro-Popular Front demonstrators outside the Supreme Soviet responded to what they perceived as the obstructionism of minority legislators by becoming increasingly hostile. Following a series of confrontations in the capital, a leading legislative

*Moldovan parliament
building, Chisinau
Courtesy
Paul E. Michelson*

*Chisinau city government
offices
Courtesy
Ernest H. Latham, Jr.*

representative of Yedinstvo was badly beaten; 100 deputies associated with the Russian-speaking Soviet Moldavia faction withdrew from the Supreme Soviet on May 24, 1990.

A new reformist government, with Mircea Druc as prime minister, took over that same day, after the previous government suffered a vote of no confidence. The many changes wrought by this government included a ban on the CPM, a ban on political parties becoming in effect synonymous with the government, and the outlawing of government censorship. In June 1990, the country changed its name from the Moldavian Soviet Socialist Republic to the Soviet Socialist Republic of Moldova and declared its sovereignty.

Increasing strain between nationalists and their opponents had become apparent since the opening session of the Supreme Soviet. In the culmination of this trend, delegates to the second congress of the Popular Front passed measures signaling a clear break with the CPM and took an openly nationalistic direction. The Popular Front's new program called for the country to be renamed the Romanian Republic of Moldova, for its citizens to be called "Romanians," and for the Romanian language to be designated the official language of the republic. The program also called for the return of areas inhabited by ethnic Romanians that were transferred to Ukraine when the Moldavian SSR was formed, and for the withdrawal of Soviet forces.

The Popular Front's promotion of this agenda, which was perceived by minority populations to be expressly nationalistic in character, inexorably factionalized the population. Many of Moldova's ethnic Romanians also perceived the Popular Front as extremist, excessively pro-Romanian, and ineffectual. The opposition was able to bring the public's general dissatisfaction with the Popular Front into focus and eventually bring about a reversal in the political fortunes of the Popular Front.

Conflict in Transnistria and Gagauzia

As the summer of 1990 advanced, the country's initially inchoate political divisions transformed themselves into competing governmental authorities. Delegates to city and *raion* councils in Transnistria and in the Gagauz region met independently with their Supreme Soviet delegates and called for regional autonomy. Republic-level officials denounced these efforts as separatist and treasonable.

As efforts to reach some form of accord foundered, more decisive measures were taken. On August 21, 1990, the Gagauz announced the formation of the "Gagauz Republic" in the five southern *raioane* where their population was concentrated, separate from the Moldavian SSR and part of the Soviet Union. The Transnistrians followed suit on September 2, proclaiming the formation of the "Dnestr Moldavian Republic," with its capital at Tiraspol, as a part of the Soviet Union.

It was under these circumstances that violence broke out in the fall of 1990. A decision by Gagauz leaders to hold a referendum on the question of local sovereignty was intensely opposed by the republic's government and by the Popular Front. Rival political forces mobilized volunteer detachments to defend their competing interests by force. Adding to the volatility of the conflict between the Gagauz and the ethnic Romanians, militia forces from Transnistria entered the Gagauz region to support the sovereignty movement there.

In the Transnistrian city of Dubasari, the militia seized the city council building as part of its preparations for a referendum on autonomy in the region. When the republic's police sought to retake the building, new forces were mobilized from ethnic Romanian regions as well as from Russian-speaking regions. In the ensuing conflict, three persons were killed and dozens more wounded.

Relations between the separatists and the republic's government were characterized by mutual denunciations and sporadic violence from late 1990 until early 1992, when conditions took a sharp turn for the worse. As efforts among Moldova, Russia, Ukraine, and Romania to mediate the conflict foundered and as the Transnistrian separatists consolidated their position with the support of Russia's 14th Army, pressure built on President Snegur to take decisive action to resolve the conflict.

In late March 1992, Snegur declared a state of emergency across the republic, and soon afterward the government made an effort to disarm the separatists' militia. These efforts were met by armed resistance, which, by May 1992, had escalated into a full-scale civil war as weapons released to the Transnistrians by the 14th Army were used against Moldovan military units.

By the close of the summer, more than 300 people had been killed in the conflict, and more than 1,000 had been wounded. A large part of the city of Tighina, which had become a focal point of the conflict, had been devastated; thousands of refugees flooded out of the region.

Easing of Tensions

While combat in the civil war remained at a bloody stalemate into mid-1992, the political situation in Moldova changed dramatically, at least partly as a consequence of popular dissatisfaction with the conflict. In the first stage of the realignment, former CPM first secretary Lucinschi was named ambassador to Russia. Lucinschi, the highest-ranking "Moldavian" outside of the country during the communist era, was able to use his connections with the Moscow political elite to promote accommodation.

Soon afterward, in July 1992, Prime Minister Valeriu Muravschi (who had replaced Mircea Druc) was replaced by Andrei Sangheli of the Democratic Agrarian Party of Moldova. Sangheli was a former CPM *raion* committee first secretary and member of the Council of Ministers. Sangheli's new government included significantly improved minority representation and promised a more efficient economic reform program, as well as a more moderate approach to the ethnic conflict.

By taking this more flexible approach, Moldova was able to reduce the level of violence involved in the separatist dispute, if not to bring the conflict to an end. But the shift in policy direction precipitated a strong backlash from the more extreme elements of the Popular Front, which felt that it was slipping from power. This and popular dissatisfaction with the failing economy forced a fundamental political reorientation.

In December 1992, President Snegur, who clearly supported the more conciliatory course, touched off a crisis by delivering a speech to Parliament in which he laid out a course of foreign policy based on the pursuit of national independence. Snegur warned against the extremes of either unification with Romania or reintegration into some form of alliance with Russia. His public position against efforts to promote unification further soured relations between himself and the Popular Front and at the same time sharpened divisions between moderates and more extreme nationalists within the Popular Front itself.

Fallout from Snegur's speech was almost immediate. In early January 1993, Alexandru Mosanu, chairman of the Moldovan Parliament, offered his resignation, citing the differences between himself and the president of the republic and complaining about tendencies within the government favoring the previous political system.

If, as some suggest, Mosanu's resignation was intended to rally support in an effort to undermine President Snegur, it failed miserably. Not only was the resignation accepted, but Parliament voted overwhelmingly to replace Mosanu with Petru Lucinschi, a leader of those very forces about which Mosanu had warned.

Political Realignment

Lucinschi's election on February 4, 1993, to the leading position in Parliament marked the peak of a process of political realignment in Moldova. By early 1993, the Popular Front, now named the Christian Democratic Popular Front (CDPF), was in near-total disarray. Moderate intellectuals (such as Mosanu), who had added tremendously to the prestige of the Popular Front during its early years, organized the "Congress of the Intellectuals" to promote a nationalistic, but less extreme, agenda. As a result, they were expelled from the CDPF in mid-May.

As a consequence of factionalism and defection, the CDPF's voting strength in Parliament was reduced to approximately twenty-five deputies. With the CDPF in decline, power shifted to the bloc of Democratic Agrarian Party of Moldova deputies (the Viata Satului legislative club), which, with support from independent deputies, was able to play a dominant role in Parliament.

Lucinschi's election and the realignment of forces among the deputies brought Parliament into much closer alignment with President Snegur and Prime Minister Sangheli's government on the ethnic conflict. As a consequence, Moldova was better positioned than it had been in the previous two years to end the infighting that had characterized its political life during that time. There was hope that Moldova's leaders would be able to resolve the ongoing civil conflict, which had, of necessity, been the dominant issue in the republic since its inception, and to proceed with the reforms that Moldova so desperately needed.

At the same time, the realignment moved Moldova's government into a more conservative position with respect to economic and political reform, marginalizing legislators who were elected as opposition candidates and vesting more power in the hands of those who were originally elected as representatives of the CPM. In particular, the realignment gave near-veto power to the bloc of Democratic Agrarian Party of Moldova deputies, many of whom were state and collective farm presidents. Although the great majority of these individuals supported democratic politics, the strength of their commitment to the transition to a market economy was questionable.

Despite the powerful combination of government, the presidency, and Lucinschi's parliamentary leadership working in harmony, the hopelessly tangled web of factions and rivalries within Parliament could not be overcome, and legislation ground to a halt. The pro-Romanian faction objected, but a vote was taken to dissolve Parliament and hold early parliamentary elections.

The 1994 Elections and Afterward

Campaigning for the February 27, 1994, parliamentary elections revolved around economic reform, competing strategies for resolving the separatist crises, and relations with both the CIS and Romania. Debate on the issues of moving to a market economy, privatization, land reform, and foreign policy was polarized.

The results of the elections quickly changed the course of Moldovan politics and stood in sharp contrast to the results of the 1990 elections. Nationalist and pro-Romanian forces were rejected overwhelmingly in favor of those backing Moldova's independence and in favor of accommodating ethnic minorities.

Under laws passed in preparation for the February 27, 1994, elections, Parliament was reduced from 380 seats to a more manageable 104. Fifty of these delegates were selected from newly drawn single-member districts, and the remainder were elected from larger multi-member districts on the basis of proportional representation. Candidates were nominated by voters (independent candidates had to submit petitions with at least 1,000 signatures), political parties, or "sociopolitical organizations"; parties had to receive at least 4 percent of the vote to be accorded seats.

The Democratic Agrarian Party of Moldova won a majority of fifty-six of the 104 seats, followed by the Yedinstvo/Socialist Bloc with twenty-eight seats. Two pro-Romanian unification parties did not do well: the Congress of Peasants and Intellectuals won eleven seats, and the CDPF won nine seats. A number

Demonstration in front of Casa Guvernului, Chisinau
Courtesy Charles King

of other parties did not get a high enough percentage of the popular vote to be represented in the new Parliament.

In March the chairman of Parliament, Petru Lucinschi, was re-elected to his post, and the prime minister, Andrei Sangheli, was reappointed to his position. In April Parliament approved a new Council of Ministers, Moldova's membership in the CIS, and Moldova's signing of a CIS charter on economic union (although the country would not participate in political or military integration within the CIS). A public opinion poll on March 6, 1994, confirmed the country's course of political independence for the future: the Moldovan electorate voted overwhelmingly for Moldova to maintain its territorial integrity.

Once the legislative logjam was broken, Parliament was able to work on a new constitution, which it ratified on July 28 and implemented August 27, 1994. The new constitution granted substantial autonomy to Transnistria and the "Gagauz Republic" while reasserting Moldovan national identity and sovereignty. Gagauzia (in Romanian; Gagauz-Yeri in Gagauz) would have cultural, administrative, and economic (but not territorial) autonomy and would elect a regional legislative assembly, which in turn would elect a *guvernator* (in Romanian; *baskan* in Gagauz), who would also be a member of the Moldovan government. This was ratified by Parliament in January 1995.

Members of the Democratic Agrarian Party of Moldova held a cautious attitude toward marketization and privatization, leading experts to believe that progress in economic reform would be slow but would be more consistent and better implemented than previously. The hard-line nationalists and the former communists could not vote as a majority to block progress.

Human Rights

The adoption of Moldova's constitution on August 27, 1994, codified certain basic human rights (including the rights to private property, individual freedom and personal security, freedom of movement, privacy of correspondence, freedom of opinion and expression, and freedom of assembly), which were observed more in the breach during the Soviet era. However, the constitution still contains language that could limit the activities of political parties and the press.

Although there is no government censorship of Moldova's independent periodicals and its radio stations and cable television stations, journalists complain that editors encourage them to soften their criticisms of government officials for fear of confrontation and possible retribution. This seems to be a well-grounded fear in Transnistria, where the authorities have cut off funding for two newspapers for occasionally criticizing some government policies and have physically attacked a cable television station for broadcasting reports critical of the authorities.

In 1994 Parliament considered a new law on the press, which journalists criticized strongly because it limited their right to criticize government policies. After reviewing recommendations from the Council of Europe (see Glossary) and the Conference on Security and Cooperation in Europe (CSCE), Parliament liberalized the law but left some restrictions that appeared to be aimed at writings favoring reunification with Romania and those questioning Moldova's right to exist.

The Moldovan Ministry of Interior and the Ministry of National Security were investigated on several occasions in 1994 to determine whether they had exceeded their legislated authority. They were accused of monitoring political opposition members and using unauthorized wiretaps. There were also claims of interference with opposition activities during the campaign preceding the 1994 elections, but there was no public investigation of those charges. The police, subordinate to the Ministry of Interior, are known to have used beatings in their dealings with some detainees and prisoners.

Reform of the judiciary (to bring it more into line with Western practices) was approved, but Parliament had not passed the laws needed to implement it by the end of 1994. For example, prosecutors rather than judges issue search and arrest warrants, there is no judicial review of search warrants, and courts do not exclude evidence obtained illegally. There are also reports that local prosecutors have brought unjustified charges against individuals in retaliation for accusations of official corruption or for political reasons.

Trials in Moldova are generally open to the public, and the accused has the right to appeal. Bail does not exist, but release usually may be arranged by obtaining a written guarantee by a friend or family member that the accused will appear in court.

Because the security forces and the government of the "Dnestr Republic" are so closely connected, human rights abuses in Transnistria are more flagrant. The worst of the abuses in Transnistria occurred in 1992, during the height of the fighting. There were reports of beatings, ill treatment, abduction, torture, and even the murder of civilians by members of the police and the Republic Guard. Requests for visits by Amnesty International and the International Committee of the Red Cross were routinely refused.

In Transnistria four of the six ethnic Romanians of the "Tiraspol Six" remained in prison as of mid-1995, following their conviction in 1993 for allegedly assassinating two Transnistrian officials. The fairness of the trial was seriously questioned by international human rights groups, and there were allegations that the defendants were prosecuted solely because of their membership in the CDPF.

Moldova has several local human rights groups, which maintain contacts with international organizations, including Helsinki Watch and Helsinki Citizens Assembly. The government does not interfere with human rights groups' operations.

The Media

The main daily newspaper in the republic, *Moldova Suverana*, is published by the government. *Sfatul tarii* is published by Parliament, which also publishes the daily *Nezavisimaya Moldova* in Russian. Other principal newspapers include *Rabochiy Tiraspol'* (in Russian, the main newspaper of the Slavs in Transnistria), *Tara*, *Tineretul Moldovei/Molodëzh Moldovy* (in Romanian and Russian), and *Viata satului* (published by the government). The main cultural publication in Moldova is the weekly journal *Literatura si arta*, published by the Union of Writers of Moldova. Other major periodicals include *Basarabia* (also published by the writers' union), *Chiparus, Alunelul, Femeie Moldovei, Lanterna Magica, Moldova, Noi*, and *Sud-Est*. *Kishinëvskiye novosti, Kodry*, and *Russkoye slovo* are Russian-language periodicals. Other minority-language periodicals include *Prosvita* and *Homin* in Ukrainian, *Ana sözu* and *Cîrlangaci* in Gagauz, *Rodno slovo* in Bulgarian, and *Undzer col/Nash golos* in Yiddish and Russian. In all, 240 newspapers (ninety-seven in Romanian) and sixty-eight magazines (thirty-five in Romanian) were being published in the republic in 1990. Basa Press, an independent news service, was established in November 1992.

Foreign Relations

In the wake of its proclamation of sovereignty in 1990, Moldova's main diplomatic efforts were directed toward establishing new relationships with the Soviet Union's successor states, establishing diplomatic links with other national governments and international bodies, gaining international recognition, and enlisting international support to resolve the conflict in Transnistria. Although substantial gains have been made in each of these areas, Moldova's foreign policy efforts have been complicated by its geographic position, its history, and the ongoing ethnic conflict within its borders.

After it declared independence, Moldova made significant progress in international relations in a relatively short period of time. The first state to recognize Moldova's independence was neighboring Romania. By early 1995, Moldova had been recognized by more than 170 states, including the United States (which extended recognition on December 25, 1991), although the foreign diplomatic presence in Chisinau remains limited.

View of downtown Chisinau
Courtesy Charles King

As of early 1995, Moldova had been admitted to several international organizations, including the CSCE (renamed the Organization for Security and Cooperation in Europe, or OSCE, in January 1995), the United Nations (UN), the International Monetary Fund, the World Bank, the European Bank for Reconstruction and Development (EBRD), the North Atlantic Cooperation Council, and the Community of Riparian Countries of the Black Sea. It also had observer status at the General Agreement on Tariffs and Trade (GATT) and the World Trade Organization (WTO), the successor to GATT.

By mid-1994 Moldova had accepted all relevant arms control obligations of the former Soviet Union. It had ratified the Conventional Forces in Europe Treaty (CFE Treaty—see Glossary), with its comprehensive limits on key categories of conventional military equipment. Even though Moldova had not acceded to the Nuclear Nonproliferation Treaty, it had indicated that it intended to do so.

Commonwealth of Independent States

The domestic political ramifications of Moldova's civil conflict in Transnistria were matched by its effect on foreign relations. Domestic sentiments limited the foreign policy flexibility of the government in dealing with the former Soviet Union. Although President Snegur signed the Minsk Agreement (which created the CIS; see Appendix B) on December 8, 1991, and the Alma-Ata Declaration (which expanded the membership of the CIS; see Appendix C) on December 21, 1991, Moldova's Parliament, strongly influenced by the Popular Front bloc of delegates, refused to ratify the agreements.

Further, along with Ukraine and Turkmenistan, Moldova refused to sign a January 1993 agreement that would have strengthened political and economic integration among CIS members. It thus embarked upon a difficult course of independence, maneuvering between Russia and Romania, both of which have strong interests in the region and both of which are more powerful than the young republic. It was only in April 1994 that the new Parliament finally approved Moldova's membership in the CIS and signed a CIS charter on economic union.

Romania

The relationship between Moldova and Romania, while generally good, is far from trouble free. Although Romania was the first state to recognize Moldova and has provided substantial support to the new republic in relation to Bucharest's means, ties between the two Romanian-speaking states are fraught with political difficulties for both countries.

The relationship between Romania and Moldova began to deteriorate shortly after Moldova's independence. Because of their different histories, with Moldova part of the Russian Empire and later the Soviet Union, Moldovans and Romanians have different attitudes about basic social and political issues, such as the extent of social payments (i.e., welfare). Many Romanians see the Moldovans as "Russified" and hold the condescending view that they are in need of assistance to overcome their cultural disabilities. This has been a source of growing resentment among the majority of Moldovans.

For his part, Romania's president, Ion Iliescu, has worked consistently to maintain a positive relationship with Russia. On the one hand, moves on his part that could be seen as destabilizing the interethnic balance in Moldova and tipping it toward civil war would be potentially disastrous for his country—both in the limited sense of setting back Russian-Romanian relations and in the more serious sense of potentially drawing Russia into a regional conflict. On the other hand, any precipitous move on the part of Moldova in the direction of Romania would immediately raise fears of imminent unification with Romania among the Russian-speaking population and among the Gagauz and would feed interethnic hostility in the republic. The March 6, 1994, public opinion poll confirmed to all interested parties, in no uncertain terms, that the populace of Moldova is not in favor of reuniting with any country.

In late 1994, President Iliescu made comments questioning Moldova's independent status. Although relations between the two countries remain cordial, these comments reflected the Romanian nationalistic parties' greater influence in national politics and in the parliament in Romania.

Russia

In the case of Russia, interethnic conflict in Moldova produced results similar to those that followed outbreaks of violence in other former republics of the Soviet Union soon after they had proclaimed their independence. Intrinsically, Moldova was probably of little interest to Moscow, but the presence of an ethnic Russian minority in Moldova altered Moscow's perspective. Moldova's ethnic Russians found the prospect of

Moldova's reunification with Romania alarming, because it would alter their status from that of a large and politically powerful force to that of a small and politically powerless minority. Moldova was geographically important to both the Russian Empire and the Soviet Union because it formed part of the border of each. In this way, it formed a barrier between Russia itself (in both cases, the ruling entity) and the outside world.

Although officially neutral, the Russian 14th Army (stationed in Transnistria) played a vital role in the conflict between the government of Moldova and the "Dnestr Republic." Its commanders permitted the transfer of weapons from their stockpiles in Moldova to the Transnistrian militia and volunteered the services of "Cossack" (see Glossary) forces that entered the region once fighting broke out (there were approximately 1,000 "Cossacks" in Transnistria in 1994). Furthermore, strong indications suggested that elements of the 14th Army actively intervened on the side of the separatists during the fighting, using their heavy weapons to turn the tide in the fighting when necessary.

Eventually, however, it became evident that the Transnistria conflict was not about ethnic issues (especially once implementation of the language law of 1989 was delayed, and the Popular Front extremists lost much of their power) but about political systems. The Transnistrian leadership wanted to return to the days of the Soviet Union and was wary of the Yeltsin government (it never repudiated its support of the August 1991 coup d'état) and the reformists.

In July 1992, an agreement negotiated by presidents Snegur and Yeltsin established a cease-fire in Transnistria, which brought an end to the worst of the fighting in Moldova. Transnistria was given special status within Moldova and was granted the right to determine its future should Moldova reunite with Romania. Russian, Transnistrian, and Moldovan peacekeeping troops subsequently were introduced into Transnistria.

Maintaining the agreement was complicated by the instability of Russia's central government and by the implications of the 14th Army's involvement for Russia's domestic politics. The 14th Army's commander, Lieutenant General Aleksandr V. Lebed', was politically very conservative and, despite repeated warnings from his superiors to restrain himself, had stated publicly that he would not "abandon" Transnistria's ethnic Russians. Like Lebed', Russia's conservatives generally considered abandonment of the ethnic Russian minority to be an anath-

Window display on Russian hostilities in Transnistria, Chisinau
Courtesy Paul E. Michelson
People waiting in line for bread, Chisinau
Courtesy Matt Webb

ema. In 1995 nationalists in Russia (whose strength was growing) were ready to protect the "rights" of Russians in the "near abroad" and would, no doubt, politically attack moderates who might be willing to end the conflict through compromise.

By 1994, however, relations between the Transnistrian leadership and the 14th Army had deteriorated to the point that both sides were accusing each other of corruption (including arms trafficking, drug running, and money laundering) and political provocation. General Lebed' also saw many in the Transnistrian leadership as not cooperating with Russian efforts to mediate the conflict and as actively hampering the peace process.

After the 1994 change in Moldova's government, compromises were made by both the Moldovan and the Russian governments to improve relations over the issue of Transnistria. The status of the 14th Army was scheduled to be reduced to that of an "operational group," General Lebed' was to be released from his position, and the number of officers was to be reduced. The two countries signed an agreement in October on the withdrawal of Russian troops from Transnistria and Tighina within three years. Moldova accepted a linkage between withdrawing Russian troops and achieving a political solution to the conflict in Transnistria. Transnistrian observers, who had feared that the Yeltsin government would strike a deal without their consent, saw the agreement as a blow to their existence as a Russian entity (and also to their illegal money-making activities) and walked out of the negotiations.

However, peace was not to come easily to Transnistria. The October 1994 agreement was a "gentlemen's agreement" that was signed by the two prime ministers and was to be approved by the two governments, but would not be submitted to the countries' parliaments. The Moldovan government approved the agreement immediately, but the Russian government did not, citing the need to submit it to the Russian State Duma (the lower house of the Russian parliament), although it still had not submitted the agreement as of mid-1995.

According to General Lebed', three years was not enough time to withdraw the 14th Army and its matériel (although an American company working in Belarus offered to buy the 14th Army's ordnance and destroy it). Some members of Russia's Duma flatly refused to consider withdrawing the 14th Army. Under these circumstances, there was little hope for the agreement to be implemented.

Ukraine

Moldova's relationship with Ukraine, another important player in the Transnistrian conflict, is also complicated. Areas that were traditionally part of the region of Moldova or Romania (northern Bukovina, Herta, and southern Bessarabia), and that continue to be inhabited in part by ethnic Romanians, were annexed by the Ukrainian SSR when the Moldavian SSR was formed. The potential claims on these territories created tension between the two neighbors in the early years of Moldova's independence, when the Popular Front made public its demands for restitution.

Another potential problem is the presence of a large ethnic Ukrainian minority in Moldova. Ethnic Ukrainians have sided with the local ethnic Russians in the dispute over Moldova's language law, and many ethnic Ukrainians have supported the separatist effort in Transnistria. However, the government of Moldova took significant measures to meet the demands of the Ukrainian minority for cultural autonomy and appears to have met with substantial success in defusing opposition to Moldova's language law.

In 1995 potential problems between Ukraine and Moldova were subordinate to what had emerged as a strong common interest in containing the Transnistrian conflict. Given their own dispute with Russia concerning the status of Crimea, Ukrainians had little interest in supporting the presence of Russian military units outside Russia.

As a more practical question, it was not in Ukraine's interest to have a large and well-equipped Russian military formation based in neighboring Transnistria. The 14th Army could reach Russia only by traversing Ukrainian territory or airspace, so its presence could only be seen as a potential source of danger and instability. Therefore, it is not surprising that Ukrainian president Leonid M. Kravchuk made several statements supporting Moldova's position in the Transnistrian conflict, protested the movement of "Cossack" volunteers across Ukrainian territory to Transnistria, and refused to recognize Transnistrian claims to sovereignty.

Turkey

Politically moderate Gagauz have received support from Turkey, which has urged the leadership of the "Gagauz Republic" to negotiate with the Moldovan government rather than resort to violence, as had been the case in Transnistria. Turkish president Süleyman Demirel visited the "Gagauz Republic" in mid-1994, urging the Gagauz to accept regional autonomy and to be loyal citizens of Moldova. Turkey pledged to invest US$35 million in the Gagauz region via Chisinau.

The West

Moldova has pursued cooperation with, and has striven to maintain good relations with, the West. It has joined a number of international organizations and has been responsive to foreign concerns about the pace of its conversion to capitalism. A January 1995 trip by President Snegur to the United States was the setting for an announcement by President William J. Clinton of additional assistance to Moldova for its privatization program and for economic restructuring. Moldova has also signed bilateral treaties with European Union (EU) members.

National Security

In October 1991, President Mircea Snegur announced Moldova's decision to organize its own national armed forces; Moldova had demanded the withdrawal of Soviet troops when it declared its independence. The decision not to participate in the joint forces of the CIS was made explicit by Parliament's rejection of the Alma-Ata Declaration of December 21, 1991.

The number, training, and quality of the armed forces and the police have varied greatly since the republic's declaration of independence. In April 1991, Moldova passed legislation that exempted its residents from service in the Soviet armed forces and granted immunity from prosecution to anyone declining to serve. A law on alternative service for conscientious objectors was passed later.

Initially, political leaders intended to keep troop levels low. Moldova's plan for the regular armed forces was to recruit Moldovan citizens to serve in the army and national police and take over positions in Soviet military structures and in the Moldovan Ministry of National Security, which replaced the Committee for State Security (KGB—see Glossary) in Moldova. This program would in effect "republicanize" the armed forces. An eighteen-month draft of eighteen-year-old males was introduced. However, students at institutes of higher education were exempted from all but three months of service, which was

Moldovan State University, Chisinau
Courtesy Paul E. Michelson
Museum of National History, Chisinau
Courtesy Charles King

deferred until graduation. Alternative service was available for those with religious objections to military service.

The Armed Forces

A transition to a professional force of 12,000 to 15,000 volunteers was planned at first, but when fighting erupted in 1991 between supporters of the central government in Chisinau and supporters of separatist regions, males between eighteen and forty years of age were mobilized, and the size of Moldova's military was temporarily expanded to meet the demands of the Transnistrian conflict. In 1994 the armed forces (under the Ministry of Defense) totaled some 11,100 volunteers, and there were plans to gradually create a professional army similar to that of the United States.

At the beginning of 1994, the Moldovan army consisted of 9,800 men organized into three motor rifle brigades, one artillery brigade, and one reconnaissance assault battalion. Its equipment consisted of fifty-six ballistic missile defenses; seventy-seven armored personnel carriers and sixty-seven "look-alikes"; eighteen 122mm and fifty-three 152mm towed artillery units; nine 120mm combined guns and mortars; seventy AT–4 Spigot, nineteen AT–5 Spandral, and twenty-seven AT–6 Spiral antitank guided weapons; a 73mm SPG–9 recoilless launcher; forty-five MT–12 100mm antitank guns; and thirty ZU–23 23mm and twelve S–60 57mm air defense guns. Moldova has received some arms from former Soviet stocks maintained on the territory of the republic as well as undetermined quantities of arms from Romania, particularly at the height of the fighting with Transnistria.

In 1994 the Moldovan air force (including air defense) consisted of 1,300 men organized into one fighter regiment, one helicopter squadron, and one missile brigade. Equipment used by the air force included thirty-one MiG–29 aircraft, eight Mi–8 helicopters, five transport aircraft (including an An–72), and twenty-five SA–3/5 surface-to-air missiles.

Other military forces also exist within Moldova. In early 1994, the government of the "Dnestr Republic" had armed forces of about 5,000, which included the Dnestr Battalion of the Republic Guard and some 1,000 "Cossacks." As of early 1994, the Russian 14th Army (about 9,200 troops) consisted of one army headquarters, one motor rifle division, one tank battalion, one artillery regiment, and one antiaircraft brigade. Their equipment consisted of 120 main battle tanks, 180 armored combat vehicles, and 130 artillery/multiple rocket launchers/mortars. Peacekeepers in Transnistria consisted of six airborne battalions supplied by Russia, three infantry battalions supplied by Moldova, and three airborne battalions supplied by the "Dnestr Republic."

Internal Security

In 1994 the national police of Moldova, modeled on Italy's Carabinieri, were under the direction of the Ministry of Interior and numbered some 10,000. Internal troops were reported to have 2,500 personnel, and the numbers of the OPON riot police (also known as the "Black Berets") were put at 900. Moldova's Border Guards were under the Ministry of National Security.

The scope and quality of Moldova's state security apparatus were difficult to determine. Like the armed forces, local assets of the former Moldavian KGB were transferred to the new government along with those personnel who wished to enter the service of the new government. These elements now function under the republic's control under the Ministry of National Security.

Crime

Crime in Moldova, as everywhere in former Soviet republics, has risen dramatically since the demise of the Soviet Union. Economic and drug-related crimes, the most visible and predictable results of the deteriorating economic situations in the newly independent countries, have simply overwhelmed the human and financial resources devoted to them. Often, however, the problem is more extensive than what is acknowledged: many crimes are not registered. For example, in early 1995 the Moldovan government stated that overall crime in Moldova had risen by 29 percent over the previous year. However, the number of motorbikes and motor vehicles "being searched for" was thirteen times the number of vehicles listed as "stolen." Illicit cultivation of opium poppies and cannabis is carried out in Moldova, mainly for consumption in CIS countries. In addition, Moldova is a transshipment point for illegal drugs to Western Europe.

*   *   *

The best historical treatments of Moldova in the pre-Soviet period are still found in general treatments of Romania. Particularly useful works include Vlad Georgescu's *The Romanians,* Robert William Seton-Watson's *A History of the Roumanians,* and Barbara Jelavich's *History of the Balkans: Eighteenth and Nineteenth Centuries.* Older, yet still useful, works focusing on Bessarabia are Charles Upson Clark's *Bessarabia: Russia and Roumania on the Black Sea* and Andrei Popovici's *The Political Status of Bessarabia.*

Much of the available information on the Soviet period is found in general works on nationalities in the former Soviet Union, such as James H. Bater's *The Soviet Scene: A Geographical Perspective;* Mikhail Bernstam's "The Demography of Soviet Ethnic Groups in World Perspective" in *The Last Empire: Nationality and the Soviet Future,* edited by Robert Conquest; *Social Trends in the Soviet Union from 1950* by Michael Ryan and Richard Prentice; and Viktor Kozlov's *The Peoples of the Soviet Union.* Sherman David Spector's "The Moldavian S.S.R., 1964–1974" in *Nationalism in the USSR and Eastern Europe,* edited by George W. Simmonds, provides more specific information concerning overall conditions in Moldavia. Michael Bruchis's *Nations, Nationalities, People: A Study of the Nationalities Policy of the Communist Party in Soviet Moldavia* is an interesting and useful account of the implementation of the Soviet nationalities policy in Moldavia by an intimate observer of the process. Bruchis describes the politics of language in Moldavia during the Soviet period in *The USSR: Language and Realities: Nations, Leaders, and Scholars* and *One Step Back, Two Steps Forward: On the Language Policy of the Communist Party of the Soviet Union in the National Republics.*

The following are useful works on the transition period and current conditions (several also include sections on the pre-Soviet and Soviet periods): William E. Crowther's "Romania and Moldavian Political Dynamics" in *Romania after Tyranny,* edited by Daniel Nelson; Nicholas Dima's *From Moldavia to Moldova: The Soviet-Romanian Territorial Dispute;* "The Politics of Ethnonational Mobilization: Nationalism and Reform in Soviet Moldavia" by William E. Crowther in the *Russian Review;* Nicolas Dima's "The Soviet Political Upheaval of the 1980s: The Case of Moldova" in the *Journal of Social, Political, and Economic Studies;* Nicholas Dima's "Recent Changes in Soviet Moldavia" in the *East European Quarterly;* Darya Fane's "Moldova: Breaking Loose from Moscow" in *Nations and Politics in the Soviet Successor States,* edited by Ian Bremmer and Ray Taras; Jonathan Eyal's

"Moldovans" in *The Nationalities Question in the Soviet Union*, edited by Graham Smith; and Charles King's "Moldova and the New Bessarabian Question" in *World Today*. (For further information and complete citations, see Bibliography.)

Appendix A

Table

Table 1. Metric Conversion Coefficients and Factors

When you know	Multiply by	To find
Millimeters	0.04	inches
Centimeters......................	0.39	inches
Meters	3.3	feet
Kilometers	0.62	miles
Hectares (10,000 m²)	2.47	acres
Square kilometers	0.39	square miles
Cubic meters	35.3	cubic feet
Liters	0.26	gallons
Kilograms	2.2	pounds
Metric tons	0.98	long tons
....	1.1	short tons
....	2,204.0	pounds
Degrees Celsius (Centigrade).........	1.8 and add 32	degrees Fahrenheit

Table 2. Belarus: Births and Deaths, 1987–90

Year	Live Births		Deaths	
	Number[1]	Number per Thousand Population	Number[1]	Number per Thousand Population
1987	162,900	16.1	99,900	9.9
1988	163,200	16.1	102,700	10.1
1989	153,500	15.0	103,500	10.1
1990	n.a.[2]	n.a.	109,600	10.7

[1] Estimated.
[2] n.a.—not available.

Source: Based on information from *The Europa World Year Book, 1994*, 1, London, 1994, 492.

Table 3. Belarus: Agricultural Production, 1990–93
(in thousands of tons unless otherwise specified)

Commodity	1990	1991	1992	1993
Eggs	3,657	3,718	3,502	3,516
Flax	52	76	61	57
Grain	7,035	6,296	7,230	7,508
Meat	1,758	1,590	1,442	1,242
Milk	7,457	6,812	5,885	5,584
Potatoes	8,590	8,958	8,984	11,644
Sugar beets	1,479	1,147	1,120	1,569
Live animals (thousands)				
Cattle	6,975	6,577	6,221	5,851
Pigs	5,051	4,703	4,308	4,181
Sheep	403	380	336	271

Source: Based on information from International Monetary Fund, *Belarus,* Washington, 1994, 72.

Table 4. Belarus: Production of Selected Industrial Commodities, 1990–93
(in thousands of tons unless otherwise specified)

Commodity	1990	1991	1992	1993
Timber (millions of cubic meters)	6.9	6.7	6.5	6.2
Plywood (thousands of cubic meters)	192	164	157	133
Mineral fertilizers (millions of tons)	6.0	5.2	4.1	2.5
Cement	2,258	2,402	2,263	1,908
Synthetic fibers	453	443	385	293
Cotton yarn	50.5	50.5	44.9	35.2
Wool yarn	40.2	34.8	30.3	28.2
Linen yarn	30.0	24.4	27.2	20.8
Electricity (billions of kilowatt-hours)	39.5	38.7	37.6	33.4
Steel	1,112	1,123	1,105	946
Tractors (thousands)	100.7	95.5	96.1	82.4
Motorcycles (thousands)	225	214	165	128
Bicycles (thousands)	846	815	724	603
Radios (thousands)	979	932	721	768
Television sets (thousands)	1,302	1,103	798	610
Refrigerators (thousands)	728	743	740	738

Source: Based on information from International Monetary Fund, *Belarus,*Washington, 1994, 79.

Table 5. Belarus: Freight Turnover, 1990–93
(in millions of tons)

	1990	1991	1992	1993
Rail freight	119	111	96	71.5
Truck freight	428	406	304	n.a[1]

[1] n.a.—not available.

Source: Based on information from United States, Central Intelligence Agency, *Handbook of International Economic Statistics, 1994*, Washington, 1994, 59; and Paul M. Gregory and Jeffrey S. Glover, "Outlook for Belarus," *Review and Outlook for the Former Soviet Union*, Washington, March 1995, 116.

Table 6. Belarus: Trade with Other Countries of the Former Soviet Union, 1992 and 1993
(in millions of Russian rubles)

Country	1992			1993		
	Exports	Imports	Trade Balance	Exports	Imports	Trade Balance
Armenia	1,071	1,380	−309	5,266	3,952	1,314
Azerbaijan	5,685	2,774	2,911	19,172	13,322	5,850
Estonia	3,242	925	2,317	10,625	4,520	6,105
Georgia	1,696	1,193	503	3,788	4,111	−323
Kazakhstan	19,340	15,165	4,175	149,290	262,559	−113,269
Kyrgyzstan	1,629	1,230	399	5,105	11,473	−6,368
Latvia	8,161	5,164	2,997	56,065	28,325	27,740
Lithuania	8,895	7,955	940	68,308	66,560	1,748
Moldova	9,073	6,356	2,717	107,529	34,509	73,020
Russia	215,833	279,248	−63,415	2,194,852	3,344,168	−1,149,316
Tajikistan	1,597	991	606	15,972	4,614	11,358
Turkmenistan	4,188	2,194	1,994	13,043	7,963	5,080
Ukraine	86,576	85,013	1,563	539,987	511,680	28,307
Uzbekistan	12,780	7,492	5,288	52,988	38,627	14,361
TOTAL	379,766	417,080	−37,314	3,241,990	4,336,383	−1,094,393

Source: Based on information from International Monetary Fund, *Belarus*, Washington, 1994, 123.

Belarus and Moldova: Country Studies

Table 7. *Moldova: Births and Deaths, 1987–92*

Year	Live Births		Deaths	
	Number[1]	Number per Thousand Population	Number[1]	Number per Thousand Population
1987	91,800	21.4	40,200	9.4
1988	88,600	20.5	40,900	9.5
1989	82,200	18.9	40,100	9.2
1990	77,100	17.7	42,400	9.7
1991	n.a.[2]	n.a.	n.a.	n.a.
1992	70,100	16.1	44,600	10.2

[1] Estimated.
[2] n.a.—not available.

Source: Based on information from Moldova, Departamentul de Stat pentru statistica al Republicii Moldova, *Anuar statistic: economia nationala a Republicii Moldova, 1990* (Narodnoye khozyaystvo respubliki Moldova), eds., N. Pasternacov and V. Frunza, Chisinau, 1991, 30; and *The Europa World Year Book, 1994, 2,* London, 1994, 2032.

Table 8. *Moldova: Population by Rural-Urban Breakdown, 1959, 1979, and 1991*
(in thousands)

	1959		1979		1991	
	Number	Percentage	Number	Percentage	Number	Percentage
Rural ...	2,242	78	2,396	61	2,293	53
Urban...	642	22	1,551	39	2,074	47

Source: Based on information from Nicholas Dima, *From Moldavia to Moldova*, Boulder, Colorado, 1991, 84; and Moldova, Departamentul de Stat pentru statistica al Republicii Moldova, *Anuar statistic: economia nationala a Republicii Moldova, 1990* (Narodnoye khozyaystvo respubliki Moldova), eds., N. Pasternacov and V. Frunza, Chisinau, 1991, 2.

Table 9. Moldova: Marriages and Divorces, 1987–90

	Marriages		Divorces	
Year	Number[1]	Number per Thousand Population	Number[1]	Number per Thousand Population
1987	39,100	9.1	11,600	2.7
1988	39,800	9.2	12,100	2.8
1989	39,900	9.2	12,400	2.9
1990	40,800	9.4	13,100	3.0

[1] Estimated.

Source: Based on information from Moldova, Departamentul de Stat pentru statistica al Republicii Moldova, *Anuar statistic: economia nationala a Republicii Moldova, 1990* (Narodnoye khozyaystvo respubliki Moldova), eds., N. Pasternacov and V. Frunza, Chisinau, 1991, 29.

Table 10. Moldova: Consumer Goods Availability, 1989, 1990, and 1991
(in units per hundred families)

	1989	1990	1991
Televisions	91	91	98
Tape recorders	38	41	45
Refrigerators	94	94	94
Washing machines	74	77	76
Vacuum cleaners	43	44	46
Sewing machines	47	45	43
Automobiles	14	15	15

Source: Based on information from United States, Central Intelligence Agency, *Handbook of International Economic Statistics, 1994*, Washington, 1994, 61.

Table 11. Moldova: Per Capita Consumption of Selected Foods,
1990–93
(in kilograms unless otherwise specified)

	1990	1991	1992	1993
Meat[1]	58	56	46	42
Milk	303	259	198	232
Eggs (units)	203	195	166	n.a.[2]
Fish	12	7	2	n.a.
Sugar	49	41	31	30
Vegetable oil	14	12	8	n.a.
Potatoes	69	69	66	78
Vegetables	112	113	95	n.a.
Grain products[3]	171	175	170	n.a.

[1] Includes offals and slaughter fat.
[2] n.a.—not available.
[3] In terms of flour.

Source: Based on information from United States, Central Intelligence Agency, *Handbook of International Economic Statistics, 1994*, Washington, 1994, 61.

Table 12. Moldova: Principal Crops, 1990, 1991, and 1992
(in thousands of tons)

Crop	1990	1991	1992
Wheat	1,130	1,056	924
Corn	885	1,501	632
Potatoes	295	291	310
Sunflower seeds	252	169	197
Vegetables	1,177	989	784
Melons, pumpkins, and squash	480	454	450
Grapes	940	774	819
Other fruits and berries	901	698	506
Sugar beets	2,375	2,262	1,970
Tobacco (leaves)	73	69	51

Source: Based on information from *The Europa World Year Book, 1994*, 2, London, 1994, 2032.

Table 13. Moldova: Freight Turnover by Mode of Transportation,
1970, 1980, and 1990
(in millions of ton-kilometers)

Year	Railroads	Trucks	Inland Waterways	Airplanes	Total
1970	10,406	1,036	110	13	11,565
1980	15,171	1,913	299	14	17,397
1990	15,007	1,673	317	19	17,016

Source: Based on information from Moldova, Departamentul de Stat pentru statistica
al Republicii Moldova, *Anuar statistic: economia nationala a Republicii Moldova,*
1990 (Narodnoye khozyaystvo respubliki Moldova), eds., N. Pasternacov and V.
Frunza, Chisinau, 1991, 308.

Appendix B

The Minsk Agreement

Signed by the heads of state of Belarus, the Russian Federation, and Ukraine on December 8, 1991.

Preamble

We, the Republic of Belarus, the Russian Federation and the Republic of Ukraine, as founder states of the Union of Soviet Socialist Republics (USSR), which signed the 1922 Union Treaty, further described as the high contracting parties, conclude that the USSR has ceased to exist as a subject of international law and a geopolitical reality.

Taking as our basis the historic community of our peoples and the ties which have been established between them, taking into account the bilateral treaties concluded between the high contracting parties;

striving to build democratic law-governed states; intending to develop our relations on the basis of mutual recognition and respect for state sovereignty, the inalienable right to self-determination, the principles of equality and non-interference in internal affairs, repudiation of the use of force and of economic or any other methods of coercion, settlement of contentious problems by means of mediation and other generally recognized principles and norms of international law;

considering that further development and strengthening of relations of friendship, good-neighborliness and mutually beneficial co-operation between our states correspond to the vital national interests of their peoples and serve the cause of peace and security;

confirming our adherence to the goals and principles of the United Nations Charter, the Helsinki Final Act and other documents of the Conference on Security and Co-operation in Europe;

and committing ourselves to observe the generally recognized internal norms on human rights and the rights of peoples, we have agreed the following:

Article 1

The high contracting parties form the Commonwealth of Independent States.

Article 2

The high contracting parties guarantee their citizens equal rights and freedoms regardless of nationality or other distinctions. Each of the high contracting parties guarantees the citizens of the other parties, and also persons without citizenship that live on its territory, civil, political, social, economic and cultural rights and freedoms in accordance with generally recognized international norms of human rights, regardless of national allegiance or other distinctions.

Article 3

The high contracting parties, desiring to promote the expression, preservation and development of the ethnic, cultural, linguistic and religious individuality of the national minorities resident on their territories, and that of the unique ethno-cultural regions that have come into being, take them under their protection.

Article 4

The high contracting parties will develop the equal and mutually beneficial co-operation of their peoples and states in the spheres of politics, the economy, culture, education, public health, protection of the environment, science and trade and in the humanitarian and other spheres, will promote the broad exchange of information and will conscientiously and unconditionally observe reciprocal obligations.

The parties consider it a necessity to conclude agreements on co-operation in the above spheres.

Article 5

The high contracting parties recognize and respect one another's territorial integrity and the inviolability of existing borders within the Commonwealth.

They guarantee openness of borders, freedom of movement for citizens and of transmission of information within the Commonwealth.

Article 6

The member-states of the Commonwealth will co-operate in safeguarding international peace and security and in implementing effective measures for reducing weapons and military spending. They seek the elimination of all nuclear weapons and universal total disarmament under strict international control.

The parties will respect one another's aspiration to attain the status of a non-nuclear zone and a neutral state.

The member-states of the community will preserve and maintain under united command a common military-strategic space, including unified control over nuclear weapons, the procedure for implementing which is regulated by a special agreement.

They also jointly guarantee the necessary conditions for the stationing and functioning of and for material and social provision for the strategic armed forces. The parties contract to pursue a harmonized policy on questions of social protection and pension provision for members of the services and their families.

Article 7

The high contracting parties recognize that within the sphere of their activities, implemented on an equal basis through the common coordinating institutions of the Commonwealth, will be the following:

co-operation in the sphere of foreign policy;

co-operation in forming and developing the united economic area, the common European and Eurasian markets, in the area of customs policy;

co-operation in developing transport and communication systems;

co-operation in preservation of the environment, and participation in creating a comprehensive international system of ecological safety;

migration policy issues;

and fighting organized crime.

Article 8

The parties realize the planetary character of the Chernobyl catastrophe and pledge themselves to unite and co-ordinate their efforts in minimizing and overcoming its consequences.

To these ends they have decided to conclude a special agreement which will take consider [sic] the gravity of the consequences of this catastrophe.

Article 9

The disputes regarding interpretation and application of the
norms of this agreement are to be solved by way of negotiations
between the appropriate bodies, and when necessary, at the
level of heads of the governments and states.

Article 10

Each of the high contracting parties reserves the right to suspend the validity of the present agreement or individual articles thereof, after informing the parties to the agreement of
this a year in advance.

The clauses of the present agreement may be addended to
or amended with the common consent of the high contracting
parties.

Article 11

From the moment that the present agreement is signed, the
norms of third states, including the former USSR, are not permitted to be implemented on the territories of the signatory
states.

Article 12

The high contracting parties guarantee the fulfillment of the
international obligations binding upon them from the treaties
and agreements of the former USSR.

Article 13

The present agreement does not affect the obligations of the
high contracting parties in regard to third states.

The present agreement is open for all member-states of the
former USSR to join, and also for other states which share the
goals and principles of the present agreement.

Article 14

The city of Minsk is the official location of the coordinating
bodies of the Commonwealth.

The activities of bodies of the former USSR are discontinued
on the territories of the member-states of the Commonwealth.

Appendix C

The Alma-Ata Declaration

The Alma-Ata Declaration was signed by 11 heads of state on December 21, 1991.

Preamble

The independent states:

The Republic of Armenia, the Republic of Azerbaijan, the Republic of Belarus, the Republic of Kazakhstan, the Republic of Kyrgyzstan, the Republic of Moldova, the Russian Federation, the Republic of Tajikistan, the Republic of Turkmenistan, the Republic of Ukraine and the Republic of Uzbekistan;

seeking to build democratic law-governed states, the relations between which will develop on the basis of mutual recognition and respect for state sovereignty and sovereign equality, the inalienable right to self-determination, principles of equality and noninterference in the internal affairs, the rejection of the use of force, the threat of force and economic and any other methods of pressure, a peaceful settlement of disputes, respect for human rights and freedoms, including the rights of national minorities, a conscientious fulfillment of commitments and other generally recognized principles and standards of international law;

recognizing and respecting each other's territorial integrity and the inviolability of the existing borders;

believing that the strengthening of the relations of friendship, good neighborliness and mutually advantageous co-operation, which has deep historic roots, meets the basic interests of nations and promotes the cause of peace and security;

being aware of their responsibility for the preservation of civilian peace and inter-ethnic accord;

being loyal to the objectives and principles of the agreement on the creation of the Commonwealth of Independent States;

are making the following statement:

The Declaration

Co-operation between members of the Commonwealth will be carried out in accordance with the principle of equality through coordinating institutions formed on a parity basis and

195

operating in the way established by the agreements between members of the Commonwealth, which is neither a state, nor a super-state structure.

In order to ensure international strategic stability and security, allied command of the military-strategic forces and a single control over nuclear weapons will be preserved, the sides will respect each other's desire to attain the status of a non-nuclear and (or) neutral state.

The Commonwealth of Independent States is open, with the agreement of all its participants, to the states—members of the former USSR, as well as other states—sharing the goals and principles of the Commonwealth.

The allegiance to co-operation in the formation and development of the common economic space, and all-European and Eurasian markets, is being confirmed.

With the formation of the Commonwealth of Independent States the USSR ceases to exist. Member states of the Commonwealth guarantee, in accordance with their constitutional procedures, the fulfillment of international obligations, stemming from the treaties and agreements of the former USSR.

Member-states of the Commonwealth pledge to observe strictly the principles of this declaration.

Agreement on Councils of Heads of State and Government

A provisional agreement on the membership and conduct of Councils of Heads of State and Government was concluded between the members of the Commonwealth of Independent States on December 30, 1991.

Preamble

The member-states of this agreement, guided by the aims and principles of the agreement on the creation of a Commonwealth of Independent States of 8 December 1991 and the protocol to the agreement of 21 December 1991, taking into consideration the desire of the Commonwealth states to pursue joint activity through the Commonwealth's common coordinating institutions, and deeming it essential to establish, for the consistent implementation of the provisions of the said agreement, the appropriate inter-state and inter-governmental institutions capable of ensuring effective co-ordination, and of promoting the development of equal and mutually advantageous co-operation, have agreed on the following:

Article 1

The Council of Heads of State is the supreme body, on which all the member-states of the Commonwealth are represented at the level of head of state, for discussion of fundamental issues connected with coordinating the activity of the Commonwealth states in the sphere of their common interests.

The Council of Heads of State is empowered to discuss issues provided for by the Minsk Agreement on the creation of a Commonwealth of Independent States and other documents for the development of the said Agreement, including the problems of legal succession, which have arisen as a result of ending the existence of the USSR and the abolition of Union structures.

The activities of the Council of Heads of State and of the Council of Heads of Government are pursued on the basis of mutual recognition of and respect for the state sovereignty and sovereign equality of the member-states of the Agreement, their inalienable right to self-determination, the principles of equality and non-interference in internal affairs, the renunciation of the use of force and the threat of force, territorial integrity and the inviolability of existing borders, and the peaceful settlement of disputes, respect for human rights and liberties, including the rights of national minorities, conscientious fulfillment of obligations and other commonly accepted principles and norms of international law.

Article 2

The activities of the Council of Heads of State and of the Council Heads of Government are regulated by the Minsk Agreement on setting up the Commonwealth of Independent States, the present agreement and agreements adopted in development of them, and also by the rules of procedure of these institutes.

Each state in the council has one vote. The decisions of the council are taken by common consent.

The official languages of the Councils are the state languages of the Commonwealth states.

The working language is the Russian language.

Article 3

The Council of Heads of State and the Council of Heads of Government discuss and where necessary take decisions on the more important domestic and external issues.

Any state may declare its having no interest in a particular issue or issues.

Article 4

The Council of Heads of State convenes for meetings no less than twice a year. The decision on the time for holding and the provisional agenda of each successive meeting of the Council is taken at the routine meeting of the Council, unless the Council agrees otherwise. Extraordinary meetings of the Council of Heads of State are convened on the initiative of the majority of Commonwealth heads of state.

The heads of state chair the meetings of the Council in turn, according to the Russian alphabetical order of the names of the Commonwealth states.

Sittings of the Council of Heads of State are generally to be held in Minsk. A sitting of the Council may be held in another of the Commonwealth states by agreement among those taking part.

Article 5

The Council of Heads of Government convenes for meetings no less frequently than once every three months. The decision concerning the scheduling of and preliminary agenda for each subsequent sitting is to be made at a routine session of the Council, unless the Council arranges otherwise.

Extraordinary sittings of the Council of Heads of Government may be convened at the initiative of a majority of heads of government of the commonwealth states.

The heads of government chair meetings of the Council in turn, according to the Russian alphabetical order of the names of the Commonwealth states.

Sittings of the Council of Heads of Government are generally to be held in Minsk. A sitting of the Council may be held in another of the Commonwealth states by agreement among the heads of government.

Article 6

The Council of Heads of State and the Council of Heads of Government of the Commonwealth states may hold joint sittings.

Article 7

Working and auxiliary bodies may be set up on both a permanent and interim basis on the decision of the Council of Heads of State and the Council of Heads of Government of the Commonwealth states.

These are composed of authorized representatives of the participating states. Experts and consultants may be invited to take part in their sittings.

Agreement on Strategic Forces

The Agreement on Strategic Forces was concluded between the 11 members of the Commonwealth of Independent States on December 30, 1991.

Preamble

Guided by the necessity for a coordinated and organized solution to issues in the sphere of the control of the strategic forces and the single control over nuclear weapons, the Republic of Armenia, the Republic of Azerbaijan, the Republic of Belarus, the Republic of Kazakhstan, the Republic of Kyrgyzstan, the Republic of Moldova, the Russian Federation, the Republic of Tajikistan, the Republic of Turkmenistan, the Republic of Ukraine and the Republic of Uzbekistan, subsequently referred to as 'the member-states of the Commonwealth,' have agreed on the following:

Article 1

The term 'strategic forces' means: groupings, formations, units, institutions, the military training institutes for the strategic missile troops, for the air force, for the navy and for the air defenses; the directorates of the Space Command and of the airborne troops, and of strategic and operational intelligence, and the nuclear technical units and also the forces, equipment and other military facilities designed for the control and maintenance of the strategic forces of the former USSR (the schedule is to be determined for each state participating in the Commonwealth in a separate protocol).

Article 2

The member-states of the Commonwealth undertake to observe the international treaties of the former USSR, to pursue a coordinated policy in the area of international security, disarmament and arms control, and to participate in the preparation and implementation of programs for reductions in arms and armed forces. The member-states of the Commonwealth are immediately entering into negotiations with one another and also with other states which were formerly part of the USSR, but which have not joined the commonwealth, with the aim of ensuring guarantees and developing mechanisms for implementing the aforementioned treaties.

Article 3

The member-states of the Commonwealth recognize the need for joint command of strategic forces and for maintaining unified control of nuclear weapons, and other types of weapons of mass destruction, of the armed forces of the former USSR.

Article 4

Until the complete elimination of nuclear weapons, the decision on the need for their use is taken by the president of the Russian Federation in agreement with the heads of the Republic of Belarus, the Republic of Kazakhstan and the Republic of Ukraine, and in consultation with the heads of the other member-states of the Commonwealth.

Until their destruction in full, nuclear weapons located on the territory of the Republic of Ukraine shall be under the control of the Combined Strategic Forces Command, with the aim that they not be used and be dismantled by the end of 1994, including tactical nuclear weapons by 1 July 1992.

The process of destruction of nuclear weapons located on the territory of the Republic of Belarus and the Republic of Ukraine shall take place with the participation of the Republic of Belarus, the Russian Federation and the Republic of Ukraine under the joint control of the Commonwealth states.

Article 5

The status of strategic forces and the procedure for service in them shall be defined in a special agreement.

Article 6

This agreement shall enter into force from the moment of its signing and shall be terminated by decision of the signatory states or the Council of Heads of State of the Commonwealth.

This agreement shall cease to apply to a signatory state from whose territory strategic forces or nuclear weapons are withdrawn.

Agreement on Armed Forces and Border Troops

The Agreement on Strategic Forces was concluded between the 11 members of the Commonwealth of Independent States on December 30, 1991.

Preamble

Proceeding from the need for a mutually acceptable settlement of matters of defense and security, including guarding the borders of the Commonwealth member-states, the member-states of the Commonwealth of Independent States have agreed the following:

The Agreement

The commonwealth member-states confirm their legitimate right to set up their own armed forces;

jointly with the Commander-in-Chief of the armed forces, to examine and settle, within two months of the date of this agreement, the issue of the procedure for controlling general purpose forces, taking account of the national legislations of the Commonwealth states and also the issue of the consistent implementation by the Commonwealth states of their right to set up their own armed forces. For the Republic of Ukraine, this will be from 3 January 1991;

to appoint I. Ya. Kalini[n]chenko Commander-in-Chief of Border Troops;

to instruct the Commander-in-Chief of Border Troops to work out, within two months and in conjunction with the leaders of the Commonwealth member-states, a mechanism for the activity of the Border Troops, taking account of the national legislations [sic] of the Commonwealth states, with the exception of states with which a mechanism for the activity of Border Troops has already been agreed.

Note: In addition, Marshal Yevgeniy Shaposhnikov was confirmed as acting Commander-in-Chief of the Armed Forces of the Commonwealth of Independent States.

Appendix D

Declaration of Independence of the Republic of Moldova

THE PARLIAMENT OF THE REPUBLIC OF MOLDOVA, constituted after free and democratic elections,

taking into account the millenary history of our people and its uninterrupted statehood within its historical and ethnic area of its national making,

considering the acts of dismemberment of its national territory between 1775 and 1812 as being contradictory to the historical right of its people and the judicial stature of the principality of Moldova, acts recalled by the entire historical evolution and the free will of the population of Bassarabia and Bukovina,

underlining the existence of Moldavians [sic] in Transnistria, a component part of the historical and ethnic territory of our people,

acknowledging that declarations by many parliaments of many states consider the agreement of August 23, 1939, between the government of the USSR and the government of Germany null and void *ab initio* and demand that the political and judicial consequences of the above be eliminated, a fact revealed also by the declaration of the international conference "The Molotov-Ribbentrop pact and its consequences for Bassarabia", adopted on 28 June 1991,

pointing out that, without the prior consultation of the population of Bassarabia, Northern Bukovina and Hertza District, occupied by force on June 28, 1940, as well as the Moldavian Soviet Socialist Autonomous Republic (Transnistria) established on Oct. 12, 1924, the Supreme Soviet of the USSR, by infringing its constitutional prerogatives, adopted the "Law of the USSR on the establishment of the Moldavian SSR" on August 2, 1940, and its Presidium issued "The Decree concerning the frontiers between the Ukrainian SSR and the Moldavian SSR", on November 4, 1940, judicial acts whereby, in the absence of any real legal basis, it was attempted to justify the dismantlement of those territories and the incorporation of the new republic into the USSR, recalling that during the recent years the democratic national liberation movement of the population of the Republic of Moldova reaffirmed its aspirations for freedom, independence and national unity, expressed in final documents of the Great National Reunion of Kishinau [sic] on 27 August, 1989, 16 December, 1990, and 27 August, 1991, laws and decisions of the Parliament of the Republic of Moldova concerning the laws reintroducing Romanian as the state language and the Latin alphabet on August 31, 1989, the state flag on 27 April, 1990, the state emblem on November 3, 1990, and the change of the official name of the republic on May 23, 1991,

taking as a basis the declaration concerning State Sovereignty of the Republic of Moldova, adopted by the parliament on June 23, 1990, and the fact that the population of the Republic of Moldova, in its own right as a sovereign people, did not participate at the referendum on the preservation of the USSR, held on March 17, 1991, in spite [sic] of the pressures exercized [sic] by the state organs of the USSR,

taking into account the irreversible processes taking place in Europe and elsewhere in the world calling for democracy, freedom and national unity, for the establishment of a state of law and the transformation towards a free market,

reaffirming the equal rights of peoples and their right to self-determination, as laid down in the UN Charta, the Helsinki Final Act and the norms of international law pertaining to the above,

considering that the time has come for the proclamation of a judicial act, in accordance with the history of our people and moral norms of international law,

PROCLAIMS SOLEMNLY,

in virtue of the right of self-determination of peoples, in the name of the entire population of the Republic of Moldova, and in front of the whole world, that:

THE REPUBLIC OF MOLDOVA IS A SOVEREIGN, INDEPENDENT AND DEMOCRATIC STATE, FREE TO DECIDE ITS PRESENT AND FUTURE, WITHOUT ANY EXTERNAL INTERFERENCE, KEEPING WITH THE IDEALS AND ASPIRATIONS OF THE PEOPLE WITHIN ITS HISTORICAL AND ETHNIC AREA OF ITS NATIONAL MAKING.

In its quality as a SOVEREIGN AND INDEPENDENT STATE, THE REPUBLIC OF MOLDOVA, hereby

requests all states and world governments to recognize the independence of the Republic of Moldova, as proclaimed by the freely elected parliament of the republic and is willing to establish political, economic and cultural relations and any other relations of common interest with European countries and all other countries of the world, and is ready to establish diplomatic relations with the above, in accordance with the norms of international law and common practice on the above matter,

requests the United Nations to admit the Republic of Moldova as a full member of the world organization and its specialized [sic] agencies,

declares that it is ready to adhere to the Helsinki Final Act and the Paris Charta for a new Europe, equally asking to be admitted to the CSCE and its mechanisms, with equal rights,

requests the USSR to begin negotiations with the government of the Republic of Moldova to terminate the illegal state of occupation and annexation and the withdrawal of Soviet troops from its national territory,

decides that no other laws should be respected on its territory but those that are in conformity with the republic's constitution, laws and all other legal acts adopted by the legally constituted organs of the Republic of Moldova,

guarantees the exercise of social, economic, cultural and political rights for all citizens of the Republic of Moldova, including those of national, ethnic, religious and linguistic groups, in conformity with the provisions of the Helsinki Final Act and documents adopted afterwards, as well as the Paris Charta for a new Europe.

SO HELP US GOD!

Adopted in Chisinau, by the Parliament of the Republic of Moldova on this day, the 27th of August, 1991.

Bibliography

Chapter 1

Adamovich, Anthony. *Opposition to Sovietization in Belorussian Literature, 1917–1957.* New York: Scarecrow Press, 1958.

Amnesty International. *Amnesty International Report, 1994.* New York: 1994.

Association of Byelorussians in Great Britain. *Letters to Gorbachev: New Documents from Soviet Byelorussia.* (2d ed.) London: 1987.

Belarus. Ministerstva zamyezhnykh spraw. Infarmatsyyny-kamyertsyyny tsentr. *Respublika Belarus': Mahchymastsi dzelavoha supratsownitstva* (Respublika Belarus': Vozmozhnosti delovogo sotrudnichestva) (The Republic of Belarus: Prospects for Business Cooperation). Minsk: 1992.

"Belorussia." Pages 104–7 in *The Dorling Kindersley World Reference Atlas.* London: Dorling Kindersley, 1994.

Belorussian Soviet Socialist Republic. Mission to the United Nations. *Statement by H.E. Vyacheslav F. Kebich, Chairman of the Council of Ministers of the Byelorussian SSR in the General Debate at the 45th Session of the UN General Assembly.* (Press Release.) New York: September 26, 1990, 8.

"Belorussian Soviet Socialist Republic." Pages 830–33 in *The New Encyclopaedia Britannica.* (Macropaedia, 2.) Chicago: Encyclopaedia Britannica, 1975.

Bird, Thomas E. "Byelorussian Literature." Pages 374–76 in Leonard S. Klein, ed., *Encyclopedia of World Literature in the 20th Century,* 1. (Rev. ed.) New York: Frederick Ungar, 1981.

Bird, Thomas E. "Orthodoxy in Byelorussia, 1917–1980," *Zapisy,* 17, 1983, 144–213.

Blum, Jakub, and Vera Rich, eds. *The Image of the Jew in Soviet Literature: The Post-Stalin Period.* New York: Ktav, 1984.

Borushko, V.F. *Belorussiya: Lyudi, sobytiya, fakty.* (3d ed.) Minsk: Byelarus, 1989.

"Bund." Page 368 in *The New Encyclopaedia Britannica.* (Micropaedia, 2.) Chicago: Encyclopaedia Britannica, 1975.

Burant, Stephen R. "Belarus and the 'Belarusian Irredenta' in Lithuania," *Nationalities Papers*, forthcoming 1995.

Burant, Stephen R. "Foreign Policy and National Identity: A Comparison of Ukraine and Belarus," *Europe-Asia Studies* [Abingdon, Oxfordshire, United Kingdom], forthcoming November 1995.

Burant, Stephen R. "International Relations in a Regional Context: Poland and Its Eastern Neighbours—Lithuania, Belarus, Ukraine," *Europe-Asia Studies* [Abingdon, Oxfordshire, United Kingdom], 45, No. 3, 1993, 395–418.

Burant, Stephen R. "Polish-Belarusian Relations," *RFE/RL Research Report* [Munich], 1, No. 37, September 18, 1992, 41–45.

"Byelorussians." Pages 131–32 in Amiram Gonen, ed., *The Encyclopedia of the Peoples of the World.* New York: Henry Holt and Company, 1993.

Byelorussian Tristan. Trans., Zora Kipel. (Garland Library of Medieval Literature Series, 59. Series B.) New York: Garland Press, 1988.

Center for International Health Information/ISTI. *Belarus: USAID Health Profile (Selected Data).* [Final draft.] Arlington, Virginia: 1992.

"Chernobyl Accident." Page 171 in *The New Encyclopaedia Britannica.* (Micropaedia, 3.) Chicago: Encyclopaedia Britannica, 1992.

"Council of Europe Rules Belarus Ineligible Due to Election Shortcomings," *Summary of World Broadcasts* [Caversham Park, Reading, United Kingdom], Part 1–Former USSR, Third Series, SU/2324, June 8, 1995, D/3–D/4.

Curtis, Glenn E., ed. *Poland: A Country Study.* Washington: GPO, 1994.

The Dorling Kindersley World Reference Atlas. London: Dorling Kindersley, 1994.

The Europa World Year Book, 1994. (2 vols.) London: Europa, 1994.

The Europa World Year Book, 1995. (2 vols.) London: Europa, 1995.

Galeotti, Mark. "The Belarusian Army—An Example of Successful Reform?" *Jane's Intelligence Review* [Coulsdon, Surrey, United Kingdom], 7, No. 6, June 1995, 258–60.

Glover, Jeffrey. "Outlook for Belarus." Pages 89–104 in *Review and Outlook for the Former Soviet Union.* Washington: PlanEcon, August 1995.

Gonen, Amiram, ed. *The Encyclopedia of the Peoples of the World.* New York: Henry Holt and Company, 1993.

Gregory, Paul M., and Jeffrey S. Glover, "Outlook for Belarus." Pages 111–27 in *Review and Outlook for the Former Soviet Union.* Washington: PlanEcon, March 1995.

Grishan, Igor'. "I eto vsë o nas," *Sovetskaya Belorussiya* [Minsk], June 4, 1992, 1.

"History of the Baltic States." Pages 670–76 in *The New Encyclopaedia Britannica.* (Macropaedia, 2.) Chicago: Encyclopaedia Britannica, 1975.

Hlebowicz, Adam. "Przyszlosc Kosciola katolickiego na Bialorusi" (The Future of the Catholic Church in Belarus), *Wiez* [Warsaw], January, 1994, 138.

Hlobenko, M., V. Kubijovyc, and O. Ohloblyn. "Belorussia." Pages 194–99 in Volodymyr Kubijovyc, ed., *Encyclopedia of Ukraine,* 1. Toronto: University of Toronto Press, 1984.

Hockstader, Lee. "Belarus Slowly Drifts Toward Moscow Orbit," *Washington Post,* January 28, 1994, A20.

"How Belarus Will Sink," *Foreign Report* [London], August 25, 1994, 5–6.

International Monetary Fund. *Belarus.* (Economic Review Series.) Washington: 1992.

International Monetary Fund. *Belarus.* (Economic Review Series.) Washington: 1994.

"In the Slav Shadowlands," *Economist* [London], 335, No. 7915, May 20, 1995, 47–49.

Kasiak, Ivan. *Byelorussia: Historical Outline.* London: Byelorussian Central Council, 1989.

Katz, Zev, ed. *Handbook of Major Soviet Nationalities.* New York: Free Press, 1975.

Kipel, Vitaut. "Byelorussians." Pages 88–107 in Barbara Cunningham, ed., *The New Jersey Ethnic Experience.* Union City, New Jersey: William H. Wise and Company, 1977.

Kipel, Vitaut, and Zora Kipel, eds. *Byelorussian Statehood: Reader and Bibliography.* New York: Byelorussian Institute of Arts and Sciences, 1988.

Klein, Leonard S., ed. *Encyclopedia of World Literature in the 20th Century.* (Rev. ed.) New York: Frederick Ungar, 1981.

Kubijovyc, Volodymyr, ed. *Encyclopedia of Ukraine.* (5 vols.) Toronto: University of Toronto Press, 1984.

"Latvia and Belarus Sign Transport and Communications Agreement," *Summary of World Broadcasts* [Caversham Park, Reading, United Kingdom], Part 1–Former USSR, Third Series, SU/2308, May 20, 1995, E/3.

Lerner Publications Company. Geography Department. *Belarus.* (Then and Now Series.) Minneapolis: 1993.

Lubachko, Ivan S. *Belorussia under Soviet Rule, 1917–1957.* Lexington: University of Kentucky Press, 1972.

Magocsi, Paul Robert. *Historical Atlas of East Central Europe.* Seattle: University of Washington Press, 1993.

Magocsi, Paul Robert. *Ukraine: A Historical Atlas.* Toronto: University of Toronto Press, 1985.

Markus, Ustina. "Belarus: Slowly Awakening to New Realities," *RFE/RL Research Report* [Munich], 2, No. 1, January 7, 1994, 42–46.

Markus, Ustina. "Belarus: You Can't Go Home Again?" *Current History,* 93, No. 585, October 1994, 337–41.

Markus, Ustina. "Belarus a 'Weak Link' in Eastern Europe?" *RFE/RL Research Report* [Munich], 2, No. 49, December 10, 1993, 21–27.

Markus, Ustina. "Business as Usual with Lukashenka," *Transition,* 1, No. 8, May 26, 1995, 57–61.

Markus, Ustina. "Lukashenka's Victory," *Transition,* 1, No. 14, August 11, 1995, 75–78.

Markus, Ustina. "Missed Opportunities in Foreign Policy," *Transition,* 1, No. 15, August 25, 1995, 62–66.

Marples, David R. "The Legacy of the Chernobyl Disaster," *RFE/RL Research Bulletin* [Munich], 10, No. 4, February 16, 1993, 4–5.

Marples, David R. "Post-Soviet Belarus and the Impact of Chernobyl'," *Post-Soviet Geography,* 33, No. 7, September 1992, 419–31.

Maryniak, Irena. "Democracy's Playground," *Index on Censorship* [London], 22, No. 3, March 1993, 4.

Maryniak, Irena. "Language and the Nation," *Index on Censorship* [London], 22, No. 3, March 1993, 6.

Maryniak, Irena. "A Matter of Duty," *Index on Censorship* [London], 22, No. 3, March 1993, 5.

McMillin, Arnold B. *A History of Byelorussian Literature: From Its Origins to the Present Day.* Giessen, Germany: Wilhelm Schmitz Verlag, 1977.

The Military Balance, 1994–1995. London: Brassey's for International Institute for Strategic Studies, October 1994.

Morris, William, ed. *The American Heritage Dictionary of the English Language.* Boston: Houghton Mifflin, 1976.

Rich, Vera. "'First Come, First Served,'" *Catholic World Report,* January 1993, 10–14.

Rich, Vera. "Jewish Themes and Characters in Belorussian Texts." Pages 100–271 in Jakub Blum and Vera Rich, eds., *The Image of the Jew in Soviet Literature: The Post-Stalin Period.* New York: Ktav, 1984.

Rich, Vera. *Like Water, Like Fire: An Anthology of Byelorussian Poetry from 1828 to the Present Day.* London: George Allen and Unwin, 1971.

"Russia, Belarus Scrap Border Checkpoints," *Washington Post,* May 27, 1995, A26.

Sadouski, John. *A History of the Byelorussians in Canada.* Belleville, Ontario: Mika, 1981.

"Scandals in Belarus," *Foreign Report* [London], January 26, 1995, 7.

The Statesman's Year-Book, 1994–1995. Ed., Brian Hunter. New York: St. Martin's Press, 1994.

The Statesman's Year-Book, 1995–1996. Ed., Brian Hunter. New York: St. Martin's Press, 1995.

"Tatars." Pages 590–91 in Amiram Gonen, ed., *The Encyclopedia of the Peoples of the World.* New York: Henry Holt and Company, 1993.

Umbach, Frank. "Back to the Future?—The Security Policy of Belarus," *Jane's Intelligence Review* [Coulsdon, Surrey, United Kingdom], 5, No. 9, September 1993, 410–14.

"Union of Brest-Litovsk." Page 257 in *The New Encyclopaedia Britannica.* (Micropaedia, 2.) Chicago: Encyclopaedia Britannica, 1975.

"Union of Soviet Socialist Republics." Pages 941–1090 in *The New Encyclopaedia Britannica.* (Macropaedia, 28.) Chicago: Encyclopaedia Britannica, 1992.

United States. Agency for International Development. "U.S. Government Assistance to and Cooperative Activities with the New Independent States of the Former Soviet Union: Quarterly Report, April–June 1995." Washington: 1995.

United States. Central Intelligence Agency. *Handbook of International Economic Statistics, 1994.* (CPAS 94–10001.) Washington: 1994.

United States. Central Intelligence Agency. *USSR Energy Atlas.* Washington: 1985.

United States. Central Intelligence Agency. *The World Factbook, 1993.* Washington: 1993.

United States. Central Intelligence Agency. *The World Factbook, 1994.* Washington: 1994.

United States. Commission on Security and Cooperation in Europe. *Report on the Belarusian Presidential Election: June 23, 1994, and July 10, 1994.* Washington: July 1994.

United States. Department of State. *Country Reports on Human Rights Practices for 1994.* (Report submitted to United States Congress, 104th, 1st Session, Senate, Committee on Foreign Relations, and House of Representatives, Committee on Foreign Affairs.) Washington: GPO, 1995.

Urban, Michael. *An Algebra of Soviet Power: Elite Circulation in the Belorussian Republic, 1966–1986.* Cambridge: Cambridge University Press, 1989.

Vakar, Nicholas P. *Belorussia: The Making of a Nation.* Cambridge: Harvard University Press, 1956.

World Bank. *Belarus: Energy Sector Review.* Washington: April 21, 1995.

World Bank. *Statistical Handbook: States of the Former USSR.* (Studies of Economies in Transformation, No. 3.) Washington: 1992.

World Radio TV Handbook, 47. Ed., Andrew G. Sennitt. Amsterdam: 1993.

World Radio TV Handbook, 49. Ed., Andrew G. Sennitt. Amsterdam: 1995.

World Resources Institute. *The 1994 Information Please Environmental Almanac.* Boston: Houghton Mifflin, 1994.

Zaprudnik, Jan. *Belarus: At a Crossroads in History.* Boulder, Colorado: Westview Press, 1993.

Zaprudnik, Jan. "Belorussia and the Belorussians." Pages 49–71 in Zev Katz, ed., *Handbook of Major Soviet Nationalities.* New York: Free Press, 1975.

Zaprudnik, Jan. "Belorussia Reawakening," *Problems of Communism,* 38, July–August 1989, 36–52.

Zaprudnik, Jan, and Thomas E. Bird. *The Uprising in Byelorussia: "Peasants' Truth" and "Letters from Beneath the Gallows" (Texts and Commentaries).* New York: Kreceuski Foundation, 1980.

Zickel, Raymond E., ed. *Soviet Union: A Country Study.* Washington: GPO, 1992.

(Various issues of the following periodicals were also used in the preparation of this chapter: British Broadcasting Corporation, *Summary of World Broadcasts* [Caversham Park, Reading, United Kingdom]; and Foreign Broadcast Information Service, *Daily Report: Central Eurasia.*)

Chapter 2

"Adunaria Republana a Alegatorilor" (Republican Meeting of Voters), *Moldova Socialista* [Chisinau], February 13, 1990, 1–5.

Amnesty International. *Amnesty International Report, 1993.* New York: 1993.

Arutyunyan, Yu. V. *Opyt etnosotsiologicheskogo issledovaniya obraza zhizni: Po materialam Moldavskoy SSR.* Moscow: Nauka, 1980.

Bachman, Ronald D., ed. *Romania: A Country Study.* Washington: GPO, 1991.

Bater, James H. *The Soviet Scene: A Geographical Perspective.* New York: Edward Arnold, 1989.

Berbekaru, G. "În Spiritul Democratizarii" (In the Spirit of Democratization), *Moldova Socialista* [Chisinau], June 13, 1989, 4.

Bernstam, Mikhail. "The Demography of Soviet Ethnic Groups in World Perspective." Pages 314–68 in Robert Conquest, ed., *The Last Empire: Nationality and the Soviet Future.* Stanford, California: Hoover Institution Press, 1986.

"Biografile Membrilor Guvernului Republicii Moldova" (Biographies of the Members of the Government of Moldova), *Moldova Suverana* [Chisinau], August 20, 1992, 1–2.

Bremmer, Ian, and Ray Taras, eds. *Nations and Politics in the Soviet Successor States.* New York: Cambridge University Press, 1993.

Bruchis, Michael. *Nations, Nationalities, People: A Study of the Nationalities Policy of the Communist Party in Soviet Moldavia.* New York: Columbia University Press, 1984.

Bruchis, Michael. *One Step Back, Two Steps Forward: On the Language Policy of the Communist Party of the Soviet Union in the National Republics: Moldavia: A Look Back, a Survey, and Perspectives, 1924–1980.* Boulder, Colorado: East European Monographs, 1982.

Bruchis, Michael. *The USSR: Language and Realities: Nations, Leaders, and Scholars.* New York: Columbia University Press, 1988.

Buckmaster, Barbara. "Bessarabia." Pages 546–47 in *Encyclopaedia Britannica*, 3. Chicago: Benton, 1965.

Center for International Health Information/ISTI. *Moldova: USAID Health Profile (Selected Data).* Arlington, Virginia: 1992.

Clark, Charles Upson. *Bessarabia: Russia and Roumania on the Black Sea.* New York: Dodd, Mead, 1927.

Clines, Francis X. "Six Killed in Violence in Moldova," *New York Times*, November 3, 1990, 7.

Comnène, N.P. *Roumania Through the Ages: An Historical, Political, and Ethnographical Atlas (La terre roumaine à travers les ages: Atlas historique, politique, et ethnographique).* Lausanne: Librairie Payot et Cie, 1919.

Crowther, William E. "Moldova after Independence," *Current History*, 93, No. 585, October 1994, 342–47.

Crowther, William E. "The Politics of Ethnonational Mobilization: Nationalism and Reform in Soviet Moldavia," *Russian Review*, 50, No. 2, April 1991, 183–203.

Crowther, William E. "Romania and Moldavian Political Dynamics." Pages 239–59 in Daniel Nelson, ed., *Romania after Tyranny.* Boulder, Colorado: Westview Press, 1992.

"Cu Privire la Alegerile de Deputati al Poporului al RSS Moldovenesti" (Concerning Elections of People's Deputies of the Moldovan SSR), *Moldova Socialista* [Chisinau], November 29, 1989, 3.

Dima, Nicholas. *From Moldavia to Moldova: The Soviet-Romanian Territorial Dispute.* Boulder, Colorado: East European Monographs, 1991.

Dima, Nicholas. "Recent Changes in Soviet Moldavia," *East European Quarterly,* 24, No. 2, Summer 1991, 167–78.

Dima, Nicholas. "The Soviet Political Upheaval of the 1980s: The Case of Moldova," *Journal of Social, Political, and Economic Studies,* 16, No. 1, Spring 1991, 39–58.

"The Dniestr Republic: The Stalinist State Format Kept in Readiness," *Soviet Analyst: An Intelligence Commentary,* 22, No. 5, 1993, 1–12.

Dobbs, Michael. "Three Former Soviet Republics Decline to Sign CIS Charter," *Washington Post,* January 23, 1993, A15.

Donos, Alexandru. "Nu trebuie sa învinga birocratii" (The Bureaucracy Does Not Have to Win), *Literatura si arta* [Chisinau], No. 4, February 1, 1990, 1.

"Eparchy." Pages 831–32 in Volodymyr Kubijovyc, ed., *Encyclopedia of Ukraine,* 1. Toronto: University of Toronto Press, 1984.

Esinencu, T., ed. *Republica Moldova.* Chisinau: Editura Universitatis, 1992.

The Europa World Year Book, 1991. (2 vols.) London: Europa, 1991.

The Europa World Year Book, 1993. (2 vols.) London: Europa, 1993.

The Europa World Year Book, 1994. (2 vols.) London: Europa, 1994.

Eyal, Jonathan. "Moldovans." Pages 123–41 in Graham Smith, ed., *The Nationalities Question in the Soviet Union.* New York: Longman, 1990.

Fane, Darya. "Moldova: Breaking Loose from Moscow." Pages 191–53 in Ian Bremmer and Ray Taras, eds., *Nations and Politics in the Soviet Successor States.* New York: Cambridge University Press, 1993.

The FirstBook of Demographics for the Republics of the Former Soviet Union, 1951–1990. Shady Side, Maryland: New World Demographics, 1992.

Fischer-Galati, Stephen. "Moldavia and the Moldavians." Pages 415–33 in Zev Katz, ed., *Handbook of Major Soviet Nationalities.* New York: Free Press, 1975.

French, Richard Antony. "Moldavian Soviet Socialist Republic." Pages 650–51 in *Encyclopaedia Britannica,* 15. Chicago: Benton, 1965.

"Gagauz Proclaim Republic; Situation 'Explosive,'" Moscow Domestic Service [Moscow], August 21, 1990. Foreign Broadcast Information Service, *Daily Report: Soviet Union.* (FBIS–SOV–90–162.) August 21, 1990, 92.

Gall, Carlotta. "Moldova, Transdnestr Agree to Pursue Peace," *Moscow Times* [Moscow] (International Weekly Edition), 2, No. 34, January 8, 1995, 20.

Georgescu, Vlad. *The Romanians.* Columbus: Ohio State University Press, 1991.

Gold, Bernard. "Outlook for Moldova," *Review and Outlook for the Former Soviet Republics.* Washington: PlanEcon, March 1995.

Grosul, Ya.S., and N.A. Mokhov. "Istoricheskiy ocherk" section of "Moldavskaya Sovetskaya Sotsialisticheskaya Respublika." Pages 425–30 in A.M. Prokhorov, ed., *Bol'shaya Sovetskaya Entsiklopediya.* Moscow: Sovetskaya Entsiklopediya, 1974.

Hockstader, Lee. "In Moldova's East Bank, Separatists Still Cling to the Bad Old Days," *Washington Post,* March 25, 1994, A31.

"Hotarîrea Sovietului suprem al RSS Moldova" (Decision of the Supreme Soviet of the Moldovan SSR), *Moldova Socialista* [Chisinau], June 26, 1990, 2–3.

"În Comisa Electorala Centrala Pentru Alegerile de Deputati al porporului al RSS Moldovenesti" (In the Central Electoral Commission for the Election of Deputies of the People of the Moldovan SSR), *Moldova Socialista* [Chisinau], March 1, 1990, 1.

International Monetary Fund. *Common Issues and Interrepublic Relations in the Former USSR.* (Economic Review Series.) Washington: 1992.

International Monetary Fund. *Moldova.* (Economic Review Series.) Washington: 1992.

International Monetary Fund. *Moldova.* (IMF Economic Reviews.) Washington: 1993.

Ionel, S. "Mitinguri în timpal Lucrului" (Meetings During Work Time), *Moldova Socialista* [Chisinau], May 4, 1990, 3.

Ionescu, Dan. "Back to Romanian?" *Transition*, 1, No. 15, August 25, 1995, 54–57.

Jane's Sentinel, The Unfair Advantage. Commonwealth of Independent States: Regional Security Assessment. Ed., Paul Beaver. Coulsdon, Surrey, United Kingdom: 1994.

Jelavich, Barbara. *History of the Balkans: Eighteenth and Nineteenth Centuries.* New York: Cambridge University Press, 1983.

King, Charles. "Moldova and the New Bessarabian Question," *World Today* [London], 49, July 1993, 135–39.

King, Charles. "Moldovan Identity and the Politics of Pan-Romanianism," *Slavic Review*, 53, No. 2, Summer 1994, 345–60.

Kondratov, E. "Moldavia Hit by Three-way Ethnic Strife," *Current Digest of the Soviet Press*, 42, No. 43, November 28, 1990, 1–7.

Kozlov, Viktor. *The Peoples of the Soviet Union.* Trans., Pauline M. Tiffen. (Second World Series.) Bloomington: Indiana University Press, 1988.

Landgren, Signe. "Post-Soviet Threat to Security." Pages 546–47 in *SIPRI Yearbook, 1992: World Armaments and Disarmament.* New York: Oxford University Press, 1992.

"La sesiunea Sovietul Suprem al RSSM" (At the Time of the Secession of the Supreme Soviet of the MSSR), *Moldova Socialista* [Chisinau], May 13, 1990, 1–3.

Lerner Publications Company. Geography Department. *Moldova.* (Then and Now Series.) Minneapolis: 1993.

Lucinschi, P.K. "Aspectete Politice al Restructurare si Activitatea Partidului Comunist Moldovenesti sub Conditiile Noi" (Political Aspects of Restructuring and the Activity of the CPM under the New Conditions), *Moldova Socialista* [Chisinau], March 3, 1990, 1–3.

Lucinschi, P.K. "Ob itogakh XXVIII s"yezda KPSS" (On the Results of the XXVIII CPSU Congress: Report of P.K. Lucinschi, First Secretary of the SS, CPM) [speech to the Central Committee of the CPM], *Sovetskaya Moldova* [Kishinĕv], August 6, 1990, 2–3.

"Mîine Iarasi la Aleger," *Moldova Socialista* [Chisinau], March 17, 1990, 4.

The Military Balance, 1992–1993. London: International Institute for Strategic Studies, 1992.

The Military Balance, 1993–1994. London: International Institute for Strategic Studies, 1993.

The Military Balance, 1994–1995. London: International Institute for Strategic Studies, 1994.

"Moldavia." Page 650 in *Encyclopaedia Britannica,* 15. Chicago: Benton, 1965.

Moldova. *Report of the Government of Moldova for the World Social Summit, 6–12 March 1995, Copenhagen.* Chisinau: 1995.

Moldova. *The Republic of Moldova.* Chisinau: Moldpres, 1995.

Moldova. Departamentul de Stat pentru statistica al Republicii Moldova. *Anuar statistic: economia nationala a Republicii Moldova, 1990* (Narodnoye khozyaystvo respubliki Moldova). Eds., N. Pasternacov and V. Frunza. Chisinau: Universitas, 1991.

Moldova. Departamentul de Stat pentru statistica al Republicii Moldova. *Economia nationala a Republicii Moldova.* Chisinau: 1992.

"Moldovan Women Force Out General," *New York Times,* June 18, 1995, 10.

Morar, A., N. Movilyanu, and I. Shishkanu. "Vvedeniye latinitsi: kak eto bylo" (The Introduction of the Latin Alphabet: How It Was), *Sovetskaya Moldavia* [Kishinёv], June 17, 1989, 3.

Morar, A., N. Movilyanu, and I. Siskanu. "Cum a fost arestata Grafia Latina" (How the Latin Alphabet Was Arrested), *Moldova Socialista* [Kishinёv], June 17, 1989, 3.

"Narodnyye deputati Moldavskoy SSR" (People's Deputies of the Moldavian SSR), *Sovetskaya Moldaviya* [Kishinёv], March 17, 1990,4.

Nedelciuc, Vasile. *The Republic of Moldova: Moldova, Basarabia, Transnistria: A Short History: State Organization, National Problem, Transnistria Conflict.* Trans., Eugenia Nadolschi. Chisinau: n.p., June 1992.

Nedelciuc, Vasile. *The Republic of Moldova: Moldova, Basarabia, Transnistria: A Short History: State Organization, National Problem, Transnistria Conflict.* Trans., Eugenia Nadolschi. Chisinau: n.p., July 1992.

Nelson, Daniel, ed. *Romania after Tyranny.* Boulder, Colorado: Westview Press, 1992.

Newton, Melanie, ed., and Vera Tolz, comp. *The USSR in 1989: A Record of Events.* Boulder, Colorado: Westview Press, 1990.

Newton, Melanie, ed., and Vera Tolz, comp. *The USSR in 1990: A Record of Events.* Boulder, Colorado: Westview Press, 1992.

"Pale." Page 689 in *Encyclopaedia Britannica,* 7. (Micropaedia.) Chicago: Encyclopaedia Britannica, 1975.

Patras, Mihai. "Migrarea: Statasul Problemului si Calea Rezolvarea lui sub conditiile auto-financiare" (Migration: The State of the Problem and the Path to Its Resolution under Conditions of Self-Financing), *Literatura si arta* [Chisinau], No. 6, 1990, 6.

Petersen, Phillip. "Moldova—Improving the Prospects for Peace," *Jane's Intelligence Review* [Coulsdon, Surrey, United Kingdom], 6, No. 9, September 1994, 396–400.

"Petru Lucinschi, Presedintele Parlamentului Republicii Moldova" (Petru Lucinschi, President of the Parliament of Moldova), *Moldova Suverana* [Chisinau], February 6, 1993, 1.

Popovici, Andrei. *The Political Status of Bessarabia.* Washington: Georgetown University, Ransdell for School of Foreign Service, 1931.

Postolachi, Vasile. "Speranta ramine în turn doi" (Hope Remains in the Second Round), *Literatura si arta* [Chisinau], No. 9, March 1, 1990, 1.

"Russia and Moldova Reach Accord on Dniester Region," *New York Times,* July 22, 1992, A9.

"Russia, Moldova Agree on Pullout," *Washington Post,* August 11, 1994, A24.

Ryan, Michael, and Richard Prentice. *Social Trends in the Soviet Union from 1950.* New York: St. Martin's Press, 1987.

Seton-Watson, Robert William. *A History of the Roumanians.* London: Archon Books, 1963.

Shaw, Geoffrey William. "Rumania." Pages 635–52 in *Encyclopaedia Britannica,* 19. Chicago: Benton, 1965.

Sheffield, Sharon S. "U.S. Agricultural Credits and Aid to Republics Total over $6 Billion." Pages 39–45 in *International Agriculture and Trade Report: Former USSR.* (Situation and Outlook Series.) (RS–93–1.) Washington: Department of Agriculture, Economic Research Service, 1993.

Shend, Jaclyn Y., Sharon S. Sheffield, and Christian J. Foster. "Projected 1993–94 Grain Imports Will Not Make Up for Fall in Output." Pages 46–65 in *International Agriculture and Trade Report: Former USSR.* (Situation and Outlook Series.) (RS–93–

1.) Washington: Department of Agriculture, Economic Research Service, 1993.

Snegur, Mircea. "Poporul Trebuie Întrebat si Ascultat" (The People Must Ask and Be Heard) [speech], *Moldova Suverana* [Chisinau], December 26, 1992, 1–2.

Socor, Vladimir. "Moldavia Builds a New State," *RFE/RL Research Report* [Munich], 1, No. 1, January 3, 1992, 42–45.

Solomon, Andrew. "Republics Heavily Dependent on Food Imports." Pages 34–38 in *International Agriculture and Trade Report: Former USSR.* (Situation and Outlook Series.) (RS–93–1.) Washington: Department of Agriculture, Economic Research Service, 1993.

Soviet Union. Ministerstvo geologii i okhrany nedr SSSR. Glavnoye upravleniye geodezii i kartografii. *Atlas Ukrainskoy SSR i Moldavskoy SSR.* Ed., V.G. Bondarchuk. Moscow: 1962.

Soviet Union. Ministerstvo geologii i okhrany nedr SSSR. Glavnoye upravleniye geodezii i kartografii. "Po Moldavii, turistskaya karta." Moscow: 1989 (map).

Spector, Sherman David. "The Moldavian S.S.R., 1964–1974." Pages 260–69 in George W. Simmonds, ed., *Nationalism in the USSR and Eastern Europe.* Detroit: University of Detroit Press, 1977.

The Statesman's Year-Book, 1993–1994. Ed., Brian Hunter. New York: St. Martin's Press, 1993.

Sukhopara, Fyodor Nikolayevich. "Moldavian Soviet Socialist Republic." Pages 301–4 in *The New Encyclopaedia Britannica.* (Macropaedia, 12.) Chicago: Encyclopaedia Britannica, 1975.

Takiy, Aleksandr. "Complex Situation Persists in Moldavia," TASS [Moscow], August 2, 1990. Foreign Broadcast Information Service, *Daily Report: Soviet Union.* (FBIS–SOV–90–190.) August 3, 1990, 61.

Tolz, Vera, and Melanie Newton, eds. *The USSR in 1991: A Record of Events.* Boulder, Colorado: Westview Press, 1993.

"Transnistria." Page 1939 in Leon E. Seltzer, ed., *The Columbia Lippincott Gazetteer of the World.* New York: Columbia University Press, 1962.

Uluk, P. "Automatizarya produktsiyey." Pages 242–43 in I. Vartichan, ed., *Yenchiklopediya Sovetike Moldovenyaske.* Kishinĕv: Redaktsiya princhipale a Yenchiklopediyey Sovetiche Moldovenesht', 1981.

United Nations. Department for Economic and Social Information and Policy Analysis. *Demographic Yearbook (Annuaire démographique), 1992.* (44th ed.) New York: 1994.

United Nations. Department for Economic and Social Information and Policy Analysis. *Statistical Yearbook (Annuaire statistique), 1990–91.* (38th ed.) New York: 1993.

United States. Central Intelligence Agency. *Handbook of International Economic Statistics, 1994.* (CPAS 94–10001.) Washington: 1994.

United States. Central Intelligence Agency. *Top Officials in Moldova.* Washington: 1992.

United States. Central Intelligence Agency. *The World Factbook, 1992.* Washington: 1992.

United States. Central Intelligence Agency. *The World Factbook, 1993–94.* Washington: Brassey's, 1993–94.

United States. Central Intelligence Agency. *The World Factbook, 1994.* Washington: 1994.

United States. Commission on Security and Cooperation in Europe. *Report on the Moldovan Parliamentary Elections, February 27, 1994: Chisinau, Northern Moldova, Transdniestria, Varnitsa.* Washington: April 1994.

United States. Department of Agriculture. Agriculture Marketing Service. Transportation and Marketing Division. *An Overview of Agricultural Transportation in the Former USSR.* (Foreign Agriculture Economic Report, No. 249.) Washington: 1993.

United States. Department of Agriculture. Economic Research Service. *Former USSR: Agriculture and Trade Report.* (Situation and Outlook Series.) (RS–92–1.) Washington: 1992.

United States. Department of Agriculture. Economic Research Service. *International Agriculture and Trade Report: Former USSR.* (Situation and Outlook Series.) (RS–93–1.) Washington: 1993.

United States. Department of Agriculture. Foreign Agricultural Service. "Moldova." Page 162 in *Foreign Agriculture, 1992.* Washington: 1992.

United States. Department of Commerce. International Trade Administration. Business Information Service for the Newly

Independent States. *Economic Overview of Moldova.* Washington: 1992.

United States. Department of State. "Fact Sheet: Moldova," *U.S. Department of State Dispatch,* 5, No. 18, May 2, 1994.

Ureche, Grigore, Miron Costin, and Ion Neculce. *Letopisetul Tarii Moldovei* (Chronicle of the Moldovan Nation). Chisinau: Editura Hyperion, 1990.

Vartichan, I., ed. *Moldavskaya sovetskaya sotsialisticheskaya respublika.* Kishinëv: Glavnaya redaktsiya Moldavskoy Sovetskoy Entsiklopedii, 1979.

Vartichan, I., ed. *Sovetskaya Moldaviya: Kratkaya entsiklopediya.* Kishinëv: Glavnaya redaktsiya Moldavskoy Sovetskoy Entsiklopedii, 1982.

Verona, Sergiu. "Moldova Republic: Basic Facts," *CRS Report for Congress.* (92–182F.) Washington: Library of Congress, Congressional Research Service, 1992.

Verona, Sergiu. "Moldova Republic: Basic Facts," *CRS Report for Congress.* (94–656F.) Washington: Library of Congress, Congressional Research Service, August 12, 1994.

"The Western States." Pages 275–94 in Daniel C. Diller, ed., *Russia and the Independent States.* Washington: Congressional Quarterly, 1993.

Wixman, Ronald. *The Peoples of the USSR: An Ethnographic Handbook.* Armonk, New York: M.E. Sharpe, 1984.

World Bank. *Moldova: Moving to a Market Economy.* (World Bank Country Study.) Washington: 1994.

World Bank. *Statistical Handbook: States of the Former USSR.* (Studies of Economies in Transformation, No. 3.) Washington: 1992.

World Radio TV Handbook, 47. Ed., Andrew G. Sennitt. Amsterdam: 1993.

World Radio TV Handbook, 49. Ed., Andrew G. Sennitt. Amsterdam: 1995.

Zagaievschi, Virgiliu. "Antirestructurarea: Schite anatomice" (Anti-Restructuring: An Anatomical Sketch), *Literatura si arta* [Chisinau], No. 4, January 25, 1990, 1–2.

Zagaievschi, Virgiliu. "Dos coiful sus caciula!" (Down with the Helmet, Up with the Cap!), *Literatura si arta* [Chisinau], No. 11, March 15, 1990, 1.

Zagaievschi, Virgiliu. "Moldova alege viitorul" (Moldova Chooses the Future), *Literatura si arta* [Chisinau], No. 7, February 15, 1990, 1–4.

Zelenchuk, Valintin Stepanich. "Populatia Moldovei în Perioada Feudalismului si Capitalismului" (The Population of Moldova in the Period of Feudalism and Capitalism). Pages 7–14 in V.S. Zelenchuk and E.M. Zagorodnaya, eds., *Populatia RSS Moldovenesti*. Kishinĕv: Editura Kartiya Moldovenyaska, 1983.

Zelenchuk, Valintin Stepanich. "Populatia Tinutului în Perioada Formarii RSS Moldovenesti si în Anii chelui de-al Doalia Razboi Mondial." Pages 21–22 in V.S. Zelenchuk and E.M. Zagorodnaya, eds., *Populatia RSS Moldovenesti*. Kishinĕv: Editura Kartiya Moldovenyaska, 1983.

Zickel, Raymond E., ed. *Soviet Union: A Country Study.* Washington: GPO, 1991.

(Various issues of the following periodicals were also used in the preparation of this chapter: British Broadcasting Corporation, *Summary of World Broadcasts* [Caversham Park, Reading, United Kingdom]; and Foreign Broadcast Information Service, *Daily Report: Central Eurasia.*)

Glossary

apparatchik—Russian colloquial word for someone who has been engaged full time in the work of the CPSU (*q.v.*) and/or the republic communist parties. Sometimes used in a derogatory sense.

August coup d'état—On August 19, 1991, high-ranking officials of the CPSU (*q.v.*) and the government of the Soviet Union (*q.v.*) announced that they had formed the State Committee for the State of Emergency and had removed Mikhail S. Gorbachev as the head of state. Leaders of most of the Soviet republics and many foreign leaders denounced the coup. Some key military commanders refused to deploy their forces in support of the coup leaders, and by August 22 the coup had collapsed. As a consequence of the failed coup, the CPSU and the Soviet central government were severely discredited, Gorbachev resigned, ten of the fifteen Soviet republics declared or reaffirmed their independence (including Belarus and Moldova), and the Congress of People's Deputies (*q.v.*) dissolved the Soviet Union and itself after transferring state power to a transitional government.

Belarusian ruble—The monetary unit of Belarus, introduced in May 1992. In March 1995, the exchange rate was 11,669 Belarusian rubles per US$1. The Belarusian ruble is convertible, within limits.

Bessarabia (Basarabia in Romanian)—Former principality, originally composed of lands owned by the Basarab Dynasty of Walachia (*q.v.*), extending inland from the Black Sea coast and bounded on the west by the Prut River and on the east by the Nistru River. In 1812 the name was extended to all the land between the Prut and Nistru rivers by the Russian Empire (*q.v.*), to which Bessarabia was awarded by the Treaty of Bucharest. The bulk of Bessarabia makes up most of the present-day Republic of Moldova.

Bolshevik—A member of the radical group within the Russian Social Democratic Labor Party, which, under Vladimir I. Lenin's leadership, staged the Bolshevik Revolution. In March 1918, the Bolsheviks formed the Russian Communist Party (Bolshevik) and began calling themselves Communists (*q.v.*). That party was the precursor of the Communist Party of the Soviet Union (CPSU—*q.v.*).

Bukovina (Bucovina in Romanian; Bukovyna in Ukrainian)—An area in the eastern foothills of the Carpathian Mountains populated principally by ethnic Ukrainians and Romanians. Over the centuries, Bukovina has belonged to various states, including Kievan Rus', Moldova, and Austria-Hungary. In 1940 the northern half of Bukovina became part of the Ukrainian Soviet Socialist Republic, while the southern half remained part of Romania.

Bund (General Union of Jewish Workers in Russia and Poland)—A Jewish socialist movement founded in Vilnius in 1897 by Jewish workers and intellectuals in the Russian Empire (*q.v.*). The Bund divided into two groups in 1920. The larger group merged with the Bolshevik (*q.v.*) branch of the communist party, while the minority remained independent until it was suppressed by theBolshevik government.

chernozem—Russian word meaning black earth. Rich, highly fertile soil.

collective farm (*kolkhoz* in Russian)—Under the communist (*q.v.*) regime, an agricultural "cooperative" where peasants worked collectively on state-owned land under the direction of party-approved plans and leaders and were paid wages based partly on the success of their harvest.

collectivization—Joseph V. Stalin's policy of confiscating privately owned agricultural lands and facilities and consolidating them, along with farmers and their families, into large collective farms (*q.v.*) and state farms (*q.v.*).

Comecon (Council for Mutual Economic Assistance; sometimes cited as CMEA or CEMA)—A multilateral economic alliance created in 1949, ostensibly to promote economic development of member states through cooperation and specialization, but actually to enforce Soviet economic domination of Eastern Europe. Members shortly before its official demise in January 1991 were Bulgaria, Cuba, Czechoslovakia, the German Democratic Republic (East Germany), Hungary, Mongolia, Poland, Romania, the Soviet Union, and Vietnam.

Commonwealth of Independent States (CIS)—Created on December 8, 1991, with the signing of the Minsk Agreement by Belarus, Russia, and Ukraine. The Alma-Ata Declaration, signed by eleven heads of state on December 21,

1991, expanded membership in the CIS to all other former Soviet republics except Estonia, Georgia, Latvia, and Lithuania. Moldova joined the CIS in April 1994. The CIS is a confederation of former Soviet republics in which "coordinating bodies" oversee common interests in the economy, foreign policy, and defense of its members.

communism/communist—The official ideology of the Soviet Union (*q.v.*), based on Marxism-Leninism, which provided for a system of authoritarian government in which the CPSU (*q.v.*) alone controlled state-owned means of production. It sought to establish a society in which the state withered away and goods and services were distributed equitably. A communist is an adherent or advocate of communism; when capitalized, "Communist" refers to a member of a communist party.

Conference on Security and Cooperation in Europe (CSCE)—Established in 1972, the group in 1994 consisted of fifty-three nations, including all European countries, and sponsored joint sessions and consultations on political issues vital to European security. The Charter of Paris (1990) changed the CSCE from an ad hoc forum to an organization having permanent institutions. In 1992 new CSCE roles in conflict prevention and management were defined, potentially making the CSCE the center of a Europe-based collective security system. In the early 1990s, however, applications of these instruments to conflicts in Yugoslavia and the Caucasus did not have a decisive impact. In January 1995, the organization was renamed the Organization for Security and Cooperation in Europe (OSCE).

Congress of People's Deputies—Established in 1988 by constitutional amendment. The highest organ (upper tier) of legislative and executive authority in the Soviet Union (*q.v.*). It elected the Supreme Soviet (*q.v.*) of the Soviet Union but ceased to exist at the demise of the Soviet Union.

Conventional Forces in Europe Treaty (CFE Treaty)—An agreement signed in 1990 by the member nations of the Warsaw Pact (*q.v.*) and the North Atlantic Treaty Organization to establish parity in conventional weapons between the two organizations from the Atlantic to the Urals. The treaty included a strict system of inspection and information exchange and remained in force, although not strictly observed by all parties, in the mid-1990s.

Cossacks—Originally peasants (primarily Ukrainian and Russian) who fled from oppression to the lower Dnepr and Don river regions to settle in the frontier areas separating fifteenth-century Muscovy, Poland, and the lands occupied by the Tatars. They later organized themselves into military formations to resist Tatar raids. Renowned as horsemen, they were absorbed into the army of the Russian Empire (*q.v.*) by the late eighteenth century. In the early 1990s, there were attempts to reestablish a Cossack military tradition in Ukraine. The "Cossacks" in Transnistria were mostly Russian mercenaries, ultranationalists, and military veterans.

Council of Europe—Founded in 1949, the Council of Europe is an organization overseeing intergovernmental cooperation in designated areas such as environmental planning, finance, sports, crime, migration, and legal matters. In 1994 the council had thirty-three members.

CPSU (Communist Party of the Soviet Union)—Since 1952 the official name of the communist party in the Soviet Union (*q.v.*). After the August coup d'état (*q.v.*), in which the party played a prominent role, Russian president Boris N. Yeltsin banned the party in Russia and ordered its property turned over to the government. The Communist Party of Belarus was banned in Belarus in August 1991, as was the Communist Party of Moldova in Moldova.

Cyrillic alphabet—An alphabet based on Greek characters that was created in the ninth century to serve as a medium for writing Orthodox texts translated from Greek into Old Church Slavonic (*q.v.*). Named for Cyril, the leader of the first religious mission from Constantinople to the Slavic peoples, Cyrillic is used by modern Russian, Belarusian, "Moldavian" (*q.v.*), and several other languages, both Slavic and non-Slavic.

"Dnestr Moldavian Republic"—An extralegal political entity, located on the east bank of the Nistru River, that declared its independence in September 1990. Established by Russian-speaking conservatives who wished to remain part of the Soviet Union. In 1995 the territory of the "Dnestr Republic" (as it was commonly known) consisted of all Moldovan land east of the Nistru River, with the exception of two enclaves bordering the river, one around Cosnita (northeast of Chisinau), and the other between Dubasari and Malovata to its northwest. In addition, the "Dnestr Republic" included territory on the west bank of the Nistru: the city of Tighina and an area to the southeast of the city that bordered on the river.

enterprise—A production establishment, such as a plant or a factory, in the communist (*q.v.*) era; not to be confused with a privately owned, Western-style business.

eparchy—An administrative district of the Orthodox and Uniate (*q.v.*) churches, usually headed by a bishop. Equivalent to a diocese in the Roman Catholic Church. A group of eparchies constitutes a metropolitan see.

ethnic Belarusian/Belorussian—Person whose ethnic heritage is East Slavic and whose native language is Belarusian/Belorussian.

ethnic Bulgarian—Person whose ethnic heritage is South Slavic and whose native language is Bulgarian.

ethnic Pole—Person whose ethnic heritage is West Slavic and whose native language is Polish.

ethnic Romanian—Person whose ethnic heritage is Latin and whose native language is Romanian.

ethnic Russian—Person whose ethnic heritage is East Slavic and whose native language is Russian.

ethnic Ukrainian—Person whose ethnic heritage is East Slavic and whose native language is Ukrainian.

European Union (EU)—Successor organization to the European Community, officially established by ratification of the Maastricht Treaty of November 1993. The goal of the EU is closer economic unification of Western Europe, leading to a single monetary system and closer cooperation in matters of justice and foreign and security policies. In 1995 members consisted of Austria, Belgium, Britain, Denmark, Finland, France, Germany, Greece, Ireland, Italy, Luxembourg, the Netherlands, Portugal, Spain, and Sweden.

exarchate—An independent church within the Orthodox Church. The exarch, head of the exarchate, is an Eastern rite bishop who ranks below a patriarch and above a metropolitan.

fiscal year (FY)—A one-year period for financial accounting purposes, which can coincide with the calendar year. In both Belarus and Moldova, it coincides with the calendar year.

glasnost—Russian word meaning openness. Public discussion of issues; accessibility of information so that the public can become familiar with it and discuss it. Mikhail S. Gorbachev's policy of using the media to make information available on some controversial issues in order to provoke public discussion, challenge government and party bureaucrats, and mobilize greater support for his policy of *perestroika (q.v.)*.

gross domestic product (GDP)—A measure of the total value of goods and services produced by the domestic economy of a country during a given period, usually one year. Obtained by adding the value contributed by each sector of the economy in the form of profits, compensation to employees, and depreciation (consumption of capital). Only domestic production is included, not income arising from investments and possessions owned abroad, hence the use of the word "domestic" to distinguish GDP from gross "national" product (GNP—*q.v.*).

gross national product (GNP)—The total market value of final goods and services produced by a country's economy during a year. Obtained by adding the gross domestic product (GDP—*q.v.*) and the income received from abroad by residents and by subtracting payments remitted abroad to nonresidents.

Group of Seven—The seven major noncommunist economic powers: Britain, Canada, France, Germany, Italy, Japan, and the United States.

International Monetary Fund (IMF)—Established along with the World Bank (*q.v.*) in 1945, the IMF is a specialized agency affiliated with the United Nations and responsible for stabilizing international exchange rates and payments. Its main function is to provide loans to its members (including industrialized and developing countries) when they experience balance of payments difficulties. These loans frequently have conditions that require substantial internal economic adjustments by the recipients, most of which are developing countries. Belarus and Moldova both became members of the IMF in 1992.

KGB (Komitet gosudarstvennoy bezopasnosti in Russian)— Committee for State Security. The predominant Soviet security police organization since its establishment in 1954 as the successor to the MVD (Ministry of Internal Affairs; Ministerstvo vnutrennykh del, in Russian). In October 1991, when Mikhail S. Gorbachev decreed that the KGB be disbanded because of its involvement in the August coup d'état (*q.v.*), the assets and willing personnel of the KGB in Moldova were transferred to the new republic's government, to the Ministry of National Security. In Belarus the new government took control of the KGB but did not change its name.

leu (pl., lei)—The monetary unit of Moldova, introduced in November 1993. The exchange rate was 4.27 lei per US$1 at the beginning of 1995. The leu is convertible.

Menshevik—A member of a wing of the Russian Social Democratic Labor Party before and during the Russian revolutions of 1905 and 1917. Unlike the Bolsheviks (*q.v.*), the Mensheviks believed in the gradual achievement of socialism by parliamentary methods.

"Moldavian" (*moldavskiy* in Russian)—Term used by the Soviet government to describe the language and nationality of the ethnic Romanians (*q.v.*) in Bessarabia (*q.v.*). Joseph V. Stalin claimed that their language and nationality were different and distinct from the language and nationality of the ethnic Romanians in Romania as a justification for creating the Moldavian Soviet Socialist Republic in 1940. In actuality, the "Moldavian language" is a dialect of Romanian. Under the Soviet regime, "Moldavia" was used as the short form for the Moldavian Soviet Socialist Republic.

Moldova—Former principality, one of two major historical regions inhabited by a Romanian-speaking population (along with Walachia, *q.v.*). Moldovan territory east of the Prut River was added to the original Bessarabia (*q.v.*), and the entire region was called Bessarabia when it was annexed by the Russian Empire (*q.v.*) in 1812. Also the name of a region in modern Romania.

most-favored-nation status—Under the provisions of the General Agreement on Tariffs and Trade (GATT), when one country accords another most-favored-nation status, it agrees to extend to that country the same trade concessions, such as lower tariffs or reduced nontariff barriers, that it grants to any other recipient having most-favored-nation status. The United States granted Moldova most-favored-nation status in 1992. Belarus was granted that status in 1993.

Nazi-Soviet Nonaggression Pact—Agreement signed by Nazi Germany and the Soviet Union (*q.v.*) on August 23, 1939, immediately preceding the German invasion of Poland, which began World War II. A secret protocol divided Poland between the two powers and gave Bessarabia (*q.v.*), Latvia, Lithuania, Estonia, and the eastern part of Poland to the Soviet Union. Also known as the Molotov-Ribbentrop Pact.

net material product (NMP)—The official measure of the value of goods and services produced in countries having a planned economy during a given period, usually a year. It approximates the term "gross national product" (GNP— *q.v.*) used by economists in the United States and in other countries having a market economy.

New Economic Policy (Novaya ekonomicheskaya politika in Russian—NEP)—Instituted in 1921, it let peasants sell produce on an open market and permitted small enterprises (*q.v.*) to be privately owned and operated. The NEP declined with forced collectivization (*q.v.*) of farms and was officially ended by Stalin in December 1929.

Old Believers—A sect of the Russian Orthodox Church that rejected the changes made by Patriarch Nikon in the mid-seventeenth century.

Old Church Slavonic—Also called Church Slavonic. The liturgical language of the Orthodox and Uniate (*q.v.*) churches in Slavic lands.

perestroika—Russian word meaning restructuring. Mikhail S. Gorbachev's campaign to revitalize the economy, communist party, and society by adjusting economic, political, and social mechanisms. Announced at the Twenty-Seventh Party Congress of the CPSU (*q.v.*) in August 1986.

Polonize/Polonization—The process of changing the national identity of non-Poles to one culturally similar to that of the Poles.

Procuracy—The agency responsible for the investigation and prosecution of lawbreakers. The Procuracy was subject to the authority of the CPSU (*q.v.*) and had limited purview over political matters. In Moldova the Procuracy (and its successor organization, the General Prosecution Office) was the subject of substantial controversy in discussions on constitutional reform in the early 1990s.

raion (pl., *raioane* in Romanian; *rayon/rayony* in Belarusian and Russian)—A low-level territorial and administrative subdivision, roughly equivalent to a county in the United States in terms of function. Originally used by the Soviet Union.

rayon—See *raion*.

Russian Empire—Formally proclaimed by Tsar Peter the Great in 1721 and significantly expanded during the reign of Catherine II, becoming a major multinational state. It collapsed during the revolutions of 1917.

Russianization—The policy of several Soviet regimes promoting Russian as the national language of the Soviet Union. Russian was given equal and official status with local languages in most non-Russian republics; it was made the official language of the Soviet Union in state and diplomatic affairs, in the armed forces, and on postage stamps, currency, and military and civilian decorations.

Russify/Russification—A process of changing the national identity of non-Russians to one culturally similar to that of the Russians. An official policy of the Russian Empire (*q.v.*) although not of any Soviet regime. However, such assimilation often resulted from the policy of Russianization (*q.v.*), particularly in the case of ethnic Ukrainians, Belarusians, and non-Russian educated elites.

Soviet Union (Union of Soviet Socialist Republics—USSR)— Founded December 1922; dissolved in December 1991. The Soviet Union included the Moldavian Autonomous Soviet Socialist Republic (originally called the Moldavian Autonomous Oblast) from 1924 until 1940, at which time the Soviet government created the Moldavian Soviet Socialist Republic on somewhat different territory until 1941. In 1947 the Soviet Union regained control until Moldova declared its independence in August 1991. The Belorussian Soviet Socialist Republic was established in 1919 and remained a part of the Soviet Union until it declared its independence in August 1991.

state farm (*sovkhoz* in Russian)—Under the communist regime, a government-owned and government-managed agricultural enterprise (*q.v.*) in which workers were paid salaries.

steppe—The vast, semiarid, grass-covered plain in the southeastern portion of Europe, extending into Asia.

Supreme Soviet—Under the communist regime, served as the highest organ of state power between sittings of the Congress of People's Deputies (*q.v.*). The Moldovan Supreme Soviet changed its name to the Moldovan Parliament in May 1991 and declared the country sovereign one month later. The name of the Belarusian Supreme Soviet remained unchanged after Belarus declared its independence in August 1991.

Transnistria (Transdnestria in English)—From 1941 to 1944, a Romanian *judet* (province) encompassing the land between the Nistru and Pivdennyy Buh rivers in the German-occupied Ukrainian Soviet Socialist Republic. Currently, the region between the Nistru River and Moldova's eastern border. In September 1990, Slavs in Transnistria proclaimed it the "Dnestr Moldavian Republic" (*q.v.*).

Uniate Church—An Eastern Christian Church that preserves the Eastern rite and discipline but submits to papal authority. The Uniate Church was established in the Polish-Lithuanian Commonwealth (which included Ukraine and Belarus) in 1596 at the Union of Brest.

Walachia—Former principality; a region in present-day southern Romania.

Warsaw Pact—Informal name for Warsaw Treaty Organization, a mutual defense organization founded in 1955, which included the Soviet Union, Albania (which withdrew in 1968), Bulgaria, Czechoslovakia, the German Democratic Republic (East Germany), Hungary, Poland, and Romania. The Warsaw Pact enabled the Soviet Union to station troops in the countries to its west to oppose the forces of the North Atlantic Treaty Organization (NATO). The pact was the basis of the invasions of Hungary (1956) and of Czechoslovakia (1968); it was disbanded in July 1991.

World Bank—Informal name used to designate a group of four affiliated international institutions—the International Bank for Reconstruction and Development (IBRD), the International Development Association (IDA), the International Finance Corporation (IFC), and the Multilateral Investment Guarantee Agency (MIGA). The IBRD provides loans to developing countries for productive projects. The IDA furnishes credits to the poorest developing countries on much easier terms than those of conventional IBRD loans. The IFC supplements the activities of the IBRD through loans and assistance designed to encourage the growth of productive private enterprises in the less developed countries. The MIGA insures private foreign investment in developing countries against such noncommercial risks as expropriation, civil strife, and inconvertibility of currency. To participate in the World Bank group, member states must first belong to the International Monetary Fund (IMF—*q.v.*).

Index

Procuracy (Moldova) (*see also* General Prosecution Office), 148
procurator general (Belarus), 71, 73, 74
Program for Privatization for 1995–1996 (Moldova), 131
Program of Activity of the Government of Moldova for 1992–1995, 131
Program of Activity of the Government of Moldova for 1994–1997, 131
prosecutor general (Moldova), 148
Prosvita (periodical) (Moldova), 166
Protestants: in Belarus, 36, 39
Prussia: Belorussian territory ceded to, 15
Prut River (Moldova), 105, 106, 113–14, 140
Prypyats' River (Belarus), 28, 59
public opinion poll (1994) (Moldova), 111, 163, 169
pushcha/pushchy (Belarus), 28

Rabochiy Tiraspol' (newspaper) (Moldova), 166
Rada. *See* All-Belarusian Congress
radio: in Belarus, 61; in Moldova, 141
Radioteleviziunea Nationala (Moldova), 141
railroads: in Belarus, 58–59; in Moldova, 140
raion/raioane (Moldova), 149, 152, 158
rayon/rayony (Belarus), 74
Red Army (Soviet), 21, 22, 23
Red Cross, International Committee of the, 165
referendum of 1990 (Belarus), 25
referendum of 1995 (Belarus), xix, xxii, 35, 70
Reform Party (Moldova), 151
religion: in Belarus, 36–39; in Moldova, 123–24
Republic Center on AIDS (Belarus), 42
Republican Party (Belarus), 77
Republican Party (Moldova), 151
Republic Guard (Transnistria), 165
Republic of Belarus, 25, 26, 66
Republic of Moldova, 110, 144
Republic's Voters Meeting (Moldova), 154
Reserve Fund (Moldova), 128
Revolution of 1905, 17
Ribnita (Moldova), 138, 156

roads: in Belarus, 59; in Moldova, 140
Rodno slovo (periodical) (Moldova), 166
Roma (Gypsy) people: in Moldova, 99, 117, 122
Roman Catholic Church: in Belarus, 36, 38; conflicts with Orthodoxy, 38; official religion of Lithuania, 14; Polish Catholics in Belorussia/Belarus, 18, 21, 32, 38, 81
Roman Empire, 105
Romania: birth rate in, 115; and conflict in Transnistria, 159; death rate in, 115; Moldovan foreign relations and, 168–69; Moldovan reunification with, xix, xxii; origins of culture, 124–25; rail links with Moldova, 140; Russia's foreign relations and, 169; trade with Moldova, 143; in World War II, 107
Romanian language: Moldovan as dialect of, 112, 121; in Moldovan education, 126–27; as mother tongue, 122; in proposed Romanian Republic of Moldova, 158
Romanian Orthodox Church, 123
Romanian people: in Chisinau, 115; condescension to Moldovans by, 167; in Moldova, xix, 105, 107–8, 115, 116, 117–119; in Moldovan political parties, 150–51; opposition from Transnistria to, 109–10; purged, 108, 119; territorial claims and, 173
Romanian Republic of Moldova (proposed), 158
Russia: Bolshevik Revolution of 1917, 18, 106; buffer zones, xix; Chornobyl' accident and, 29; Civil War, 121; cultural influences on Moldova, 125; customs union with Belarus, 57, 80, 87; electricity to Belarus from, 56; ethnic Belarusians in, 30; military ratio, 83; mediation in Transnistria, 159; and Minsk Agreement, 66; monetary and economic union with Belarus, 57, 80; nationalism in, 172; objection to NATO expansion, 88; relations with Belarus, 79; relations with Ukraine, 80; Revolution of 1905, 17; Russian State Duma, xxv, 172; Russo-Japanese War, 17; as trading partner with Belarus, 63; as trading partner with Moldova, 143; treaty of 1995 with Belarus, 68–69

112, 116, 172; demonstrations in, 156; as municipality, 149; railroads at, 140; Russians in, 119; violence in, 159–60

Tineretul Moldovei/Molodëzh Moldovy (newspaper) (Moldova), 166

Tiraspol, 115–16; bread rationing in, xxv; as capital of Moldavian ASSR, 107; as capital of "Dnestr Moldavian Republic," 110, 159; demonstrations in, 156; industrial development in, 129; as municipality, 149; Russians in, 119

Tiraspol Six, 165

Topal, Stepan, 110, 111

topography: of Belarus, 26, 28; of Moldova, 113

trade (Belarus): with CIS nations, 61–64; with non-CIS nations, 63

trade (Moldova), 131, 132, 135, 142; with CIS nations, 142, 143; with former Soviet republics, 141–43; with non-CIS nations, 143

trade unions, foreign, xxiii

Transnistria (*see also* "Dnestr Moldavian Republic"; Russian 14th Army), xix–xx, 145, 170; autonomy under constitution of 1994, 163–64; cease-fire of 1992, 111, 145; civil war of 1992, 159–60; elections of 1994 in, 111; energy resources in, 138; ethnic minorities in, 117, 119; and Gagauz conflict, 159; history of, 105, 125; human rights in, 165; industrial development, 129; Jews in, 121; media censorship in, 164; Moldovan military and, 170; peacekeeping forces, 111, 170, 177; as pro-Russian, 152; separatism, xix–xx, 154; standards of living in, 128; topography of, 113; Ukraine and, 173

transportation: in Belarus, 58–60, 82; in Moldova, 140

Treaty of Brest-Litovsk (1918), 18

Treaty of Bucharest (1812), 106

Treaty of Iasi (1792), 106

Treaty of Riga (1921), 19

Treaty on Collective Security (1992) (CIS), 82, 88

Treaty on Friendship and Cooperation (1995), 68–69

Turkey: joint ventures with Moldova, 143; relations with Moldova, 173–74

Turkish people: in Moldova, 105, 106

Turkmenistan: and CIS, 168

Ukraine: Chornobyl' issue and, 80–81; CIS agreement and, 168; conflict in Transnistria and, 159; connected to Moldova by landline link, 141; ethnic Belarusians in, 30; independence of, 25, 64, 65; and Minsk Agreement, 66; Moldavian Autonomous Oblast and, 106–7; rail links with Moldova, 140; relations with Belarus, 80–81; as trading partner with Belarus, 63, 143; under Lithuania, 14; military ratio, 83; nuclear disarmament, 87; zone of cooperation, 88

Ukrainian language, 33, 122, 141

Ukrainian people: in Belarus, 31, 32; in Moldavia/Moldova, 99, 105, 107, 115, 116, 117, 119, 124, 173

Ukrainian Soviet Socialist Republic, 106

Ulmanis, Guntis, 82

underemployment: in Belarus, 56

Undzer col/Nash golos (periodical) (Moldova), 166

unemployment: in Belarus, 43, 56; in Moldova, 133

Unemployment Fund (Moldova), 128

Ungheni (Moldova), 138, 140, 141

Uniate Church, 36; history of, 14–15; in Moldova, 124; use of Belarusian/Belorussian language, 38–39

Union of Belorussian Youth, 22

Union of Brest (1596), 14–15

Union of Krevo (1385), 14

Union of Lublin (1569), 14

Union of Soviet Socialist Republics. *See* Soviet Union

Union of Writers of Moldova, 166

United Democratic Party of Belarus, 75–76

United Nations: Belarus's membership in, 78; Moldova's membership in, 165, 168; Transnistrian conflict and, 112

United States: assistance to Moldova, 135–36; relations with Belarus, 78, 80; trade unions and Belarus, xxiii; immigration from Belorussia, 16, 30; trade with Belarus, 63; trade with Moldova, 143; visit by Snegur, 174

United States Central Intelligence Agency, 79

Contributors

William E. Crowther is Assistant Professor of Political Science, Department of Political Science, University of North Carolina, Greensboro, North Carolina.

Helen Fedor is a Senior Research Specialist for Central Europe and Central Eurasia with the Federal Research Division, Library of Congress.

Jan Zaprudnik is a former commentator on Soviet and international politics with Radio Liberty.

Published Country Studies

(Area Handbook Series)

550–65	Afghanistan	550–36	Dominican Republic
550–98	Albania		and Haiti
550–44	Algeria	550–52	Ecuador
550–59	Angola	550–43	Egypt
550–73	Argentina	550–150	El Salvador
550–111	Armenia, Azerbaijan,	550–28	Ethiopia
	and Georgia	550–167	Finland
550–169	Australia	550–173	Germany, East
550–176	Austria	550–155	Germany, Fed. Rep. of
550–175	Bangladesh	550–153	Ghana
550–112	Belarus and Moldova	550–87	Greece
550–170	Belgium	550–78	Guatemala
550–66	Bolivia	550–174	Guinea
550–20	Brazil	550–82	Guyana and Belize
550–168	Bulgaria	550–151	Honduras
550–61	Burma	550–165	Hungary
550–50	Cambodia	550–21	India
550–166	Cameroon	550–154	Indian Ocean
550–159	Chad	550–39	Indonesia
550–77	Chile	550–68	Iran
550–60	China	550–31	Iraq
550–26	Colombia	550–25	Israel
550–33	Commonwealth Carib-	550–182	Italy
	bean, Islands of the	550–30	Japan
550–91	Congo	550–34	Jordan
550–90	Costa Rica	550–56	Kenya
550–69	Côte d'Ivoire (Ivory	550–81	Korea, North
	Coast)	550–41	Korea, South
550–152	Cuba	550–58	Laos
550–22	Cyprus	550–24	Lebanon
550–158	Czechoslovakia	550–38	Liberia

550–85	Libya	550–184	Singapore
550–172	Malawi	550–86	Somalia
550–45	Malaysia	550–93	South Africa
550–161	Mauritania	550–95	Soviet Union
550–79	Mexico	550–179	Spain
550–76	Mongolia	550–96	Sri Lanka
550–49	Morocco	550–27	Sudan
550–64	Mozambique	550–47	Syria
550–35	Nepal and Bhutan	550–62	Tanzania
550–88	Nicaragua	550–53	Thailand
550–157	Nigeria	550–89	Tunisia
550–94	Oceania	550–80	Turkey
550–48	Pakistan	550–74	Uganda
550–46	Panama	550–97	Uruguay
550–156	Paraguay	550–71	Venezuela
550–185	Persian Gulf States	550–32	Vietnam
550–42	Peru	550–183	Yemens, The
550–72	Philippines	550–99	Yugoslavia
550–162	Poland	550–67	Zaire
550–181	Portugal	550–75	Zambia
550–160	Romania	550–171	Zimbabwe
550–37	Rwanda and Burundi		
550–51	Saudi Arabia		
550–70	Senegal		
550–180	Sierra Leone